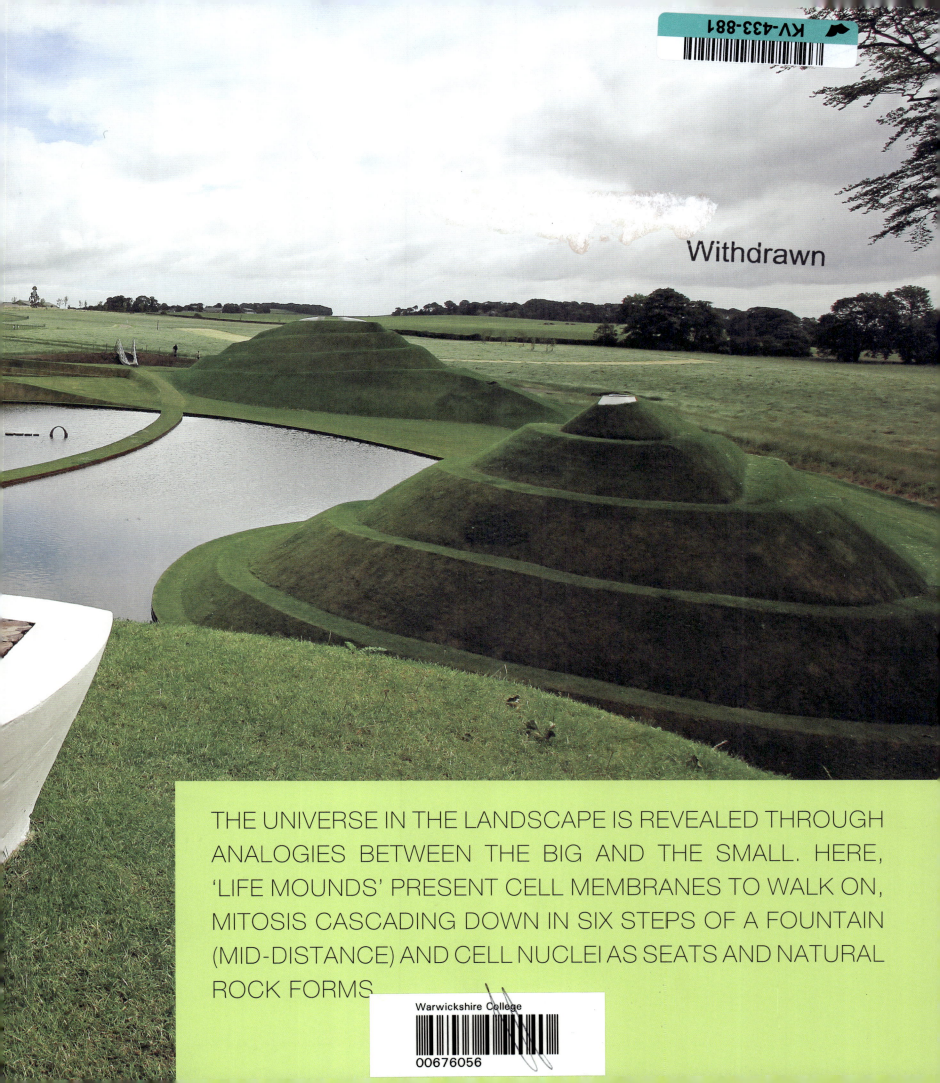

THE UNIVERSE IN THE LANDSCAPE IS REVEALED THROUGH ANALOGIES BETWEEN THE BIG AND THE SMALL. HERE, 'LIFE MOUNDS' PRESENT CELL MEMBRANES TO WALK ON, MITOSIS CASCADING DOWN IN SIX STEPS OF A FOUNTAIN (MID-DISTANCE) AND CELL NUCLEI AS SEATS AND NATURAL ROCK FORMS

THE UNIVERSE IS WRITTEN IN THE LANDSCAPE AS A MIXTURE OF EPIGRAPHY, BLACK AND WHITE CORIAN CUT AS A CONTINUOUS TEXT, AND A BIRCHBONE GARDEN OF SIGNS AND SPIRALLING SYMBOLS. PLANTS, WRITING, BONES AND WRITHING HOSEPIPE UNDERSCORE DEATH AND LIFE CAREFULLY INTERTWINING.

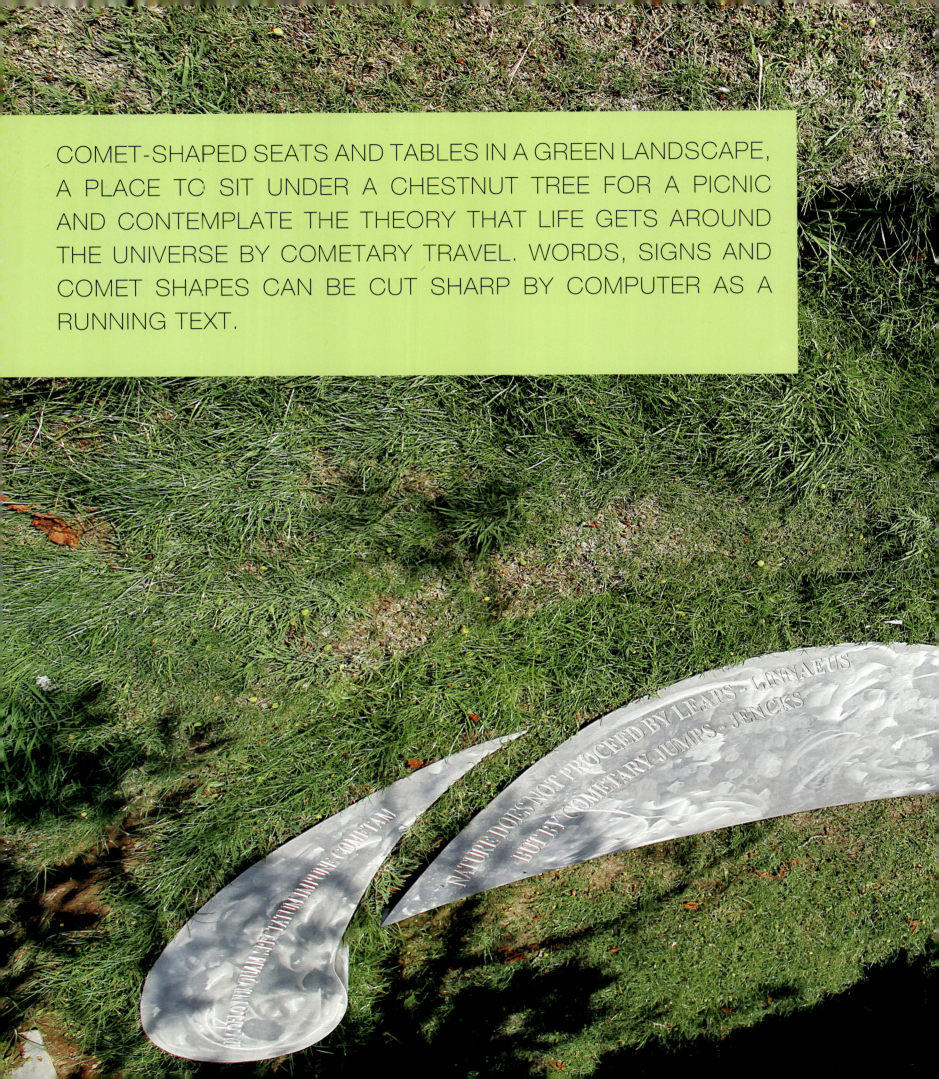

COMET-SHAPED SEATS AND TABLES IN A GREEN LANDSCAPE, A PLACE TO SIT UNDER A CHESTNUT TREE FOR A PICNIC AND CONTEMPLATE THE THEORY THAT LIFE GETS AROUND THE UNIVERSE BY COMETARY TRAVEL. WORDS, SIGNS AND COMET SHAPES CAN BE CUT SHARP BY COMPUTER AS A RUNNING TEXT.

NATURE DOES NOT PROCEED BY LEAPS · LINNAEUS

BUT BY COMETARY JUMPS · JENCKS

GIOVANE

Rebus area

0

12

Nascita

0'00"
_nascita dell'universo

5'00"
l'atomo

24

28

1

41

gennaio

febbraio

NATURAL RHYTHMS OF TIME ARE MARKED IN THIS GARDEN AS HEARTBEATS, DAYS OF THE YEAR, LIFE AND THE UNFOLDING OF THE UNIVERSE OVER 13.7 BILLION YEARS. THE SYNCOPATION OF VARIOUS TIMES IS CONVEYED THROUGH WRITINGS, SIGNS, REBUSES AND FORMS.

THE
UNIVERSE IN THE LANDSCAPE
LANDFORMS BY CHARLES JENCKS

FRANCES LINCOLN

FOR JOHN
MY SON
FOR HIS
GENEROSITY
OF SPIRIT

Writing and design are different kinds of pleasure that engage different parts of the mind. And the tenacious skill of getting things built to a designer's intention takes a willpower and conviction in short supply. So my gratitude for any qualities you might find in this book and these landscapes goes to friends, clients and other designers. First to my immediate helpers, the Head Gardener at Portrack, Alistair Clark, who continues to aim for the highest standards of garden realization; to Margherita Brianza, who struggled, as I did, to realize Spirals of Time, in Milan; and to Madelon Vriesendorp, who has constantly helped make models, draw and chat, with good humour – the muse of difference.

Nicky and Robert Wilson, whose landforms you see on the cover and elsewhere, were the ideal clients that one reads about in fiction, those who care for an artist's intentions and then make sure they are carried through, but adding their own expertise in the process.

This book was first mooted by my agent and long friend, Ike Williams, and by my publisher, John Nicoll, whom I have also long admired. Their faith in the project, and patience, has been a considerable impetus, and once again I am beholden to my PA, Gillian Innes, who did the initial layout, and Michael Brunström, who carried out the final design and editing. God, if not in the details, is in the integrating of idea and image, and the prescient semicolon. Many at Frances Lincoln Ltd will have helped in the birth and delivery of this second child, the younger sister of *The Garden of Cosmic Speculation*. To them, and my wife Louisa Lane Fox, and my son John Keswick Jencks – constant critics – special thanks for making some of the design less bad. My daughter Lily Clare Jencks and I are embarked together on the Cern Project that ends the book, as the team Jencks2 – a collaborative duo of architecture and landscape I hope continues in the future.

All the photos in this book are my own, except where otherwise noted.

Frances Lincoln Ltd
4 Torriano Mews
Torriano Avenue
London NW5 2RZ
www.franceslincoln.com

ISBN: 978-0-7112-3234-1

Printed and bound in China

1 2 3 4 5 6 7 8 9

CONTENTS

PART ONE
LANDFORMS

1: THE UNIVERSE IN THE LANDSCAPE

Content-driven

To see the universe in a landscape is an imaginative act that does not require special qualifications. It is a natural way of viewing things and is common to all ages. Probably every culture has made a garden in the image of a larger nature. Children play with such comparisons between the very big and small and, since the ancient Egyptians, gardens have been designed as if they were an idealization of the cosmos. And since the eighteenth century the British have made a landscape tradition of seeing all of nature 'as a garden'. Moreover, the comparison between the large and small, the macrocosm and microcosm, has been well versed in literature since William Blake wrote these lines, in 1803:

> To see a World in a Grain of Sand
> And a Heaven in a Wild Flower
> Hold Infinity in the palm of your hand
> And Eternity in an hour.

Seeing the world in a grain of sand or holding eternity in one hour is a basic metaphorical act that takes imagination and willpower. For me it is essential in creating landforms, sculptural earthworks that relate us to the rest of nature and the cosmos. Landforming, according to this definition, is the art of using nature to speculate on nature, to play with its shapes, manipulate it aesthetically and find uses for the result. Sometimes nature does not bend to our will, but even when it doesn't, it often sculpts the earth much better than we could possibly imagine. The Grand Canyon is an example. Also, as every gardener knows, nature can die or grow awry, be a mess and thus spoil a concept of design. Whatever the results, nature and we are on a par, fatefully engaged, different but equal, and parts of a dialogue – the subjects of this book.

Landform Ueda, Scottish National Gallery of Modern Art, Edinburgh (2002). 'Strange attractors', wave patterns that are attracted to a single or multiple basins, are a recent concept of science, underlying many self-organizing systems such as the heart and the weather. Here the Ueda attractor and Henon attractor (shown in the water) lie behind the paths and twists.

The landforms shown here are part of a larger project that I will touch on from time to time, one that is explored in the prequel and twin to this book, *The Garden of Cosmic Speculation*. They use nature to think about the ultimate forms and laws of nature, which I call Zero Nature, because these elements and laws underlie reality before anything grows: such things as gravity, DNA, black holes and galaxies. These forces I believe form the basis for a universal iconography, that is, a system of icons and symbols that is virtually eternal. My work explores how this system can be brought to life and made intelligible and aesthetic, if not always beautiful (for ugliness in the right place is also important). These landforms and gardens are part of a larger project, which I have outlined elsewhere and on which many others, artists and scientists, are engaged.[1] This larger 'Universe Project' could be a positive influence on the art of the next millennium. But, among other things, my writing and landforms are intended as a critique of the reigning mode of art current today, which is a kind of economic-driven fashion.

My work differs from this in being more content-driven. Nearly every design has some concept of nature or the cosmos behind it, motivating the patterns and rhythms. In the first section of this book these patterns relate to waveforms and the basic organizational types called strange attractors, the whirlpool motions that underlie hurricanes and the pulsating waves of our heart and mind. Landforms usually are built of earth and turf, and these elements usually self-organize in broad waves of contours pulled around an attractor basin. Paths, with continuous curves and sharp edges, form the basic grammar. As a style, it could be called Contour Gardening, in which the hidden contour lines of a map are made expressive at the surface by sharp paths, metal lines, planting or a combination of all these. As an art it underscores the strange attractors that clays and gravel tend to form from earth moving or the movement of a river. So the content-driven work in these first chapters is focused on the organizational forms themselves. The units of the universe are here the basic patterns of dynamic matter.

In the second section, the themes switch to a pursuit that is universal only to *Homo sapiens*, that is: identity. Here I base landforms on characteristics that define local, national and cosmic

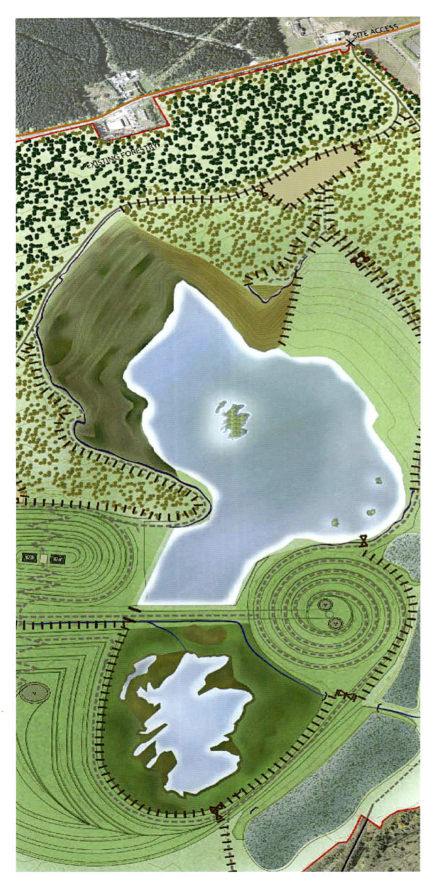

Scotloch, The Fife Earth Project, Fife (2009). A lake in the shape of Scotland's coast, a fractal landscape, is at the centre of several large mounds that represent the continents the Scots settled.

history. In a park in Milan, the content focuses on the city's past and the notion of time. In the landforms in Scotland it is driven by national identity and the way the Scots spread around the world in a creative diaspora from their motherland. In Germany it deals with the destruction of communities and their possible 'memories of the future': memories that will be sustained if these traces of identity are transformed and rebuilt as lakes and landforms.

The third section concerns further forces of destruction – war, murder and death – themes that have long had a place in landscape iconography. Garden art is necessarily concerned with the annual end of life and its planned or unplanned extinction (gardening is the editing and the constant re-organization of chaos). In these landforms and gardens I am looking for new adequate metaphors, for visual and existential elements that convey the impact, beauty and even humour of death. The fourth section, however, returns to the theme of formidable life, its overpowering nature. Here it is fecundity and the invention of living forms that are the theme, the way they may manage to outsmart the Grim Reaper and roar back on its corpse. In these works the subjects are the spread of life by comets, panspermia, an idea gathering adherents; or the natural metaphors of life in its basic units – DNA and the cell – life as basically unsuppressible. My conclusion, the fifth part, is another conjecture. It explores the way all of this, especially our relation to the cosmos, has implications for the rest of culture and not least design. Most of my own work is content-driven, and seeks to derive new form-languages from this content.

Of course some notable artists, even brand-driven ones, are engaged by such themes. On occasion, Damien Hirst creates a convincing tableau of life and death, as in *The Tranquillity of Solitude (For George Dyer)*, in which three sheep are placed inside vitrines, in their death throes, but depicted most poignantly. However, since the late 1990s much of this art has been market-driven, one-skull-deep, without any interest in exploring the basic units of the universe except those units of exchange. 'What I paint is money,' as Andy Warhol used to say when he started the most recent trend of inflationary culture, 'making money is art, and work is art and good business is the best art.' Some artists, and garden artists, have resisted this. As Ian Hamilton Finlay used to say, emphasizing the critical: 'Certain gardens are described as retreats when they are really attacks.' It is necessary to attack with gardens the monoculture of fast money, but also to criticize with irony; for who knows where they too will evolve? In global culture money has now become a universal cipher, a metaphor for inter-changeability. Hence I have used it too (see page 233), but as a macrocosmic sign of organelles within the cell, not as the Warholian motive. Like the mitochondria in our body, money is a form of condensed energy.

Thus my work is a gentle polemic aimed at the reductive mentality of the market and also the scientists who fashion simplistic metaphors – 'big bang', 'selfish genes', 'wimps and machos' – those figures of speech dreamed up to stimulate an adolescent culture. But it is concerned more with drawing novel conclusions than criticizing the present, opening up new metaphors. I think Finlay, a friend of many years from Scotland, was right when he said gardens can be attacks (as they were in the eighteenth century) but for me they promise alternative ways of seeing.

Metaphors to See By

There is a case to be made that all we can see and know is relationship, that we can only understand one object, anything, in terms of another thing. This is certainly true of experiencing the new and the unknown. For a while, a new thing is always perceived in terms of past experience, as if our nervous system were a lazy old fogey unable to rouse itself from dogmatic slumber. The reason for this conservative streak is that thought and perceptions are comparative, or radically metaphorical. A 'meta-phor' is literally the 'carrying over' of one idea to another, or the using of one object for another function, or 'seeing as'. For instance, seeing the landscape as 'like' a garden means finding the elements they have in common. A famous example that changed landscape design in the eighteenth century was the English 'ha-ha': a way of hiding a fence by sinking it below sight. That illusion elicited the gasp when stumbled upon – 'ah-ha'! William Kent, with this invention, 'leapt the fence, and saw that all nature was a garden'. He saw how the garden could be extended with the ha-ha all the way to the total landscape. Metaphor, in this case, consisted of seeing the garden as continuous with nature, and in my case here, the reverse: seeing the universe as shrunk down and discovered in the landscape. Shrinking macrocosm to microcosm.

Consider the metaphors I have criticized, ones that most scientists use when discussing the ultimate questions: how the universe started (our 'big bang' birth), what motivates us (selfishness) and in what the ultimate stuff of dark matter may consist ('weakly interacting massive particles' – wimps – or 'massive compact halo objects' – machos). Ultimate reality is compared to fairly unpleasant things; it is not a club worth joining. When scientists were confronted by the radically unfamiliar, the big questions, they had a choice and unfortunately settled on reductive answers. This has implications for the rest of society as the basic stuff of the universe is 'seen as' a theatre of warfare, an alienating view of our relationship to nature and the cosmos.

As Virgil said, 'we make our destinies through the gods we choose'. We invent, sometimes absent-mindedly, the figures of speech through which we grasp things, and then these words or phrases shape behaviour. In *Metaphors We Live By* (1980), linguists George Lakoff and Mark Johnson have shown how powerful this mode of perception can be. Everyday metaphors of the body

Water War Garden, Chaumont (2004). Water spills over channels whose chaotic rise and fall creates a drumbeat of war. Other interactive features include waterpults and a chaotic waterwheel seen in the distance.

Comet Bridge, Portrack (2009). A bridge connecting two parts of a garden transforms the iconography of a comet into seats, railings and a flaring tail, among other natural signs of these interplanetary visitors. One theory gaining credence today is that comets are behind the spread of life throughout the universe.

and human relationships pervade all thinking, not just rhetorical speech, and they drive us in certain directions. They insinuate themselves into language and then colour, if not determine, thought. You can write off the contemporary age, a hedge-funder might say; it is driven by monster metaphors and they will drive it mad. Luckily this is not true, and metaphors only inflect not control thought, for my 'driving' one is just another figure of speech, not a hard-wired command that must be followed. But they do influence culture and, like a nation, make it more or less worth inhabiting.

Consider the Big Bang Selfish Macho Universe – to pile high the standard models. In pondering these clichés and criticizing the ones that arose from the Newtonian model – above all the clockwork universe – I realized they shared a mechanistic quality based on the deep metaphors of control, predictability, determinism, sameness, lack of change and death. Of course the romantics had railed against this view of nature for two hundred years, but to little effect, because the science was against them. It was only when the chaos and complexity sciences came on stream in the 1970s that a more dynamic framework started to supplant the Newtonian, and it led me to a metaphor that was counter to clockwork: the idea of a 'jumping universe'. This became the title of a book, *The Architecture of the Jumping Universe* (1995), which presented the surprising and creative jumps in organization through which the cosmos has developed. And then it became the visual metaphor of steps, platforms and ascent up through history, in the Universe Cascade at Portrack. The story of the universe, its history over 13.7 billion years, was translated into the content for each platform, carrying the major stages of evolution. These plateaux are, in evolutionary time, a jump from one epoch to another. The choice of the metaphor was a critique of the usual notion that evolution *only* proceeds slowly and smoothly, step by step. Catastrophes and the fast creative responses are equally important.

One day it happened that a TV film crew was shooting near this cascade with the Astronomer Royal, Martin Rees (who is now head of the Royal Society), on a programme series he was making. We met at the base and, since Martin was a friend, we sat down together on the edge of a small turf mound (representing one of a series of universes) and had a chat. I asked him a question that had been preoccupying me for a long time, about whether there are discernible directions in cosmic history, some progress, some growth in complexity. In spite of obvious periods of regress and catastrophe, I posed the question: 'Is the universe going anywhere or – as Winston Churchill said about history – is it just one crazy thing after another?'

Rees fielded it completely, shifting to the subject of metaphor: 'I think we have got to celebrate the wonder, mystery and

LEFT: The Universe Cascade: a metaphor of the jumping universe, among other visual analogies. Water falls down, time jumps up. The steps, rocks and platforms tell a story of increasing complexity, a history in fits and starts, setbacks and catastrophes. Cosmogenesis is the narrative of an increasing organization and larger scale, but it is not the smooth Darwinian history that is usually recounted.

ABOVE: Martin Rees in *The Garden of Cosmic Speculation*, ZDF-Arte Production, produced by Achim Menges, directed by Christoph Schuch (2005).

beauty of the universe, and what I like so much about what we see in this garden is that you have devised lots of metaphors and analogies for the features of the universe, and the idea of multiple universes, and the idea of time and evolution etc. This is very valuable because I *don't* believe we can ever have more than an incomplete and metaphorical understanding of the deepest aspects of reality. That's why, although in some senses a religious person, I am not in favour of dogmatic religion, and suspicious of anyone who claims to have more than a vague and metaphorical understanding of deeper reality. I know it is hard understanding even a hydrogen atom. I think because of the limitations of our brains we have to learn in a limited way through metaphors that encapsulate *part* of the truth, and what I think is wonderful is that here you've devised so many metaphors which are both enlightening and aesthetically sublime.'

This displacement of my question was gratifying, especially because Martin Rees comes to the issue of metaphor and meaning as a leading representative of science. I too believe metaphor is essential for understanding, but obviously only one mode of thought and not as detailed as algorithmic cognition. And as Rees mentioned, it always contains extraneous material. All metaphors are false in some respect, and capture the salient quality of things better or worse. The so-called Universe Project, mentioned above, is hence both a critical and creative search for better metaphors, those more cogent than the reductive ones we have inherited from modernism. The 'big bang' relates us to the origin event, our birth as it were, in Pentagon language. But this moment was not 'big' (it was a quark-sized event expanding in a microsecond to the size of a grapefruit, which is not huge either) and it was not a 'bang' (no one heard it). As a metaphor it is equivalent to saying your mother was a firecracker. Rather, at the beginning of time it was the 'Hot Stretch' of space, for a few microseconds expanding faster than the speed limit of the universe, the speed of light. The radiation was indeed hot but it was the stretch that really mattered. According to inflation theory this runaway expansion of space balanced the many forces to miraculous precision, at least miraculous enough to keep it going in delicate equilibrium for the next 13.7 billion years, and get us here.

In spite of my efforts for ten years, no one has paid much attention to the 'Hot Stretch' – no doubt there are better metaphors. But one doesn't always fight hoping to win; sometimes it is enough to laugh, and there is some black humour in the Pentagon language. In Italy in the 1960s, James Bond, another avatar of the firecracker view, was called 'Kiss Kiss, Bang Bang'. No doubt his view of life prevails among those who favour multiple universes.

The Universe Project is the implicit agenda of artists, scientists and those with a cosmic view who recognize the way the traditional religions have been overtaken by developments of the last two hundred years. It refers to explicit discoveries in the sciences, especially recent ones that emphasize the self-organizing universe, the complexity and chaos sciences that reveal patterns of life and the way, for instance, the weather or a galaxy organizes itself. But the orientation it aims at is cultural, not scientific. It is critical and spiritual in the broad sense of those terms. As the reader will find here the metaphors of science are often criticized.

The Universe Project is also the implicit goal of many scientists, such as Stuart Kauffman (*At Home in the Universe*, 1996), who wish to draw metaphysical conclusions from their research, but it also drives artists who search for a timeless art based around universal or deep patterns. The project thus cuts across the usual divides of theism and atheism, prehistory and modernism, to mention only two splits of recent history. What does 'recent' mean in this context? Well, religion and science are only some 5,000 years old while *Homo sapiens* has been speculating on cosmic events and existence for at least 80,000 years. This long-time dimension of our species is relevant for several reasons. It puts in perspective the present ideological struggles, which are shown to be somewhat provincial by comparison. It also reminds us that many cultures in prehistory had a cosmic orientation that understood the importance of a larger nature and, like us, saw it as chaotic and benign, emergent and unpredictable, creative and repetitive.

There are many dimensions to the Universe Project beyond the scientific and spiritual, and two are relevant here: the role of metaphor in art and the landscape, and the importance of patterns in design and nature. For both subjects see the text opposite, but for references to pattern formation, see the important work of mathematicians and such popular writers as Ian Stewart and Philip Ball. They have elucidated much of the recent investigations into nature's art and pattern-making, following the epochal work of Ernst Haeckel in the nineteenth century and D'Arcy Wentworth Thompson in the twentieth. See for instance Ian Stewart's *What Shape is a Snowflake?: Magical Numbers in Nature* (2000) and Philip Ball's *Nature's Patterns: A Tapestry in Three Parts* (2009) among their many publications. Both of these authors, mathematician and generalist, are key authors for the new paradigm. A recent summary of this movement in design and art is found in Mark Garcia, 'The Patterns of Architecture', *Architectural Design* (November/December 2009).

I have discussed the Universe Project many times. See *The Garden of Cosmic Speculation* (2003, 2005), pp. 186–7, and also an article of that name published in *Science & Public Affairs* (December 2008), pp. 6–7, or a fuller discussion in 'Cosmogenesis and the Universe Project' in *Critical Modernism: Where is Post-Modernism Going?* (Wiley-Academy, London, New York, 2007), pp. 145–81. See also my 'Towards an Iconography of the Present', published in *Log: Observations on Architecture and the Contemporary City* (New York, Fall 2004), and *The Iconic Building: The Power of Enigma* (2005), especially the last chapter.

A NOTE ON THE UNIVERSE PROJECT

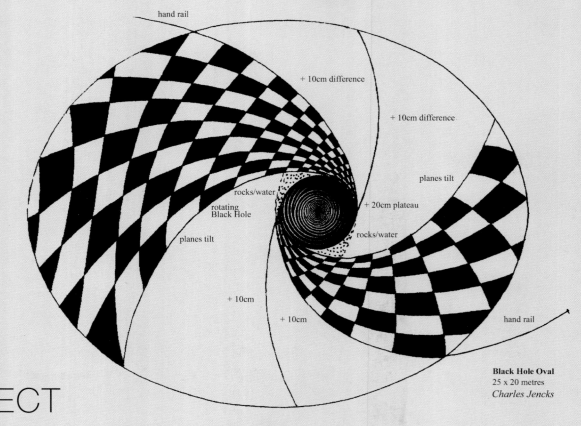

Black Hole Oval
25 x 20 metres
Charles Jencks

ABOVE: Black Hole Terrace, Portrack (1995–6). The extreme warp of space and time by gravity is visualized as distortions of a grid, and the metaphor of blackness by black rips in the environment.

RIGHT: Wu Chi, Olympic Forest Park, Beijing (2008). A large oval of space is tilted by a river. Visitors spill into either side towards a central rotating black hole where a turntable, with a visual illusion of a vortex, provides a further sensation of gravity.

Is Black Hole a Good Metaphor?

Another of the most important units of the universe (if one sees the origin of things as a unit of time) is the 'black hole'. This is also an event or self-organizing process that arises in time, but out of supergravity. Characteristically black holes occur with the extreme compression of matter as stars collapse under their own gravity. They exist at the centre of every galaxy and billions more may lie away from the centre also. But, like the atom and DNA, they are fundamentally creative units. Therefore for art and landscape they become possible icons of lasting importance, elements for a new iconology.[2] My first designs on the theme of a black hole, in 1995, brought out the salient qualities of its blackness and holeness. Black rips in the landscape underscored the way it lacerates space apart, sucks holes between us and distant galaxies so that no light escapes and we cannot see them (we see only their disturbance of the void). This violence, blackness and warping of spacetime became the visual metaphor of a dining terrace. However, as I was designing it, I became aware that, although a good metaphor in some respects, it missed the creative powers of these suction giants. Because they hold galaxies together, and create stars and planets in their embrace, I gave them the moniker 'Invisibilia': the mother of stellar things. Again, this act of naming has not overwhelmed the lexicographers, nor has there been a rush of nomothetes at L'*Academie Française* to rename these generative units. But wait another thousand years; take the long view and black holes will get a better press, because they are not just destructive.

In effect, such content-driven design is double design, working as much on the meaning as on the form and function, criticizing and creating metaphors, looking for new languages to express new insights, from science and elsewhere, that relate us to the universe in a more sensuous and positive light. Science is the oldest unbroken vision of the universe, but glasses always need a clean.

When the China Sculpture Institute asked me to design something for the 2008 Olympic Park in Beijing, we settled on the warped landform of a black hole, but also came up with an interactive, spinning centre: the singularity into which all curved lines of force pull space and time. Once again, real gravity is used to draw in the participant – you fall towards the centre – but once there you can now spin a turntable. This has spirals of black and silver that wobble and seem to suck you inwards. We also debated the meaning of the concept because the Chinese were no more pleased with 'black hole' than I was: a metaphor for the economic sink, social catastrophe and unattractive body parts. After some discussion we settled on *wu chi*, variously translated as 'energy everywhere' and 'the mother of everything', suggesting the quantum vacuum all around us that is always seething with energy, the creative void where particles come in and out of existence all the time. This last idea may be esoteric and invisible, but the supergravity is very much present and felt in the warped diamonds of metal and green, and the slope. In effect, *wu chi* pulls everything towards the centre of our galaxy and here, at the sculptural centre with the turning vortex,

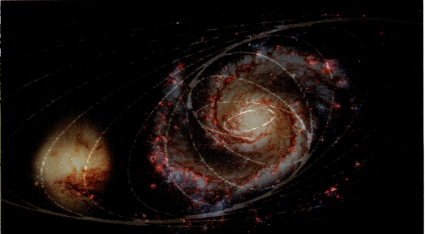

The Whirlpool Galaxy, admired since the eighteenth century for its stunning self-organization, is now understood to be tied to a smaller gallaxy, and they are mutually stripping each other of energy and matter. This striking relationship, also evident in binary stars and black holes, is diagrammed in drawings, and it becomes the idea behind several projects, including a roundabout, jewellery and landforms (under construction at Crawick). Note another recent discovery seen in the overlaid lines: the double arms of the Whirlpool are actually not permanent structures, but created by a travelling density wave that moves through the stars and gases in space.

the visual illusion works like a whirlpool. Other signs, indeed nearby plaques with writing, explain some of the meanings of these unfathomable creatures. Supplementary systems and epigraphy are part of the mixed genre that is landforming.

Spirals, helices, and patterns of recurrent curves have been my constant source of inspiration because they are so prevalent in nature and are also good structural forms. The ubiquitous spiral underlies weather patterns; it constitutes many strange attractors where two forces compete, one pulling towards the attractor basin – the central hole of blackness – the other at an angle to it. It underlies galaxies and bodies that rotate around a moving centre, because the recurrent circle-plus-linear movement generates a spiral. 'Spirals of time': this image of universal self-organization became the major metaphor of my landforms – of roundabouts, parks, DNA sculpture and jewellery. Most of my designs deploy it in a particular way, with self-similar, contiguous lines, where one trajectory of the spiral transforms the previous one into an almost-repeating swirl. The fractal patterns of flow, like those in a turbulent river, are nearly the same. They create a type of vibrating lines and an aesthetic I call Linearism.

You can see them best in moving liquids, such as soapsuds in the bathtub going down the drain, or through a telescope trained on the red spot of Jupiter, where many turbulent lines bubble in both harmony and agitation. The eye of a hurricane generates spiral swirls around its attractor basin, furrows of white and black clouds. Photographs of these shapes from the ground and the air reveal the ubiquitous shapes, and collecting such extraordinary cloud patterns has emerged as a popular pastime

LEFT: A digitized black hole dress design: a warped landscape with spirals and attractors warping a similar geometric pattern. Morphing geometries in a smooth continuum is natural to computer design (Charles Jencks, Gillian Innes).

BELOW: Fractal Terrace, Portrack. The Platonic notion of nature, that the ultimate forms are regular solids, is seen to the left side. To the right is the recent fractal view of nature proposed by Benoît Mandelbrot. The terrace metamorphoses from primary forms to the more prevalent idea that nature is *mostly* made from irregular but self-similar elements. Since the underlying geometry seems to include both types, the rectangles turn to squares and then morph to rhomboids, irregular forms and then scale down to fractals. Note that, from a diagonal view, a spiral emerges quite spontaneously

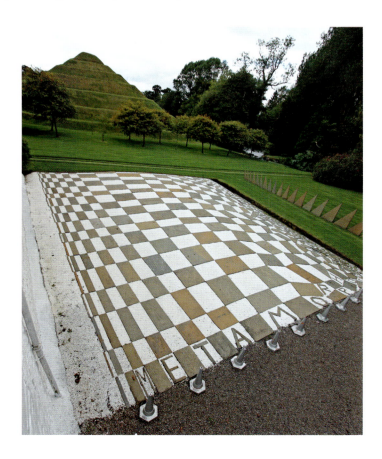

Cosmic Codes

The search for universal patterns of nature is also a major movement in the arts and architecture, cutting across ideologies and styles. Aided by computer design and digital production it is one of the strongest trends, especially in the fashion industry, where patterns of cloth and synthetic material can be manipulated with a virtuosity not easily attained in the past. The art of nature's fractals has been revealed not only by the computer but also by photographs of the infinitely small – the organization of the cell and the clustering of atoms – and by the very large – the edge of the universe shown by the Hubble telescope. In such ways, it is no exaggeration to say, our sensorium has gone cosmic in space and time. For instance, we now measure the second as the duration of 9,192,631,770 cycles of a radiating caesium atom. The microcosm and macrocosm are becoming second nature incorporated into an extended nervous system. Hence the Universe Project also stems from technical and informational evolution to which we are subject, like it or not.[3] Necessity pushes us in this direction – but compulsion is a bore. Much better is to be pulled by pleasure.

The most enjoyable way of assimilating its meaning is through games, art and fashion. Our creative play with patterns mirrors nature's recreation with the zebra's stripes. They both focus on the expressive plane of communication. The animal stripes apparently are meant to entertain members of the same species, while confusing all those of an alien one. Art is always about the abstraction of its own language. This self-concentration results in a superior form of ornament, but I feel the results go deeper when they are content-driven. Thus my design for a garden terrace plays with the language of rectangles to make a point about the geometry of the universe. They slowly turn into squares, then into rhomboids and finally into self-similar fractals, before they sink into the ground and re-emerge as a row of carefully graded teeth. This is an abstract game of black stone versus white pebble. They morph across the path of the visitor with the words 'metamorphosis' also changing in synch, but from a diagonal view other meanings emerge. In effect, as a consequence of designing rectangles to turn into fractals, other undesigned patterns appear quite spontaneously (once again it is the spiral), an unexpected bonus, a by-product of play. The last chapter will address this benign aspect of the universe.

But it is the content that also gives the shapes more power – here, the reference to nature's underlying geometry. Opposite opinions divide the field on what this geometry might be. For 2,000 years, people thought the ultimate forms of nature were Plato's regular solids, a supposition backed up by Euclidean geometry and other discoveries. Then, around 1900, irreducible chaos was uncovered by scientists such as Henri Poincaré, and various non-Euclidean geometries emerged. Today most classical and modern architecture is still built on the pattern of Plato's solids and is 'self-same' in its repetitions. But we now suspect that the geometry of nature, or at least most of it, is fractal, crinkly, irregular, grainy and 'self-similar' in pattern. The scientist and mathematician Benoît Mandelbrot wrote *The Fractal Geometry of Nature* in 1977, applying the new geometry successfully to clouds, coastlines, rocks, lightning and the stock market. Ever since these convincing demonstrations I have wondered if the two views could be presented together. The Fractal Terrace is the forced marriage, a continuous morph from Plato to Mandelbrot, from one worldview to the other.

For a long time we believed that nature's art was written in the language of mathematics. God, for Plato, the Jews and Christians, was a geometer using equations and an architect's compass, an idea that persists to the present day in the theory of superstrings (even if the geometry is madly laid out in eleven dimensions, and God is an impersonal, cosmic code). Mathematics and geometry are deep, but could it be that the patterns of the universe are deeper still? Could superstrings truly constitute the rock bottom, ultimate reality? Here opinion splits into perhaps equally valid parties, because it is possible that they could all be different versions of each other, at the same level of profundity. Whatever the case, the great race is on to decode these patterns, to diagram and transform them into art and architecture, to celebrate Nature the Great Artist.[4]

I have collected unusual and beautiful rocks for many years and, like the Chinese collectors, used them as partial compositions in small landscapes. They became miniature models for thinking about the larger landforms. At both of these scales I keep a parity between nature's art and my own, sometimes supporting the beauty or ugliness of the rock, sometimes contradicting it. These 'Metaphysical Landscapes' are a microcosm of the landforms, a type of bonsai, where words, signs, mathematics and mass-produced elements of industrial civilization all find a place, a very mixed media. For the Chinese collector, the rock patterns are always aesthetically superior, or striking. They can be repulsively so, like the celebrated yellow-wax rocks, or deeply attractive like a crystal. Either way these inherent qualities demand respect and honouring. You cannot approach nature's art today without mixed feelings, without the weight of history behind you, the knowledge that nature destroys wantonly while it creates. But, at the same time, there is always the surprise of an unknown novelty, the moving experience of seeing something beautiful for the first time. Depressing knowledge and innocent pleasure – both I find eternally present in nature's art.

Since the 1960s, land artists have played on this duality, and operated in the ambiguous area between the natural and artificial. Richard Long and Andy Goldsworthy, in different ways, have worked so spontaneously sometimes that they look as if they were part of unconscious nature, arranging earth or leaves as a termite might. Often they leave things in their primal state, but then mark their constructions with geometric forms that come from Euclid, creating lines, ovals,

A Metaphysical Landscape (2001). Beauty, in the centre, is admired right and left by ugliness and normality. Rocks are engaged in various kinds of discourse, while on the Platonic plane pure geometric solids surround a crevasse with writing, right, and are, in turn, surrounded by visual illusions – a parable.

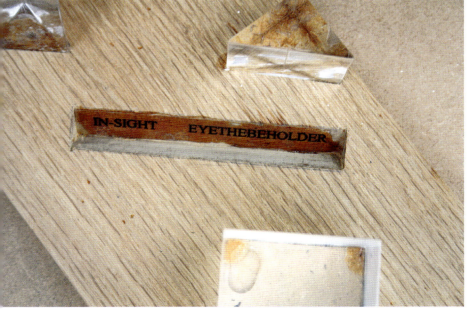

ellipses and arches. Significantly, Goldsworthy's father was a professor of applied mathematics at the University of Leeds. Their drama between innocence and knowledge, however, is underplayed. Most land art is created as a seamless passage between the cosmos and us, as if we were related to it in a straightforward way.

By contrast, my own rock art and landforms heighten the difference between nature's art and ours while giving them each a place. The Chinese have mounted wonderful-looking stones for millennia, called 'scholar's rocks', and made their pedestals look as natural as the minerals they hold (when in fact both are often highly worked). By contrast, the pedestals I devise have an equality with the rock, admit their artificiality and might even be put on top of the stone. Why? To celebrate our continuity with, and difference from, the cosmos; to accentuate the parity and highlight the different levels of nature.

We are at a place in cultural history when it is no longer possible to think of an easy harmony with the world, or a simple one. We discover the laws of nature, like $E=mc^2$, which sets us apart; we invent ways to suspend these laws momentarily, like flying. We augment our body with prosthetics – eyeglasses and computers – and in this way co-evolve with nature. We create a 'Second Nature' with our culture, and then further ones with waste. The global economy generates this layer most visibly in the land and sky around a city, by-products of the primary motive, which is survival. Just as perspiration results from the primary activity of exercise, so our work now creates an unconscious 'Fourth Nature', existing independently of intentions, like the weather. Because this is now such an important part of the landscape, I have addressed Fourth Nature, below, and turned it into a modest, if sometimes primitive, art. For the most part it is industrial scrap. The idea develops from older usage.

In the first century BC, Cicero named wilderness 'First Nature', and went on to designate farms, orchards and useful animals like sheep, cows and horses as forming a second type. The landscape writer John Dixon Hunt points out such useful distinctions in *Greater Perfections: The Practice of Garden Theory* (2000), and describes the sixteenth-century addition of 'Third Nature'. Characteristically this type is the garden, seen as 'nature improved by art'. Accepting this model as clarifying significant differences, I propose that we add another one at each end. Today we cannot escape the knowledge of a level *below* the growing variety of nature (what most people understand by the word 'nature' is something alive), that is, the laws of nature – gravity, electromagnetism, the strong and weak forces, etc. This is what I have termed 'Zero Nature'. Also, and just as inescapable, there is the waste that we now mass-produce.

Landforms, in the sense I am using the term, acknowledge these different types of nature and sometimes feature their contradictions or collisions. The small bonsai rock arrangements I have mentioned, the 'metaphysical landscapes', also heighten these various layers and they too use writing or epigraphy to underscore our difference from, and similarity to, the cosmos. The kind of cosmogenic art that interests me engages the mind, as well as the senses, and makes a claim on the deep truths that are revealed today through science (among other pursuits). It manifests such things as the diagrams of nature – the forces, constants, mental constructs and truths of the universe – and these may appeal only to those who take the trouble to decode them. In this sense it is a step beyond the seamless integration of land art and the Chinese scholar's rock, both of which I have found inspiring.

For those willing to go this step there are several rewards, including the pleasure of becoming involved in a plot. Hunt the symbol, track the narrative, follow Ariadne's thread, figure out the different layers of meaning. Even misreading is important as a motivating pleasure, because once you know there is a plot, new intentions will be discovered that were unsuspected. A garden and landform, like the universe in general, always create more meaning than intended. We live not only in a minimalist universe (a repressive one based on scarcity) under the slogan of Mies van der Rohe – 'less is more' – but also in a generous one. According to an epigram of the Nobel physicist Phil Anderson, it is an open and creative universe where 'more is different'. Add more of anything to a system and it will self-organize to a different level of meaning: true in physics, true in a garden. Thus a garden becomes a place of increasing meaning, asking to be read.

The enjoyment of decoding iconography used to be expected in a garden where it was meant to slow down perception, to make one pause and meditate, to sit down to read the signs both literal and metaphorical. This was true in the Italian Renaissance where the phrase 'festina lente' (make haste to go slow) was inscribed on stone. It was more pronounced in the Chinese garden, where inscriptions were carved into plaques on a wall, or written in giant characters painted over a pavilion entry, or placed in front of a classic view. These supplementary signs were like the colophons on a Chinese painting, barnacles of meaning that accreted with time as many visitors added opinions, changing interpretations ('more is different').

In one landform devoted to the 'Cells of Life' at Jupiter Artland in West Lothian (see pages 216–43), I used many different signs that relate to the cell's miraculous achievements: when it divides, turning one cell into two, or during fertilization, turning two cells into one. We are so used to this miracle, and it is taught in the schools as mitosis, among other things, that we take it for granted. We discount the extraordinary truth behind it. So, one of the areas of these mounds is devoted to a Mitosis Rill, which celebrates the double transformation. It uses a fountain and rocks, with conventional symbols of cell division. It employs models, epigraphy, numbers and flowing water to dramatize the shifts: two into one, one into two. Several key issues are raised by this approach.

Cosmic Inflation Pillows – eggs, stones, rocks and epigraphy – tiny landforms.

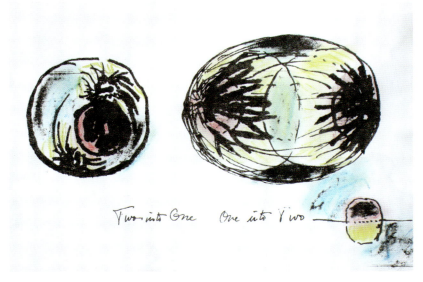

Cells of Life, using causeways, mounds, fountains, words and rocks to depict some of the extraordinary aspects of life. The way cells divide is portrayed in the Mitosis Rill, right, a fountain with six small waterfalls showing the major stages of cell division, how one cell becomes two. The nucleus at the centre of each cell becomes a seat with phrases underlining some relationships between the macrocosm and the microcosm. Particularly the Liesegang rocks, with their red target shapes, show parallels between the big and very small, the red crystals and the cellular organelles. 'One into Two' remains the overriding metaphor of life's power and creativity.

The Architecture of the Universe?

The first issue is comprehension. As they walk over the mounds, I do not expect everyone to decode these signs or understand the iconography all at once. As Walter Benjamin famously wrote of architecture: unlike a symphony, it is often experienced inattentively, and the landscape is often positively appreciated when it too is background ambience. One pleasure of being in the countryside is simply being without a purpose, or perhaps perceiving with a non-artistic frame of mind. At Jupiter Artland, one can drive a car between the mounds at 15 mph, and by design this vehicular track plays a role in the story of the 'cell walls'. So, the Renaissance garden rule – 'festina lente' (make haste to go slow) – is hardly enforced.

Some people will want to take more time, or come back when less pressed, and for them a second glance and a more extended text is provided. They can sit down on the cell seats, where there is writing and imagery that comment on the units of life – for instance, the difference between the animal and plant cell. It takes a little time to see the relationship between the model of the cell and the red spots of the Liesegang rocks, and not much education beyond introductory biology. But for those who make the effort, there is the celebration and the metaphor. The invisible microcosm of life is here blown up thousands of times, and its workings compared to the macrocosm of rock nodules. The similarities in colour, relative size and relationship are fascinating. The self-organizing cell is equated

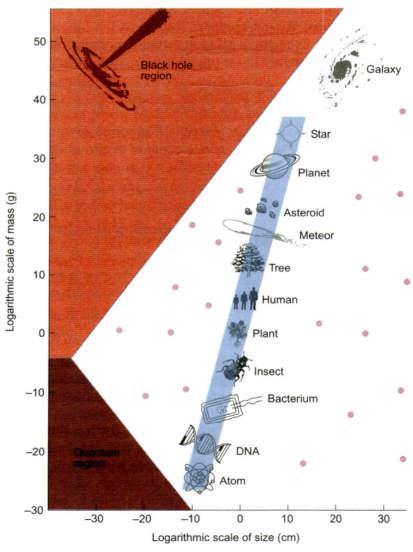

The conic sections (circle, parabola, etc.) are an old idea of universal architecture: pure geometrical shapes with a counterpart mathematical expression. The Greeks discovered the truth that well-aimed cuts of a cone could produce the well-formed figures of the circle, ellipse, parabola and hyperbola. Two other idealized forms also result, the point and line (not shown here). Thus six integral shapes come with one object, the cone, an excess of beauty at no extra cost.

The Architecture of the Universe. The pattern that connects, the blue line of cosmic density; the exceptions in red, inside a black hole, or the quantum regions; and large things that rotate like galaxies. Pink dots show the all-over expected variety of densities that don't exist. The density of atoms, the ratio of mass to volume, goes virtually all the way up and down. After John Barrow, *The Artful Universe* (Oxford University Press, 1995).

to the self-organizing Liesegang rock. You can sit your own bottom cells down on these rocks and think about it. As Le Corbusier said, 'in a work of art there are hidden masses of implications that reveal themselves to those who care'. This does not mean everybody all of the time or even anybody most of the time, but at least somebody some of the time.

The second key issue is the matter of choice. Which of the myriad elements of the universe are worth celebrating, or dredging up from the collective amnesia? As Braque said, 'reality only reveals itself when illuminated by a ray of poetry. All around us is asleep.' We are drugged by commerce and necessity. The truth is that we have become inured to some amazing cosmic elements by the way they are diminished within a utilitarian framework, discounted as last year's fashion, as dead stock. If familiarity breeds contempt, then over-familiarity with scientific terms – the atom, the cell, DNA, mitosis – often learned in school by rote, drains these universal units of their potency. We forget, or never perceive, that they are as close to magic as to be indistinguishable from it. Hence the Surrealist call to de-familiarize ourselves with the usual framing. Salvador Dalí, in his better moments, had a lifelong commitment to do that with the extraordinary insights of recent science. Four-dimensional space, quantum theory and DNA were some of the concepts he worked over. The Universe Project exists on many levels of contemporary science and the arts, but the third key question becomes: how do we choose the pertinent elements?

Obviously one answer is ready made: we cut reality into its ontological categories. As Plato said, the good carver cuts the chicken at the joints, the bad one hacks through the middle of the bones. So the customary divisions of science already furnish a well-sliced bird: obviously, the atom, DNA and the stars. Another standard of choice comes from the arts, and concerns aesthetics and the generic distinctions of geometry. Think of the famous conic sections as a type of universal architecture. If Plato sliced a cone at four or five well-aimed, geometric angles, he would get a perfect circle, ellipse, parabola and hyperbola – that is, 'architectural integers', intelligible figures. Here an old distinction helps, the opposition separating the mass of building from the rarity of architecture, the background noise from the foreground music, the 90 per cent from the 10 per cent. While no one will be happy with a permanent set of such oppositions – architecture versus building (the absolute hierarchy was overthrown in the nineteenth century) – the general distinction is worth reinventing when it comes to cosmic events. Every rock has some interesting feature, but only one in a million is distinctively formed and worth collecting. Likewise, every galaxy is interesting, but very few have the aesthetic quality of the great Whirpool Galaxy, discovered in 1773. In effect, most of the universe is building, and we have to discern the very small percentage that is more significant. The architecture of the universe is the metaphor of choice.

This architecture can be conceived not just in terms of the generic and well-formed shape, but also as the relationship between things, the underlying order that unites the microcosm to the macrocosm. Such structure has an eternal beauty that can be brought out best in a diagram. John D. Barrow, in his fascinating book *The Artful Universe* (1995), which analyses several of the ways nature is an artist, also shows the pattern that connects the very small to the large. A line of constant density unites the atom with the insect, the human with the planet and the star, and almost connects us all to the collection of galaxies. We are in the middle of this logarithmic scale of mass and size, a Cinderella location from which to observe this harmonic order. The balance between atomic forces of repulsion and gravity's forces of attraction creates the delicate equilibrium. As the diagram opposite shows, the exceptions are those things that depend on motion for structure, like galaxies, and those parts of the universe where the force balances are set very differently – the black hole and the quantum world. As Barrow points out, one expects that nature would explore all possibilities (as it does usually) and occupy all regions, that is, develop a variety of balance (shown in the pink spots). But it doesn't. There are only certain things allowed by equilibrium, and this creates grand architectural orders.

Landforms: The Hybrid and the Meaningful

Landforming has been a human activity for a long time. But before I propose a narrower definition for my own landforms, it is important to see how they fit into the recent history of land art developed since the 1960s for, in two ways, they extend that tradition: towards hybrid amalgamation and towards meaningful symbolism.

In the 1970s Rosalind Krauss, an art historian, addressed a confusion reigning in contemporary art: the impossibly wide and messy usage of the term 'sculpture'. In response, she wrote 'Sculpture in the Expanded Field' (1979), a seminal paper that exposed the fundamental problem with wit and logic. Pointing out the conservative nature of the label 'sculpture', which is applied indiscriminately to every kind of art that is not painting, she illustrates this sad fact with an amusing paradigm. It works on negative logic. Barnett Newman's revealing epigram sets the tone of permissive gobbledegook: 'Sculpture is what you bump into when you back up to see a painting.' This of course could be, and was, anything: a negative territory that was being explored, which jumped over habitual categories. 'Sculpture' was being used to describe things such as Christo's *Running Fence* and wrapped buildings, Robert Smithson's *Spiral Jetty* of 1970, a wooden maze by Alice Aycock constructed in 1972 and various earthworks and 'marked sites', such as a sunken, framed hole in the ground executed by Mary Miss in 1978. Sculpture was that which was absent. Also some of this was being discussed as 'land art', for instance work by Richard Long, because it certainly was art and clearly was in and of the land.

But Rosalind Krauss was not happy with such a partial renaming of the new field; she wanted to explore all the new categories at once and construct a kind of hyperspace of possibilities. Hence she devised a model that included Barnett Newman's not-painting (i.e. sculpture) and not-architecture and not-landscape, among other not-axes. This hyperspace becomes the 'extended field' for us to think about and place such things as Sol Lewitt's not-sculpture, that is, his exploration of mathematical white grids – what she calls 'axiomatic structures'. The diagram (opposite, above) is helpful and rightly warns us about assimilating every departure from a profession to previous categories. This is why her article became so important for thinking about contemporary practice. But it raised two fundamental problems. You cannot define things by what they are not, for the obvious reason this includes an infinite number of categories. Secondly, it overrates the negativity in recent 'not-sculpture' which is *not* trying to exclude so much, but rather aiming to be positively hybrid. Often it is not *against* sculpture or architecture or landscape, but a partial synthesis of each field.

This is particularly true of my own landforms. They are combinatorial, and their aim is not to get away from past genres but to mix them, the better to communicate an idea. Being content-driven, they have to combine different fields, since sculpture, architecture and landscape on their own may not be enough to get a concept across. Supplementary fields are needed – such as painting or epigraphy, or any mixed media for the job at hand. Landforming, or at least mine, is thus more like opera than it is like exclusionary art. Compared to minimalist art, landforms might be thought messy, impure and polyglot. But these, largely aesthetic, terms miss the point, which is that they intend to signify many things beyond aesthetics, and must use various signs to do so.

The landform, as I am using the term, operates between the categories because it combines various signifying material. In my case, it brings together the different levels of nature, those I have mentioned above: the laws of nature, from industrial waste through to basic cosmic realities. Reconfiguring Krauss's diagram (opposite, below) reveals some of the positive combinations. The top left shows one of the strongest hybrids today, landscape urbanism, a movement that has emerged around the world but is typified by West 8 in Holland. Their work often combines the social and economic necessities of a public park, and this is true of my Parco Portello in Milan (pages 63–85) and the Fife Earth Project in Scotland (pages 118–27). The top right of the diagram shows another current mixture, the iconic building that emerges from signifying forces of architecture and urbanism in the cityscape. The structure may have to become a gateway or identifying image, one purpose of Northumberlandia, outside Newcastle (pages 48–59). Like 'sculpitecture', a word Antony Caro uses about some of his own large metal constructions (lower right), it might be a hybrid of sculpture

Richard Long, *Tame Buzzard Line* at Roche Court, Wiltshire (2001). A line, 35m long by a thin 71cm wide, points in the landscape at the terrace steps. The white and grey flint is dramatically set off by grass, but this strong form has no discernible reference other than its materiality and the enigmatic title (Are there tame buzzards here?). The typical sign of Land Art leaves the meaning up to you, a theme of Colin Renfrew's book about prehistory and contemporary art.

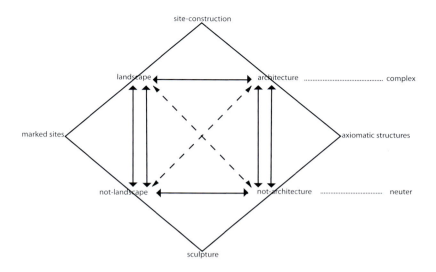

Diagram of expanded definitions of sculpture, after Rosalind Krauss, 'Sculpture in the Expanded Field', October, 1979.

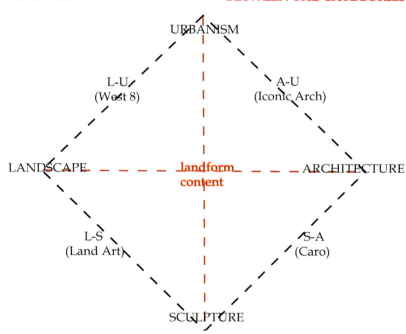

Landform: Between the Categories. Being content-driven, as they often were in the past, my landforms combine disciplines often separated by specialization. This diagram is in two-dimensions and shows only four fields, but clearly other incommensurate areas should be included – epigraphy and signage above all. A hyperspace diagram would be necessary to show the usual combinations.

and architecture (such as my Rail Garden in Scotland). Or (bottom left), it may combine landscape and sculpture, the usual hybrid case of land art. This diagram hardly exhausts all the combinations of a landform with other media, but it does illustrate the motivating force that pulls the genres together: content.

The Garden of Scottish Worthies (discussed more fully below pages 86–117) illustrates the hybrid landform driven by content. Because it was created as a result of having to move a railway line, its subject became industrialization and movement: the train that still runs here. It signifies progress and thus the Enlightenment. Because it is constructed from the fourth type of nature, industrial waste – old bridge sections, rails and concrete ties – it contrasts this with the other three kinds. Because the Scots were particularly involved in the eighteenth-century Enlightenment, and led the world in several respects, each of the Worthies becomes personified as an industrial railway car, given a name, dates and several relevant epigrams. Thus the garden combines epigraphy, land art, sculpture and an urban scale (if not architecture): a typical mixture that classifies it as existing between the categories. It is not a negation of them. My argument is that this is in the larger tradition of landforming going back centuries and millennia, an idea taken up in the following chapters and addressed in the conclusion.

Notes

1. See, for instance, *The Garden of Cosmic Speculation* (Frances Lincoln, London, 2003, 2005), pp. 186–7, and also an article of that name published in *Science & Public Affairs*, London, December 2008, pp. 6–7. The Universe Project is the implicit goal of many scientists such as Stuart Kauffmann (*At Home in the Universe*, 1996), who wish to draw metaphysical conclusions from their research, but it also drives artists who search for a timeless art based around universal or deep patterns. The Universe Project thus cuts across the usual divides of theism and atheism, prehistory and modernism, to mention only two splits of recent history. Recent? After all, religion and science are only some 5,000 years old, while *Homo sapiens* has been speculating on cosmic events and existence for at least 80,000 years. See also 'Cosmogenesis and the Universe Project', Chapter 5 of *Critical Modernism: Where is Post-modernism Going?* (Wiley-Academy, London, New York, 2007), pp. 145–81.

2. The Universe Project in search of a new iconography worth celebrating is the subject of *The Garden of Cosmic Speculation*, op. cit., and my work; see also my 'Towards an Iconography of the Present', published in *Log: Observations on Architecture and the Contemporary City* (New York, Fall 2004); also *The Iconic Building: The Power of Enigma*, (Frances Lincoln, London, 2005), especially the last chapter.

3. See 'Cosmogenesis and the Universe Project' in *Critical Modernism: Where is Post-modernism Going?* (op. cit.), especially pages 145–86.

4. Mathematicians and such popular writers as Ian Stewart and Philip Ball have elucidated much of the recent investigations into nature's art and pattern-making, following the epochal work of Haeckel in the nineteenth century and D'Arcy Wentworth Thompson in the twentieth. See, for instance, Ian Stewart, *What Shape is a Snowflake? Magical Numbers in Nature* (2001), among his many publications, and Philip Ball, *Nature's Patterns: A Tapestry in Three Parts* (Oxford, 2009), among his numerous works. Both of these authors, mathematician and generalist, are key authors for the new paradigm. A recent summary of this movement in design and art is Mark Garcia, 'The Patterns of Architecture', *Architectural Design* (2009).

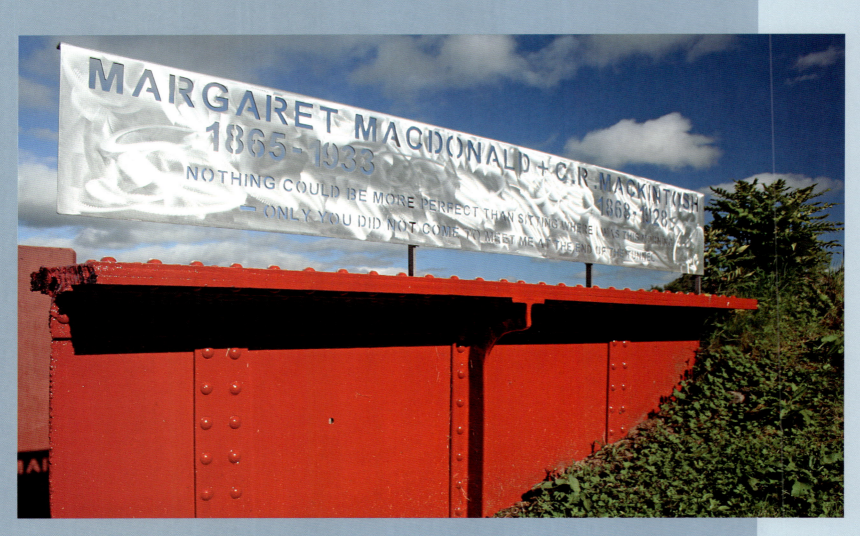

MARGARET MACDONALD 1865 - 1933 + C.R. MACKINTOSH 1868 - 1928.
NOTHING COULD BE MORE PERFECT THAN SITTING WHERE I WAS THIS MORNING
— ONLY YOU DID NOT COME TO MEET ME AT THE END OF THE TUNNEL.

A hybrid landform: The Garden of Scottish Worthies, Portrack (2004). This combines architecture (a new bridge, above left), epigraphy, 'moundettes', planting, and industrial waste including an old train (below right): Fourth Nature. Because of its place, next to a rail line, the underlying theme of this garden became progress and the Scottish Enlightenment. Content leads naturally to multiple systems of expression, between the categories.

2: LANDFORM UEDA

For more than 5,000 years landforms have served myriad functions: as mounds for burial, as sacred places and as high lookouts of defence. Since the 1970s land artists have extended this genre while, during the same period, archaeologists have looked closer at the evidence and come up with the notion that ancient landforms – Stonehenge is typical – were part of a huge 'ritual landscape'. Today landforms are even more hybrid and once again sites of pilgrimage. But the traveller is now more in search of Destination Art than a sacred ritual (unless Trial by Art Opening is experienced as a sacramental passage).

The Landform Ueda, outside Edinburgh's National Gallery of Modern Art, serves many functions. It shields the building and lawn from road traffic to the north. It acts as a gateway announcing the two museums which are on either side of a heavily used street and fitting into Terry Farrell's masterplan for the entire site. As a set of terraces, it was designed as an outdoor gallery from which to view sculpture on its pathways – from above, below and in movement – although it has yet to be used this way. As a walk-on sculpture, it was intended to communicate ideas of self-organizing nature, cosmic orientation and scientific insight into 'strange or chaotic attractors' (explained below). Finally it was meant to be a pleasant place to sit by the water and stroll, a respite from hectic city life and museum fatigue.

I pictured the landform on a sunny day crawling with people, a contemporary equivalent of Seurat's *La Grande Jatte*, with everything going on at once. Fashionable youngsters out on a Sunday walk, some fishing or eating lunch; others having a drink or chasing kites: recreation, bustle, contemplation. No fishing is allowed, but festivities do go on in summer months; it's a highly social place. When it opened in August 2002 I climbed on to the gallery roof and photographed fathers chasing their children across the terraces, lovers lying on the grass, other games – it was working.

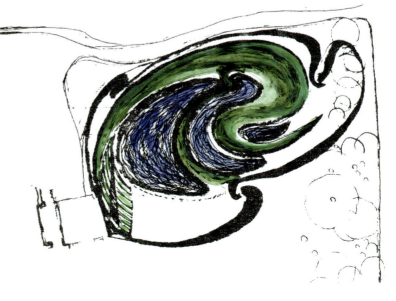

LEFT AND RIGHT: Landform Ueda was conceived to enliven a flat lawn and shield noise from the side road. It faces two ways, to the gallery and across the road to its sister, the Dean Centre. The connecting 'S' form also derives from two chaotic attractors, the Ueda and Henan (named respectively after Japanese and French scientists). With Terry Farrell & Partners and Ian White Associates. Construction supervised by Duncan Whatmore and Alistair Clark.

COMPETING SCHEMES

Given the sensitivity of the site and the requirement to buffer traffic, I modelled four schemes in competition with each other. Immediately apparent was that the highest part of the mound should be in the northernmost corner. Here it would be furthest from the gallery, at the lowest point of the site, and provide a natural focus for movement from the gallery terrace. It would cast a shadow on the road, not on the grass lawn, and it would be identifiable as a gateway or landmark from the main road.

THE DOUBLE-S

The dynamic Double-S has the virtue of protecting the trees and providing maximum surprise. It is envisioned to rise 35 or 40 feet at the northernmost point with paths that wrap over, giving two twists and exciting drama to movement. We soon realized, however, that it would extend too far into the site and compromise the space in front of the gallery.

THE GALAXY

The double spiral of paths allows visitors to go up and down in a continual flow, without even meeting. The problem is that it is too predictable – there is no discovery.

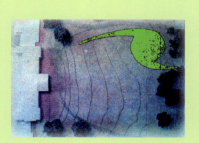

RESPECT THE GALLERY AND ITS SPACE

The next question concerned the particular forms. Which are the most dynamic and interesting and which enhance the site and impinge on the gallery the least? The neo-classical gallery relates to the grass lawn in a straightforward way: it commands this space as a villa does a flat parterre and one should respect this arrangement. The big problem with the existing grass lawn was its flatness and lack of focus – the amorphous space needed a strong counter-form.

THE SINGLE-S

The third scheme, pushed further to the north, impinged less on the flat green lawn and had one twist of movement. It is similar to the Snake Mound at Portrack, but there are two disadvantages: there is no causeway, a very important dramatic feature, and water would have to be at two levels, because of the drop in the site.

THE STRETCHED-S OR SERPENT

With its single twist affording two orientations, its causeway and the accentuation of the shape by the water, this was the best solution. It complemented the gallery, enhanced the space in front, impinged the least and did not disturb the existing trees. It also contained the sloping lawn, gave focus to movement from the terrace, acted as a gateway and buffered traffic to the north. As a landform it provided a route between the Dean Centre and the gallery connecting up a path that Terry Farrell's masterplan foresees extending to a very large area: a river walk by the Leith, the old cemetery and a garden by the Dean Centre. A great advantage, which would be unique, was that it would provide a path for viewing sculpture in the open air, from many positions – a dramatic promenade.

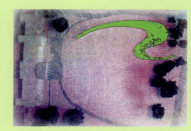

WALK UP THE MOUND

You first cross a fence, and a threshold of river-washed stones set in an S-curve, and then walk over the phrase 'festina lente' cut in aluminium. 'Make haste to go slow' is the admonishment for those entering, as it was in the Renaissance garden. The idea then was to slow visitors down by making them think hard about the ornament and symbolism. Here they have to decode the swirls in the aluminium sheet, the S-curves of the strange attractor underfoot. Also present are signs of the cardinal points, the sun and inner planets (on the man-hole cover) and other symbolic ornament. From here you descend to the steps for seating, or coast down the ramp and turn left, then mount a gently rising, thin arm of the mound. This invites you up slowly and branches into several paths. The arm has a slight curve. Nothing is ever straight, heightening the flat terraces in their relative movement. The high point, and culmination, is just before the switch-back, and it cups the view from the gallery containing the whole site and flat lawn. Here the view opens in all directions, and there's a choice. You can slowly descend on the S-curve, appreciating the water following the path on both sides, or else switch back and descend on a steeper slope to the road. The superiority of this design over the others is the way it gradually discloses the temple front of the gallery, then the whole building, thus providing a certain expectation and discovery.

STRONG WAVEFORMS IN NATURE: THE RESULT OF CONTRARY FORCES

Landforms relate us directly to the adjacent nature, that is, the sky above them and the earth below. They have become basic signs of the cosmos, both logically and historically. They also indirectly relate to recent discoveries, especially the new science of complexity, non-linear dynamics. Since constructed mounds are shaped by machines they naturally form linear, viscous shapes which resemble what are known as 'strange attractors' or 'chaotic attractors'. Two of the most interesting are the Lorenz Attractor, the 'Butterfly Effect', with its fortuitous-shaped wings forming a figure eight or butterfly and the Ueda Attractor, which has S-curves and switch-backs. Both attractors have inspired these and other designs.

Strange attractors also typify the shapes that underlie natural processes of self-organization. Occasionally, when a very few contrary forces are at work in nature – producing both positive and negative feedback – strong waveforms can result. Sometimes this form is hidden, as in the rocks of the Alps, where only the vertical section through the Simplon Pass shows its existence. Sometimes a strong form can emerge, such as the trains of vortices visible when a solid object is drawn through stationary liquids such as oil. Similar shapes, such as the red spot of Jupiter and its surrounding vortices, emerge because of planetary rotation. Occasionally sharp forms arise because of contrary forces of liquidity. For example, the veins of sand on the beach are caused by the ebbing of the tide versus the differential stickiness of sand. Lastly, invisible waveforms occur everyday over our heads in weather patterns, air currents that curl where streams of warm and cold air meet. (Drawings after Theodor Schwenk, *Sensitive Chaos: The Creation of Flowing Forms in Water and Air,* Rudolf Steiner Press, London, 1965.)

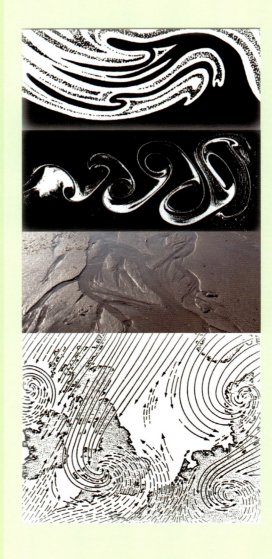

STRANGE ATTRACTORS

Landform Ueda has been developed in accordance with an analysis of certain forms occurring in nature and, in particular, those relevant to chaos theory. The Ueda and Henon Attractors – strange attractors generated by a series of simple transformations – have been used as inspirations for the modelling. There are three basic types of attractor. A pendulum oscillating in a series of ovals or circles is called a 'periodic attractor', because its trajectory almost repeats the same spacetime line over every oscillation, or period. As it runs out of energy the pendulum moves toward the centre of gravity, and thus aims at a stable 'point attractor'. Most living systems, and even non-living whirlpools, have a periodic attractor basin that changes slightly over space and time. These show order in chaos and are hence known as 'chaotic, or strange attractors'. The pulsations of the heart and the fluctuations in the brain as it contemplates a complex thought are the two strange attractors of most concern to us. In the late 1970s, the Japanese scientist Yoshisuke Ueda studied a 'chaotic pendulum', a non-linear electronic circuit with an external drive. From the simple chaotic swing of the pendulum, a complex, ever-changing pattern results, one that has similarities and switch-backs, S-curves and basins, embedded in its structure. This fascinated me because of its complex mixture of surprise and pattern, the way it symbolized not only order in chaos but also the way riverbeds and flowing material self-organize. S-curves and bulges have since become the inspiration for landforms that symbolize the growth of cells, the spiral of galaxies and the workings of thought and feeling.

VIRTUAL REALITY SIMULATION

A three-dimensional computer study of the landform was set up to explore the detailed nature of the volume encompassed by the form, and to assess the impact that this would have on the landscape adjacent to the Gallery of Modern Art. These gave a picture of the landform and here, in this rendering by Co-Evolution, one can also see the underlying spatial and structural dynamics. Digitizing landforms helps design but, given the broad variance of constructing with earth during rainstorms, it is only one more supplemental system. Redrawing, re-modelling and re-laying out with tape are just as important (see overleaf).

CHILDREN FOLLOWED BY GPS

One day on a school outing a swarm of children were tagged with GPS devices and told they could run all over the mound and explore it. The result of this tracking is eerily similar to the initial sketches of my first designs, continuous fluid motions left by the pencil. This aerial calligraphy fortuitously relates to the Nasca Lines in Peru that form various human figures, plants, animals and geometric structures. When seen first from an aeroplane, in the 1920s, they presented an archaeological mystery. How could people in AD 500 construct, on such an unfathomable scale, a figure that could not be perceived on the ground? We now believe the Peruvians danced and walked their forms into the desert, over many generations, in a kind of repeated, sacred ritual. As an article in *New Scientist* put it, the geoglyphs such as trapezoids were made by 'prayer walking' (24 January 2009). This in turn recalls the songlines of Australian aborigines, the White Horses of Britain and, for me, children running around a landform leaving electronic traces in the sky. Ritual landscape?

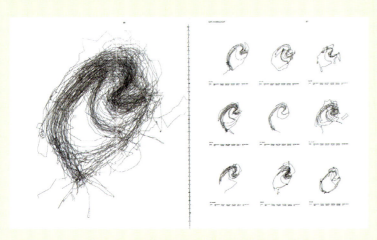

TEN POINTS OF LANDFORMING:
VISUAL TROPES, MOWING AND SAFETY

Over twenty years of constructing mounds I have come to understand some possibilities and limits of landforming, and here offer a few pointers. Some of these look extremely obvious, yet are often disregarded.

1 Self-evidently landforms are to walk on and look at, so their shapes should be changing, full of surprise and allow a certain discovery along the way. Mistakenly many mound designers subtract the paths. These walkways are the key to articulating lumps of earth and a necessity for safety, especially for gardeners doing the grass cutting. Walking the landform is *the* prime experience – in, over, between, through the earth – a visceral and haptic experience best felt in the morning or evening when the sun sculpts the earth from an angle. The ancient verbal tropes, 'mother earth' and 'earth snake', are recurrent and spontaneous reactions to these forms.

2 Different kinds of people enjoy them, especially children. But signs or indicators are necessary to keep visitors from abusing them, or else they must be robust enough, especially at the vulnerable path edges. If paths are their secret to success, then they must pulsate in width to become plateaux at certain points, and shrink to minimum lines at other places.

3 Visually landforms are best seen in contrast with water, or white gravel, which forms a counter-pattern to the green turf. Indeed contrast is their prime quality. So different levels, paths and materials can give the essential differentiation, especially apparent in the strong, raking sunlight.

4 Sharp edges with sweet curves define the light, but such curves are deceiving for those brought up in an orthogonal world. They must be examined from many angles. This takes experience and skill that has to be developed on site. Judging curves from many angles is not the same

as experiencing the right-angled world of a Western city. The sharp edges define the paths and the raking light of morning and evening, when they make the landform come alive. Mistakes of two kinds are often made: a) not getting the superincumbent paths in correct relationship so that they ascend in synch or parallel to each other; and b) not getting the edges sharp, smooth and continuously curving. This is why site supervision throughout the construction is important, with constant fine-tuning. Because earth sculpting is an imprecise art, with a tolerance of 3 or 4 feet (versus a quarter of an inch in architecture), it is necessary to revisit the site with maps, plans and models.

5 Revisiting the construction site to improvise from mistakes makes landforming closer to action painting than the controlled system of architectural blueprints. Simulating an end state that one wants is an amusing challenge. Just as the diggers and dumpers create the form one wants, they erase the layout on the ground. While it is possible to overcome this representational problem with GPS construction, an easier method is to re-stake the mistakes with light bamboo shoots. Then, once the shapes are re-determined, and perhaps changed, one can outline the result using various curved implements. Coloured hosepipes or highly visible tape give a visual idea of the desired lines. Then spray paint is usefully applied to the earth for the fine-tuning. Computerized landforming is often tried, and I love the imaging; but dirt, unlike I-beams, still refuses to be digitized.

6 Landforms often work best when they have a clear and distinct shape. One reason is that gardens and landscapes fill up with an extraordinary array of supplementary things – signs, curbs, fences and rubbish bins.

Another reason is that simple geometries are robust in use, and remain after shrubs, trees, animals (not to mention gravity) have eroded their form. Good landforms often result from necessities – excess earth and mining – and necessity produces generic forms and standard visual tropes. One archetype that results from structure plus the movement of people is the spiral around the most stable form – the cone. Another archetype is its first cousin, the zigzag path up the side of a pyramid. Sometimes nobility results from these brute necessities. Recall the stepped pyramid at Sakkara, or the ziggurat of Ur. Hence I have derived a fundamental diagram, a kind of 'Mound Zero', based on a series of such constraints that include safety and minimal grass-cutting, by sheep.

7 Thus landforms have to be robustly designed to be maintained, but as far as I am concerned they should have some ambiguous or unusual shapes to challenge the mind, some deeper meaning that gives them interest. Inherently symbolic and evocative, they will be read as a dramatic text about earth and our relation to it. Maintenance is mentioned below, but cutting grass by machine or robot often determines the aesthetic limits. The width of the machine and its continuous motion are two constraints, but these limits can actually lead to aesthetic tropes: for instance, what I would call the 'Tilted S'. Here one goes down a slope, only to reverse near the end of the 'S' to ascend, because the mower and walker need to do this. A series of 'Tilted S's can be a pleasant surprise.

8 The height and steepness of a mound should be as great as is consistent with health and safety, and with the stability of slopes. Contrast with the surrounding landscape is the usual strategy, but ambiguous

morphing between the natural and artificial is an alternative. Landforming as a hybrid media thrives on the addition of sculptural edges, or metal and gravel accents.

9 Maintaining landforms is essential but can be done in varying ways, with differing costs and outcomes. In general, there are four methods. a) High-maintenance areas, such as golf courses, putting greens, lawn tennis courts, with short and thick grasses, need constant upkeep. b) Medium-maintenance areas, for mid-sized, close-cropped fine grasses, as in Landform Ueda and parts of Portrack, need cutting sixteen times per summer (or every two weeks, depending on the weather). c) Low-maintenance areas, such as the archaeological site at Avebury, with slow-growing grasses on large and bold forms, need cutting four to six times in summer or once a month, and, as at Avebury, sheep are also employed. d) Very-low-maintenance areas, such as the pyramids on the M8 outside of Edinburgh, or the Flying Flock at the Fife Earth Project, are entirely grazed by sheep. Because of the bold forms this works adequately, though edges are lost and new sheep paths may be formed. Grass cutting is best done by a mixture of methods: ride-on lawnmowers, strimmers and fly-mows are best for the small areas, and remote-controlled robots for the broad banks.

10 The aesthetics and meaning of landforms thus depend crucially on the way the paths articulate the volumes and wider context where it lies. Considered abstractly, the landform is a superior form of contour mapping, an essentialized version of hills and mountains. As a miniature that is big enough to walk over, it relates to our body and the earth, a haptic symbol seen in motion and as the weather changes.

ABOVE: Cheviot Hills and landform.

RIGHT, ABOVE: The Cerne Abbas Giant is a Celtic fertility symbol with a club.

RIGHT: The White Horse, near Uffington Castle, Berkshire. As you walk the white chalk, as people have done since perhaps the fifth century BC, you are not aware of traversing a figure. The horse is visible only from a distance and even then very obliquely.

3: NORTHUMBERLANDIA

Empathy and Projection

Approximately 5 miles north of Newcastle on the A1, the city gives way to a rolling landscape, and then, in the distance, the Cheviot Hills. I was asked to mark this transition with a symbolic gateway to the north, a landform that would be striking and related to the area. Perhaps it should be a recognizable sign of regional identity? That was my first idea, but the client, a coal

company called Banks, and a friend, Matt Ridley, asked for something more, a striking and attractive form with a strong presence, and that thought led me to the human body. People empathize with images of the face and torso. As Degas put the question, rhetorically: 'We were created to look at one another, weren't we?' It is said that more neurones are hard-wired for facial recognition than for any other specialized shape, and no one needs to be taught the pleasures of looking at a shapely body. But today, with over-exposed celebrity and under-exposed modesty, such shapes may be more effective when they are suggested. Anything at the scale of the landscape needs to be first a part of nature before becoming part of another plot. Not just an arm and a leg but a pathway and a plateau. The seamless mixture of the body and landscape allows the imagination the freedom to roam, yet also gives a general direction in which to aim. Especially important for high summits is a visible goal, to pull one up the hill, something recognizable.

On this stretch of motorway the far-off hills do not have much impact, especially when viewed at 60 miles per hour, but they can be pulled into the foreground by similar curves of a body. Hence the design called Northumberlandia, the woman as a traversable landform gesturing at the natural ones in the distance. In the first millennium BC, images of the human and animal body were walked into the landscape. For instance, in Britain, paths of white chalk generated the White Horse of the Berkshire Downs and, later on, the Cerne Abbas Giant, images that are completely visible only from an aeroplane. No doubt they were conceived symbolically from above, as explicit body figures, as if people could fly over them mentally. But on the ground the reality is much more suggestive and abstract, because one can perceive them only obliquely, as partial figures. This mixture of suggestion and partial representation works well, as it does in such contemporary figures as Antony Gormley's Angel of the North. As to the several white horses in the south, a good guess as to their use is that they were traversed seasonally, perhaps in some kind of ritual, as the local farmers marched to a tune or a chant. The body in the landscape plays a continuous and major role throughout history because people unconsciously project their own moods and shapes on to living nature.

ABSTRACT BODY SHAPES AND CONTOUR MAPPING

In the Newcastle area during the Roman occupation local goddesses were celebrated, such as Coventina and the Alaisiagae, and there were other regional precedents for anthropomorphic shapes, but as mentioned above my goal was to make them part of other contexts. Here they relate to the distant landscape or disappear into causeways and broad plateaux. From any one viewpoint there is always more than one image and use. Moreover, since the scale is so huge compared to us (Northumberlandia is a quarter of a mile long), the presence of a woman will often slip below consciousness as one perceives a set of rhythmical contours. Nevertheless, this figure identifies a place, giving a name and use to what was a flat agricultural landscape, and then an opencast site for mining coal.

There are three basic methods of suggesting anthropomorphic shapes in the landscape: contour mapping, volumetric profiling and path marking. Sometimes these strategies overlap and become the same, when for instance the outline of a leg also becomes underlined in white as a public walking route. At other times they conflict or work in counterpoint suggesting several different readings. Multiple meaning is also supported by different uses. Perhaps one will punt on the small lakes, or fish among the bullrushes, or picnic in the shade of the existing Moore Plantation, where one enters. Along the top of the landform a linear walk will afford views of the coal production as it continues. The landform can obviously become a peaceful place from which to survey the distant Cheviot Hills and for those with an interest in seeing ancient landforms, it could be on a tour that takes in six of the local henges: those at Milfield Basin, Milfield North and South, Coupland, Ewart, Akeld and Yeavering.

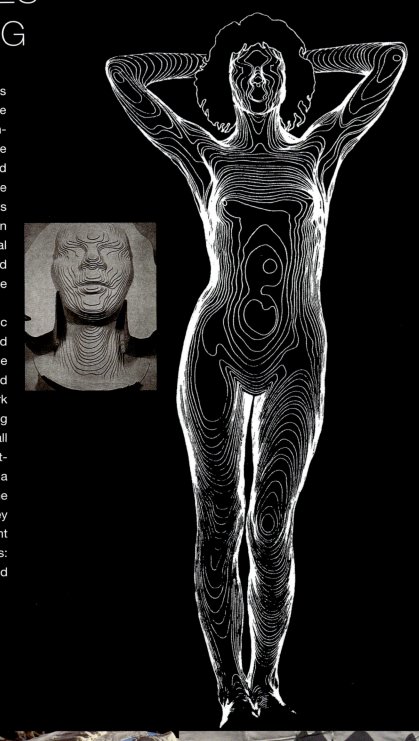

LEFT: Since the 1970s and improvements in digital cutting, contour mapping of the body has become more refined. Here Klaus Linkwitz and Hans Preuss in *Study in Relief* (1970) transform 'Susan' into delicate flat planes and her entire contour portrait is made by Gerhard Nagel in *Stereophotogram* (1970). Digital milling machines have since become even more accurate, but in an important sense this last stage is not very relevant for landforms. Volumetric curves are less pertinent for walking than contours. Safety, visibility and pleasure of movement become the key issues, as pathways take precedence over volumes.

LEFT BELOW: Northumberlandia conceived as a contour map and set of pathways. Since the landform is so big relative to us, she will be read first as horizontal strata, rather like the Grand Canyon, and a series of superimposed pathways or plateaux. Some of the first schemes played with readings of this sort, with the linear outlines and pleasing ambiguities of contours.

TOP: In the early models the muscles, skin and volumetric outline were investigated.

RIGHT: I discovered that if one turned the map of Northumberland upside-down, and outlined the county, an eighteenth-century lady emerged. She was incorporated in several models.

BELOW: Punting on the lake.

OVERLEAF: A pastel rendering of the contour map solution.

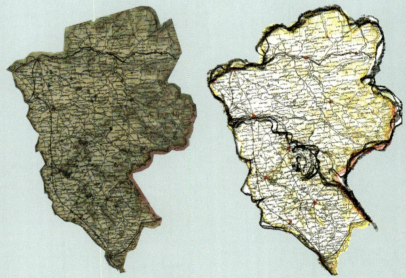

THE HAND, THE PROFILE AND ANTHROPOMORPHISM

The green models, right, compare the two basic ways of treating the human figure as landform, the abstract, contour model versus the naturalistic and volumetric one. Inevitably, the synthesis of these types led to further questions, both of meaning and safety. If the profile of the face is the main attraction and goal of movement, how do you make it recognizable from a distance but not dangerous to walk on? The answer was to place most of this area off limits to walking, behind a wall of planting.

After the face, the hands became the expressive parts to accentuate. The white model above shows that one approach to Northumberlandia is across a causeway, by the side of her fingers. Here, and on the other side, the hands are conceived in a welcoming gesture, with open palm. It's a sign with a long Buddhist and Christian history, and even Nietzsche, otherwise critical of such usage, proffers such a symbol of the Open Hand. After reading his *Thus Spake Zarathustra*, where this image is described, Le Corbusier adopted it as the symbol for his new city at Chandigarh in India. Because it rotates cheerfully in the wind, welcoming visitors like a friendly bird, I photographed one of Le Corbusier's followers, the architect Charles Correa, giving the same gesture, near right, the customary wave or hi sign. In the final model, lower right, the right hand points at the entrance mounds, while the left one opens up with generosity. Pointing at a significant symbol and remaining silent, as T.S. Eliot implied, remains a potent deictic gesture.

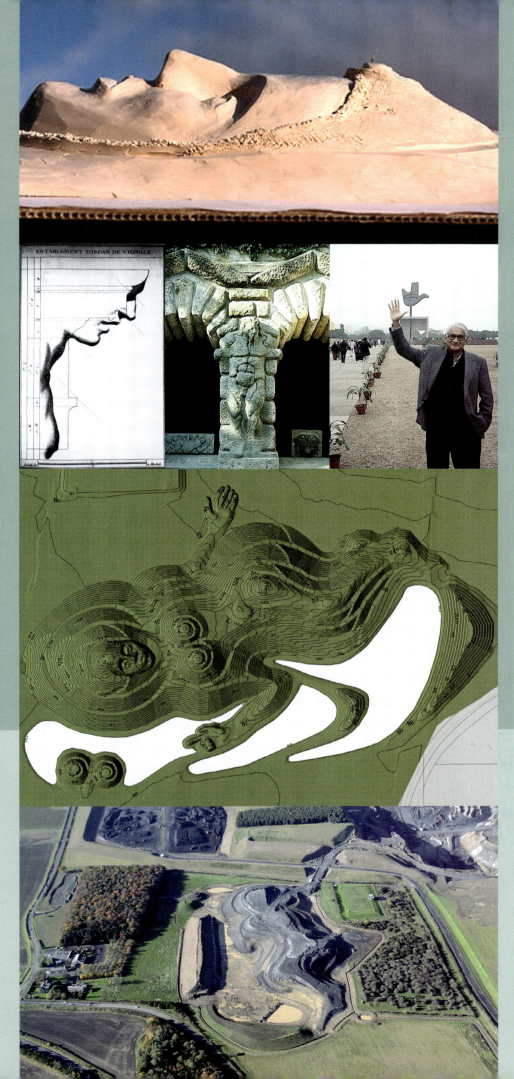

Translating the face into stone is, of course, an old art that goes back to the ancient Egyptians. In the garden this translation can be very effective when done with large and rough stones that also serve a structural role. To the left, centre, one can see how the Italian artist Primaticcio doubly coded the male body with building elements, rugged boulders and voussoirs, so it seems to disappear and reappear. This ambiguous equation was created during the 1540s at Fontainebleau, in the Grotte des Pins. Later, the French theorist Jacques-François Blondel (1705–74), far left, followed the same classical analogy when he compared the entablature with the nose, mouth and chin. He even turned this metaphor into a point of judgment. Good proportions of the body and building, he claimed, had the same basis, and thus if one were well-tuned and empathetic, one could feel goodness in the profiles of a cornice. If that idea is absurd the point of empathetic projection nevertheless remains valid and underpins the whole classical language of architecture. Many architects have proved the point, from Michelangelo to Geoffrey Scott to Le Corbusier. For us, anthropomorphism amounts to a universal feeling, as faces leap out of the clouds, bushes and mouldings of a building.

Northumberlandia under construction, November 2010.

COMPUTERIZING LANDFORMS

Arguments for and against digitizing landforms are equally convincing. Since shaping a lot of earth is expensive, computer modelling is used to rationalize the process. One can calculate the volumes of soil, the angles of ascent and slippage, the pathways and profiles all in one program. Then these parameters can be manipulated and recalculated. Flexibility, cost and control are the advantages. The main disadvantage is that digital modelling is still cumbersome and crude, with the result that computer programs start to generate shapes and pathways. When it comes to details and sculptural subtlety, a physical model in plasticine still has the edge. In five very large projects using the computer I have seen digital necessity take precedence over the eye and mind. Yet these schemes would not have materialized except for this control, and there are compensating virtues. Paths, heights and the danger of slope angles can be analysed together quickly. It is only a matter of time before the software, and its users, become more adept at manipulating the digital putty. For the present, however, the computerization of landforms has to be supplemented by further simulation and the work modified in construction and on the site. The beautiful renditions on these pages, worked out with Mark Simmons, have their own fascinating aesthetic of yellow layout triangles and polychromatic slope angles.

LEFT: Like the Angel of the North, this anthropomorphic shape generated some contentious speculation, such as the danger of walking on a 100-foot breast.

RIGHT: As the computer elevation reveals, most visible are landforms, so only aeroplanes, flying low directly overhead, could actually attain the shock that journalists so ardently desire.

BEFORE PLANTING

Views of Northumberlandia before the paths, planting and significant areas have been designed. The entrance through Moore Plantation, above, frames the goal of movement and highest point at 34 metres, the forehead. Two intervening mounds, visual puns on the breasts, veil the face and relate to other landforms to left and right. Further similarities between causeways, elbow and hand can be seen in the aerial perspectives of Madelon Vriesendorp, opposite. The parity between repeated landforms and representational parts sets up a carefully orchestrated balance.

In the final model, right, every plateau from the foot to the forehead is both a human form and a landform, a goal and viewpoint for the next stage. Hence the double readings and ambiguities. Is the first helix an ankle bone or a pyramid of rocks? Is the next one a knee joint or a zigzag of divergent paths? Is the third a hip joint or three paths converging on a spiral? A pubic mound or another vesica? Breast or double helix of white paths? A nose and eye-ridge or a ramp-like wedge of rock? The forehead or the culminating dome? Exploring this female Gulliver is, at the same time, a walk through a *giardino segreto*. Multiple meanings and ambiguity are particularly important today when celebrities saturate the media, for who wants to contemplate, daily, the Colossus of Tony Blair? The woman of the north is something other, and more generous, suggesting an ancient dance with her switching posture and pointing to her second, the approach.

PART TWO
IDENTITY

4: SPIRALS OF TIME

A Public Park in Milan

The Parco Portello, located in north-west Milan, started life, like the Parc André Citroën in Paris, as the offspring of a car factory: the old Alfa Romeo plant. Initially conceived in 1906, the Portello factory was on the outskirts of the city, which then grew quickly to swallow it. Milan is the most industrious of Italian cities, and things move very fast here, especially fashion and furniture, which always race ahead of the global market. Yet slowness, and the 'slow food' movement, is cultivated also, and when I was asked to get involved in designing, I reminded the patron behind the park of the way Milan's cathedral proceeded at a snail's pace. Napoleon, when he came into the conquered city in 1805, allegedly warned the citizens either to finish the façade, a ramshackle affair that had bumbled along through many redesigns for 500 years, or he would blow it up. The threat worked and the Gothic face was completed. Marco Brunelli, the owner of the hypermarket to the north-east of the site, replied that he had been trying to construct his park since the mid-1990s. My first designs started in 2002 and for the next eight years redesigns became necessary for countless Machiavellian reasons, not all of them municipal. Perhaps Italian cities need the threat of a Napoleonic bomb to concentrate the mind. Slowness, indeed stalemate, frustration and compromise, notoriously plagues the construction of contemporary architecture. In Rome Zaha Hadid struggled for more than ten years to complete her new museum, while David Chipperfield, also from Britain, has not finished a Venetian cemetery after more than twelve years of design work. Nonetheless, when it comes to city parks, there is something to be said for the Renaissance garden phrase 'festina lente' (make haste to go slow), and friendships have space to develop amid the struggle. Moreover, one should take time to conceive and experience nature, especially when surrounded by such a fast-paced city as Milan. From this site Alfa Romeo won many Grand Prix, and gave birth to the first celebrity drivers: Enzo Ferrari and Juan Manuel Fangio. But why race through the green place that is, in the end, the result of speed?

In a public park, time should slow down, and be extended by the unhurried reflection on nature and, I thought, the symbols and signs of time itself. 'Time Spirals' or the 'spirals of time' was an 'ambigrammo' I had conceived that could be read two ways and upside-down, rather the way time recurs within each memory of the past, and in a somewhat different form. Also the visual metaphor of time combines the circle with the straight line. Why? Because, like a planet revolving around a sun, there are two forces of movement at work, the local and the interstellar gravity. Or another analogy: the seasons recur, like a circle, but the overall climate also changes, slowly or fast. Put the circle and line together and you get the spiral of time, the theme of the park, 'Time Spirals'. This combination we see with hurricanes, DNA, galaxies and many other kinds of vortex including the whirlpool.

A double-helical mound, opposite, is topped by its DNA sculpture, the culmination of spiral movement. Spirals are a natural and cultural sign of time, as the growth of ammonite rings, left, has often symbolized. The ambigrammo, above, which when read upside-down, changes its meaning slightly, in the way memories are always somewhat different from each other. Re-remembering is really what the act of recollection is, the way we make sense of things by putting them in a string of previous thoughts.

A CHANGE OF PLAN

Thematically the park is unified by the narrative of time, and visually by the geometry of circles, arcs and crescents. Overall Parco Portello presents the history of Milan in its three large landforms (Prehistory, History and the Present) and a more individual relationship to time in the small garden. Thus personal time is contrasted with the many rhythms of time marked in the paving and planting.

As mentioned, this scheme itself took a lot of time to design, a saga of ups and downs, of intrigues and counter-plots that might well occupy an entire book. Perhaps as many as ten basic layouts were proposed and modified, but an outline of the main plot can be followed in the change of the plans. The landscape firm that was initially involved, Andreas Kipar and his company LAND, had reached a proposal, by January 2002, that featured a picturesque park bisected into two halves because of a future underground roadway. This subterranean passage for vehicles was to come and go like a plague, finally shrinking the park to its present size, squeezed to the west.

Then in March 2002 I was asked by Marco Brunelli to design Portello and, as one can see by the plans, came up with three and then four basic mounds shaped like question marks (or their inverse). These protected communal and semi-private spaces, small flower gardens and recreation areas, children's playgrounds and, at the centre of it all, a contemplative space with water and a causeway. Pathways defined these landforms visually into sculptural bodies and, if one slipped on a steep bank, the paths lessened the fall, always a consideration for safety in public parks. In the final scheme, however, these paths were turned into crescents of planting, and the main walkway was up the spine of Mounds One and Two. You ascend through an avenue of laurel and thuja, so the land-forms are now defined by strong lines of colourful growth – rather than the paths or metal sculpture I have employed in the past.

A children's garden is just to the north of Mound Two, a kiosk to its north-east, and then an area for bowling and the small Time Garden by the hospital. A reflecting lake with its causeway defines the curves of Mound One. As usual, water and turf are in sharp contrast, to bring out their mutual qualities. As some of the plans show explicitly, solid and void were manipulated in opposition to each other, to achieve the best balance between the large amount of earth we had to accommodate and the various activities needing flat ground. It was a matter of pushing and pulling, like making pastry with plasticine, and remains of these viscous, strange attractors can be seen in some of the hundred drawings.

Throughout the ten-year process we were steered as a group by the practised hand and eye of Ennio Brion, whose family worked with Carlo Scarpa on the famous Brion Cemetery. During this time I was immensely helped, and encouraged, by the ever-resourceful Margherita Brianza, a designer of skill and integrity. To her should also be given much credit for Parco Portello.

Parco Portello, Milan, Early plans and plasticine models, Charles Jencks, May 2002–November 2002, 2003–5, and penultimate solutions 2009. Parco Portello was overseen by the office of Andreas Kipar, LAND, and some of the designers there, Giuliano Garello and Marco Grazioli, and the overall group was steered by Ennio Brion. Bottom drawing by Margherita Brianza and LAND; plasticine model with Madelon Vriesendorp.

THE UNNATURAL URBAN PARK

However natural it may look, an urban park must be conceived and maintained as an artifice. The basic social and economic lessons that I learned about this artefact, summarized below, were presented to Marco Brunelli. For the public to be attracted to a park, it needs not only strong visual themes but different kinds of use. One of the greatest dangers is crime and drugs and, as sociologists have found, the best way to discourage these is to attract a wide and constantly changing audience. Thus an urban park also needs an exquisite garden where one can escape from the city and find peace. In our design this sheltered area became the Time Garden at the north, next to the hospital, a place to relax among flowers, to sit at tables, play chess and stroll on the enclosed 'Time Walk'.

SOME LESSONS OF CITY PARKS

From a study of city parks in the West, certain lessons emerge that usually bear fruit. They can be summarized as economic and social propositions with aesthetic and philosophical implications. In terms of success, use comes first and ideas and form second, but in the end they are equally important. The ten lessons I have learned about city parks are:

1 High public use of an urban park can double the land value of surrounding areas, and cut crime.

2 The key to high use is usually that by women with their children.

3 But use by local people can be just as important. Most visitors will be women and local people.

4 Intervisibility between areas in an urban park allows people to feel confident and safe, as does seeing ways into and out a space or garden. Thus many entrances and exits are desirable. The formal layout of the whole should be clear, but also complex and intimate in parts.

5 To attain high use, a park will need, during the first opening years, the management and scheduling of events – fashion shows, stage events, open-air films, art installations, games and contests. These events create both a sense of ownership, and loyalty, and expectation of future use.

6 Further functions underscore this ongoing commitment – a children's play area, a café or kiosk, different places of exercise for old and young – which soon creates continued loyalty. A city park is like a good theatre to which one returns.

7 Local small gardens within the park, of different character and quality, are essential. The response to nature as an individual, sensual and intimate experience must be encouraged and satisfied. Sunbathing, killing time and romantic encounters are typical activities.

8 In small gardens lots of tables and seats should be provided, for joint activities such as chess, and for reading alone.

9 Highly visible attractors should be provided: striking sculpture or landforms that give identity and continued aesthetic interest. Landforms must have shade, sculpture and something to attract people to make the journey to their top, or they become barren. Complex details and meaning, at several points, should engage visitors and make them slow down. One visits an urban garden to contemplate and relax in a 'place apart'. As the Renaissance garden advised: 'festina lente' (make haste to go slow).

10 The art of nature and the nature of art make one reflect on the fundamental delights and perplexities of life. Like the church and museum, the city park is an institution essential to spiritual and communal life, to the public realm.

These propositions do not ensure a successful urban park, but disregarding their truth can court trouble. They are the *sine qua non* that guarantees nothing, pointers not recipes.

LOGOS OF PORTELLO

A family of logos, instead of a single brand, can create identity while avoiding repetition. Here the self-similar, crescent shapes and letters P are derived from the alliteration of the name, Parco Portello, and the causeway over water. The basic crescent form, and its complementary shapes, also led to an alphabet, a kiosk and several details. For instance, a large painted sign, next to the highway on the south, announces the park to the city and also becomes a supergraphic that disguises the concrete extract of the underground road. The name 'Parco Portello' and the 'vegetable-shaped' extract above it, also in green, displace the grim industrial necessities towards more organic meanings. Prefabricated crescent tiles, nestling into each other, were also to be based on the logo. A green logism thus accentuates the artificial nature of urban nature.

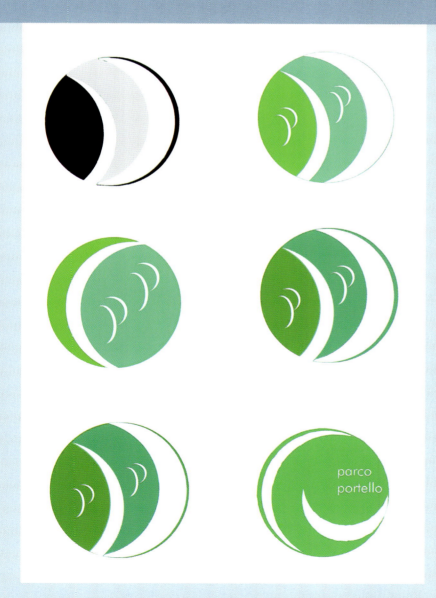

The heart of the garden has water, shade and protection from the highway noise, and the housing blocks on the other side of the Mound One. A place of quiet contemplation.

TIME WALK

4 Seasons
4 Ages

Primavera
Azaleas
Giovane
Pre-history

Estate
Choisca
Maturo
Historie

Autunna
Ceanothus
Adulto
Present

Inverno
Mahunia
Anaiano
Future

Lunar month 28 days

THE TIME GARDEN – RITMO DEL TEMPO

Nature is like a museum full of clocks that ring at different times. Indeed, life marches to a tune of various rhythms internalized in the nervous system. Depending on the situation this can be pleasant or maddening, but a garden is a place where these rhythms are to be enjoyed, celebrated and contemplated. They certainly dominate life. For instance, grunion fish off the coast of California have an innate clock which tells them when to spawn. This neural timepiece is set by the rhythms of the moon and the cycle of high tides. Tides rise to their highest point in the spring, leaving the grunion spawn out of reach of predators, so that is the right moment for these fish to let go of their eggs. Lunar months are a little more than 28 days, and this apparently sets one important rhythm. Women display a cycle that lies close to the lunar period, as do many other animals that have menstrual cycles. Several biorhythms are fine-tuned by cosmic cycles, but many more of them are only approximately regulated. Our circadian rhythms of sleep settle on a 25-hour cycle of slumber and wakefulness, and we have six or so up-and-down periods in a 24-hour day. Many reasons are adduced for the approximate nature of biological clocks – they are easier to reset than precise ones – and they may have several different functions needing to be resolved. But as a metaphor, and stimulus, nature's clock works on our body sometimes like a slave-driver ringing neurological bells, and other times like a dance partner. Either way it can be turned into rhythmical architecture and ornament. Indeed, time's image *is* ornament.

In the Time Garden, black and white steps mark the rotation of the earth, turning every 24 hours in its night and day cycle, the fundamental rhythm. Also manifest are the four seasons (marked on the side of the red walls), the 28 days of the lunar month (marked in the rings on either side of the Time Walk), the 12 months of the year (words cut in steel), the 365 days of the year and the major events of the universe, unfolding over 13.7 billion years (in steel plates). Each rhythm of time has a specific shape, a very personal form, from our heartbeat and individual step to the oscillations of day and night. Everything in nature marches to its singular tune, and together they make the music of time. Like a Japanese Zen garden, the Daisen-in, this one depicts an individual's journey over time, with steps, pebbles, planting, rebus figures and 'dry water' (in the form of *rizzada*, the zigzag waves of the heartbeat). This small garden is further protected from the activity of the larger areas by a steep bank of pampas grass and red berberis.

SYNCOPATED TIME

Placing different rhythms of time on top of each other creates syncopation. However, nature's clocks do chime in unison when they are orchestrated by the black and white of night and day, or the monthly cycle of 28 days and the changing crescents of the moon. Because these basic rhythms dominate nature they are the visual ordering principle here. They create the line of the Time Walk and the 28 divisions of the circles, on either side of the line. But, as can be seen in the plan below, and various details opposite, further clocks run at different speeds. For instance, the usual heartbeat (*battito cardiaco*) pulses at a rate a little faster than a second, and this obviously depends on your emotion or exertion. Nature's different times thus create a kind of syncopated music and this is shown in the intriguing sketch from about 1300 (bottom right). Based on a manuscript of *c*.470 by Anicius Boethius, showing a monochord for three parts, it is a beautiful illustration of the crescents of time – overlapping, interlacing and syncopated. The music of the spheres is the big conductor, while the music of the living provides the variation and delight.

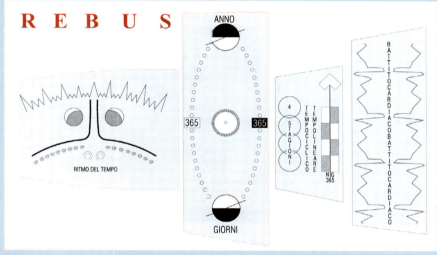

WALKING

You enter from the west, through a short walk with planted borders and roses to either side. These frame the rest of the garden, giving protection and a place to sit. Then you reach a transition with the words 'RITMO DEL TEMPO' set in concrete. The rhythm of time is a steady drumbeat; the four seasons, marked in four circles, are identified by steel words set in the concrete walls: Inverno, Primavera, Estate, Autunno. Underfoot the four ages are marked – Prehistory, History, Present and Future. The pathway has black and white stones: 'day/night', 182¼ + 183 steps = 365¼, each step is the day of a solar year. The twelve months are presented to either side and marked in steel 'blades' that have their names laser-cut, as voids: 'gennaio, febbraio, marzo' etc. Between them are grass and box 'moundettes' (for sunbathing). These rise and fall like the basic rhythm of time, and opposite them are four banks of hardy shrubs, with colour and perfume that are present in the four seasons of the year. *Mahonia japonica* comes out yellow in Inverno; azaleas turn bright in Primavera; choisya is white in Estate, and ceanothus turns blue during Autunno. Thus each season has its strong colour and scent. But life is punctuated by one-off events, here the seats and diagonals of the trees and grasses. Some major events of the universe, over its 13.7 billion years, are also marked in metal plates – for instance, the origin, the creation of atoms, galaxies and the earth. The syncopations are broken by other variations, four rebus areas and veiled faces, puzzles that children enjoy.

T I M E W A L K

12 Months - aluminium blades
Each stone circle - 24 hours

4 Puzzles - 4 rebus
Rizzada - times rhythmn & heartbeat

THE ALFA KIOSK

As mentioned, the former Alfa Romeo factory worked the site from 1906 to the 1980s, and therefore the green park owes its existence, partly, to this earlier time. Large amounts of earth had to be cleared from other constructions, and the factory ground also de-polluted and sealed. The mounds resulted from the excess earth, and the iconography of speed resulted from the racing cars. The park was in effect created as a mixture of codes and ages, various speeds of growth and decay. As Victor Hugo wrote about cathedrals: 'Great buildings, like great mountains, are the work of ages. Often art undergoes a transformation while they are pending completion . . . Time is the architect – a nation is the builder.' Or, in this park, *variable* times are the constructor. How to combine these with a feeling for nature? This became a pressing question when I was asked to design a kiosk next to Mound Two, the area given over to the memory of Alfa Romeo.

The solution is a green building with an undulating roof that is meant to nestle into the ground as if it were another mound, yet appear with echoes of a sports car, the undulating Disco Volante. The building's iconography and plan are generated by the summer and winter sunlines, the two extreme conditions. The south façade has two different sunshades: vertical lines that are closely spaced to give more relief in the hot months, and widely spaced lines for the winter. The roof structure also undulates with straight lines forming a hyperbolic parabola. Thus the structure, elevation and plan all merge usually contradictory meanings: the straight lines of the machine, mass production and speed, and the curved lines of nature and planetary movement. Indeed, a 'solargraph' taken by Justin Quinnell for half a year, opposite below, shows the path of the sun between its highest point on 21 June 2008 and its lowest on 19 December 2007. Literal sunlines find their counterpart in the hanging sunlines of the façade and sides of the kiosk. For a long time I have been inspired by the possibilities of using the slightest change in such lines to create the illusion of movement – Linearism – the subtle play of light, shade and colour across a landscape. Gates and fences at Portello continue the illusion of a travelling wave. In these works the shape of time is stretched from pointillism, and the overall pattern, to Linearism. It has many unexploited possibilities.

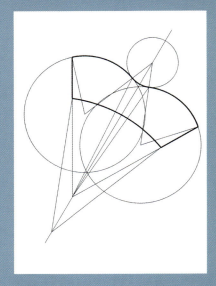

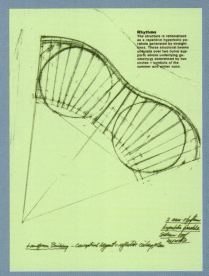

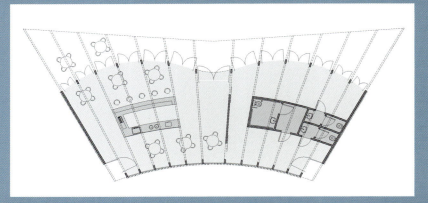

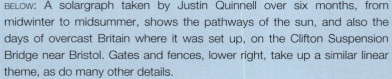

BELOW: A solargraph taken by Justin Quinnell over six months, from midwinter to midsummer, shows the pathways of the sun, and also the days of overcast Britain where it was set up, on the Clifton Suspension Bridge near Bristol. Gates and fences, lower right, take up a similar linear theme, as do many other details.

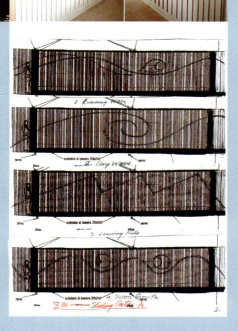

MOUND ONE: PREHISTORY

In a public park, attracting people to the top of the mounds is the challenge – enticing them to walk a considerable distance and, what's more, to return again and again. Unless one provides shade, a place to sit and drink, some interesting plants and something of a mystery – sculpture, a work of art, a view – they will not come back. The success of a city park, as pointed out, rests on continuous use by different kinds of people, on the social art of attraction. Two basic attractors here are the overall narrative and the formal coherence: the *ritmo del tempo* and the order of crescents, continuous undulations and axial views.

Mound One, closest to the west highway, is a welcome beacon for visitors because it is on one of the main routes into Milan, the approach from the international airport, Malpensa, and such large institutions as the New Milan Trade Fair. On the outside the landform is a green gateway to the city and, on the inside, it provides a good visual and acoustic buffer for the heart of the scheme, the reflecting pool. Thematically, Mound One signifies early time, prehistory, and the first large structures of the universe: the spiral galaxies. Mr Brunelli asked for 'a sense of velocity', naturally present in the lines of planting and curved pathways.

My first designs marked the beacon, the high centre, with up-lights placed in seats, which would bounce a directed beam off a reflector and provide a circular glow at night. A primitive oak pier was the basic element of this wood circle oriented to the cardinal points. It marks the turning points of the year, and at its centre is a pyramidal sundial. Stone circles and the paradoxical double orientation of Stonehenge were inspirations. The latter caused a great controversy over which way it was oriented – to the rising sun of the north-east or the setting one to the south-west – until experts granted that because of its propitious location it could be both.

Later designs of mine took this form of prehistoric marking and other key rhythms of time. The sun's rise and fall are framed by tall rocks and the break in planting. Benches, *rizzada*, gravel, shrubs and a progressive emergence of fractal-cut stones mark eight crucial shifts in time. But the same forms are also mapped to the waves of a spiral galaxy, another natural sign of duration. This cosmic image of passing time has been known since at least the nineteenth century, when the Whirlpool Galaxy was discovered. But recently a surprising truth has emerged about the spiral arms. They are not the constant rotation of stars and planets, as they appear, but rather a density shock wave that travels through space pulling and pushing all the matter to every side. In effect, not rotating chains of stars but rotating density waves of star formation. This formal order, like a creative traffic jam caused by a travelling wave of people stepping on their brakes, brings the bodies into existence. It is an extraordinary event of the universe and one marked here by the fractal stones progressing towards the seats.

Alternating bands of red shrubs – photinia and berberis – underline the movement of the pathway, while a swell of red azaleas underscores the arms of the central spiral. Seen from above, from a cerebral helicopter, one can discern the way the mound embraces the quiet part of the garden and the water. Its causeway swings in a counter-curve of movement. There are crescents of time, rhythms not too far from the monochord of the fifth century (see page 72).

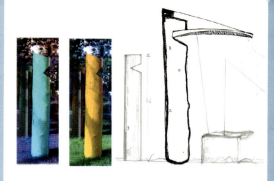

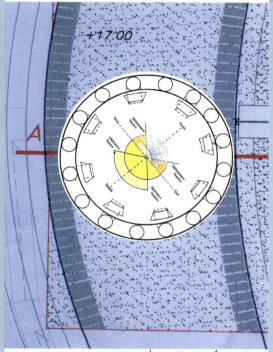

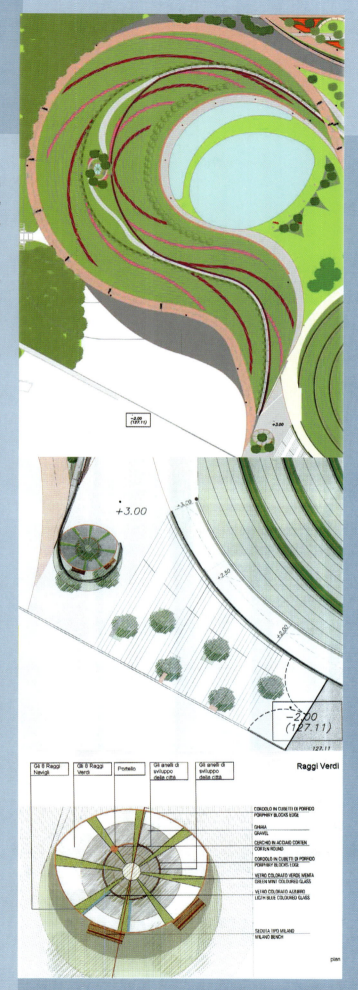

NARRATIVE FLOW

The main entrance to the park is from the south, Viale Serra, up a wide public stairway that mixes seats and trees in an interesting diagonal rhythm. The Spanish Steps in Rome, and monumental steps outside cathedrals and museums, have shown that these informal seating areas can be an active public realm, and a pleasant place to observe city life. At the top you reach a small crescent mound and, under the same trees (*Wallichiana*) you find an abstracted map of Milan depicted on the ground in stones and glass, its inner rings of transport, and the eight greenways for the city that Andreas Kipar has proposed. Parco Portello, and the visitor's location, is picked out on the north-west route. From here the geometry of planting and pathways leads further up to Mound One, prehistory, and then Mound Two, history, and finally the third landform, the double helix, the present period of time. Running the entire route of all three mounds, as joggers will do, takes ten minutes; walking and contemplating stops time.

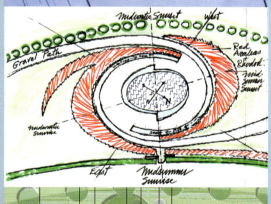

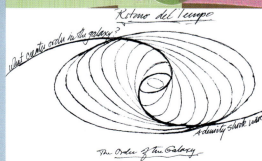

MOUND TWO: HISTORY

You descend the first mound and ascend Mound Two in a counter-curve of laurel, thuja and photinia. This small crescent divides the heart of the garden from the children's area and the Time Walk to the north. Thematically the narrative has shifted from prehistoric Milan to the known periods – the Roman, Early Christian, Medieval and Renaissance epochs. All these produced extraordinary cultures, and they culminated in the industrial powerhouse of the Italian north, and such factories as Alfa Romeo. Mound Two, an artificial hill constructed out of waste, was meant to mark this impressive history, but over eight years several of my designs were shelved by the patron and others. Curiously some of their residues remain, traces of previous ideas like the palimpsest of Milan itself: signs of velocity, a water garden and waterwheel, a homage to Leonardo but one that is based on chaos theory. A zigzag pathway and hedge of choisya set up the basic rhythms of time, which were taken up in the beating drums, reminiscent of the War Garden (pages 156–7). The two fundamental types of time, circular and linear, are frozen into the curves and angles of the *parapetti* which rise and fall with the curve of the hill.

Later designs morphed into a recollection of the Alfa Romeo factory, its moments of triumph and destruction, its role in the two wars and some of the cars it produced. Up-lighters, pennants and seats now create a steady beat between the thuja. The shape of speed is taken up in the shrub-lines of choisya and the fountain sculpture, a set of spinning wheels throwing water in spiral jets.

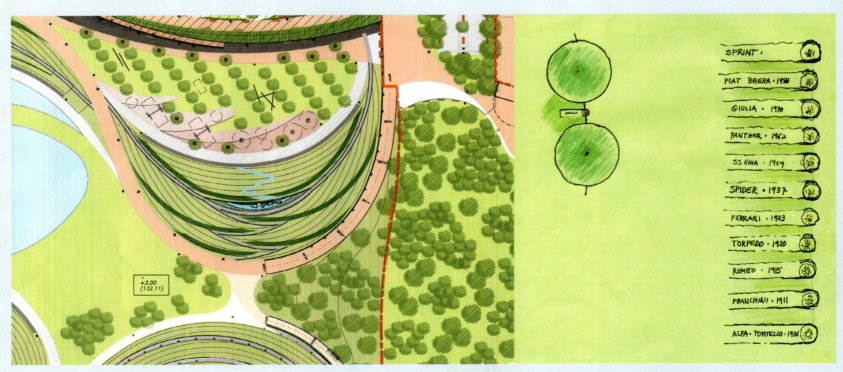

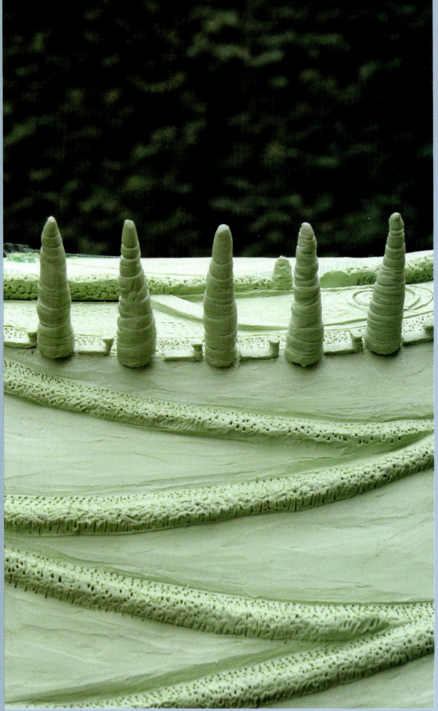

MOUND THREE: PRESENT

The largest mound, at 22 metres, faces south towards the centre of Milan, a double helix of earth that culminates in a sculpture of DNA. The pathways spiral upwards to be visually continued into the sky by the trees to one side, and the aluminium steps of the sculpture to the other. A basic opposition is set up between the metal and trees – silver versus green – and underlined by the contrasting pleasures of a city park: shade and water, several places to sit and eat, or read, a table (holding the electric box), a drinking fountain and something to look at. The big view is over the city or, in the other direction, the layout of the park, and the thing that has brought it into being, the molecule of life that has been decoded in the present time, DNA. One might ask where this overall narrative of time, and the route over three mounds, develops after the present, and what the future (mound) might be like; intimations are found as one looks down and across at the beginning of the climb.

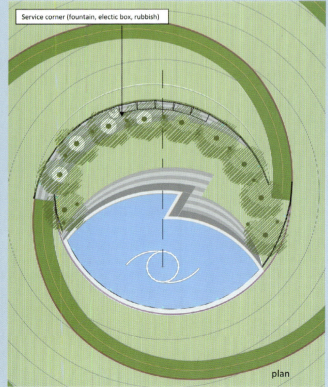

Service corner (fountain, electic box, rubbish)

plan

5: IDENTITY SCOTLAND

If envy is a flower one should never water, then identity is a bloom needing constant attention. It thrives on pride and wilts with contempt. It can be expunged by brainwashing, but, contrary to flowers that bloom, it gets stronger the more you beat it. In 1296 Edward I invaded Berwick, the Border city of Scotland, and slaughtered 7,500 men, women and children. He then went on to brutalize more of the country, becoming infamous as the Hammer of Scotland. But the more he hammered the more he forged identity, creating the very nationalism his terror was meant to extinguish.

Identity is an unlikely mixture of traits, which tends to disappear if you look at it too closely, blurring into myths and symbols that fade with the penetrating light. At the same time it gives form and pleasure to life, its character and differences. Tribal and national identity are constructed, as the cliché has it, from opposite materials and separate realms, one part climate, other parts culture, history and self-reflection, the stories that are told, the labels and signs that are applied. But, in spite of the fashion for branding

and nationalism, no one controls it – though many people try. The Victorian Scots were particularly keen on forging their self-image based on the wars of independence, building a 200-foot monument to William Wallace near Stirling Castle. Sir Walter Scott culminated this tradition of history as myth. The romantic novel became the most potent form of self-reflection until film took over.

Much earlier, after Roman civilization had left the British Isles, identity depended on asserting rights of continuity, the legitimacy of ownership and rule. For English and Scottish kings this meant proving one's provenance, the length and strength of one's bloodline. Best to have a family tree that went back to Adam and Eve or, failing that, to be the summation of a king list that originated with Noah. This is what John Balliol produced when Edward I was hammering Scotland in the 1290s. At that time Balliol needed to prove an ancestry, more royal and biblical than that of the English kings, and he did this using the lists of Constantin II, King of the Scots 900–43. The coronations extending over 1,976 years went backwards through thirty kings of Dalriada to sixty-five Pictish kings, all the way through 113 to Noah. The key figure in this identity-forging bloodline was Scota, who gave her name to the whole enterprise. Scota came from Egypt looking for a promised land and, always heading north, ended up in Scotland. The daughter of the Pharaoh

LEFT AND BELOW: The map of Scotland, in red ballast, is divided by the four main faults cutting Scotland into different geological epochs.

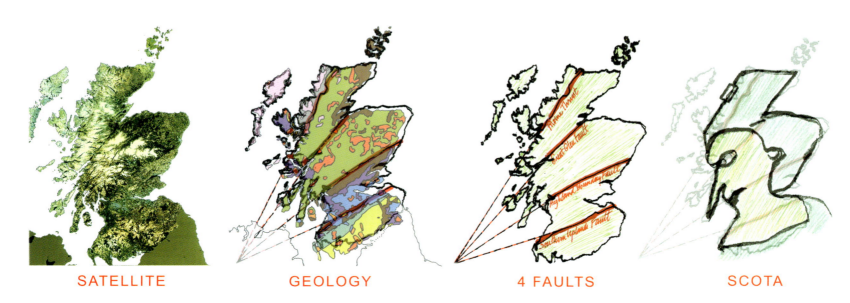

SATELLITE   GEOLOGY   4 FAULTS   SCOTA

of the Oppression (Ramesses II, 1304–1237 BC), she showed her mettle by wandering for 1,200 years with a block of sandstone on her back. It weighed 152kg and was the venerable Jacob's Pillow, which became the Stone of Destiny. Hence the stone-worship, or petromania, that has always been a hallmark of the Scots, a confirmation of their underlying geology. Hence Edward I's stealing the Stone of Scone, and then the 1950s counter-theft of rock.

From the east coast of Ireland, Scota looked with hope across the seas to a green and mountainous landscape, and thence took her sacred relic. The direction was north-east, where all lines and lochs point, even the fault-lines going back a billion years. However exaggerated the myth of her wanderings it obviously relates to the Scotti Tribe who travelled part of her way, from Ireland. This is a well-worn path. Prehistoric trade routes, extending from what is now Spain to Norway, united this edge of the Atlantic into what has been called by the archaeologist Maria Gimbutas 'Old Europe'. It was a great stone civilization fanning through the glens and lochs, following the geological traces laid down over aeons, always heading north. The perennial injunction was 'Go north!' (until you run out of land).

Thus, when presented with the opportunity of building by the River Nith, facing the distant landscape, I thought of these mythic and geological beginnings. The pretext was a collapsing train bridge, which needed immediate attention, and to my delight it faced north over the water. This led to a conceptual ordering. The four great faults of Scotland, up which people trekked and rivers and canals were made, could be projected on the ground backwards, to meet at infinity (or at least in Ireland). The identity of Scotland as geology, climate and the bloody line of history then became a starting point. 'Go north!' became the forced perspective of the old bridge in its new role cantilevering way out over the river. It gives dramatic views of the passing trains, the distant mountains and the occasional salmon.

The Garden of Scottish Worthies

In 2002 Railtrack came to me with a problem. The Portrack Railroad Viaduct over the River Nith in Scotland, which runs across our property, was in danger of collapse. The structural failure was not imminent but, in spite of repairs over the years, inevitable. Modern and ever heavier trainloads of coal were vibrating the bridge beyond its 1845 capacity. Reinforcing gusset plates had been added, but the cracks kept increasing. There were other pressing concerns. In the previous few years Railtrack had suffered some financial misfortunes and human catastrophes. They and their lawyers were in no mood to court further trouble and so it was in this context that I entered into a discussion on how we could both benefit by necessity. A new bridge was imperative and this meant moving the rail line 30 metres to the east.

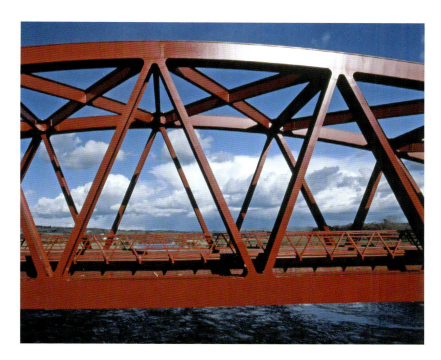

LEFT ABOVE: The Old Rail Viaduct, to the right, new railway line to left.

LEFT BELOW: Four-arch bridge 1840–2004 needing repair (and crazy Railtrack sign?) – Worthies march along with nature.

ABOVE: Zigzag Bridge close up showing the smooth curves and joints of Italian product design.

But this entailed further problems. They had to persuade several landowners for the new right of way. They had to excavate and reconstruct a large part of the existing landscape beside the Nith and construct a single-span 90-metre rail bridge. Faced with so many hurdles they were in the mood, as the saying goes, 'to negotiate towards yes'. For my part it was an opportunity to rethink garden design.

The train track connecting London and Glasgow had long been considered an eyesore and hazard by those adjacent to it. Noisy, polluting with sparks and occasional fire in the days of steam, railroads were an intrusion into the rolling hills of Dumfriesshire. Inevitably, the tracks were planted out by my father-in-law, John Keswick, with a double row of poplar trees, which give a rushing sound in the wind and appear as a stately row of columns. They acted as a screen and a tall avenue in perspective. Everything was done to camouflage the industrial reality. Since the train was seen as a sore in the heart of nature further eyesores were added near by, including a junk heap and a midden for farm waste. If beauty entices people to reproduce it, as Leonardo averred, then garbage attracts more garbage.

Types of Nature

Yet other thoughts were in the air. 'The Machine in the Garden' was one striking metaphor of critics, and Surrealists had adopted it in the 1960s. Land Artists such as Robert Smithson had attempted to turn landscape detritus into something else. And I believed that industrial waste produced as a natural consequence of economic growth could be understood as a kind of Fourth Nature, as emergent as the first three. As discussed on page 27, two types of nature had been named by Cicero and extended to a third in the sixteenth century by Italian philosophers. The garden historian John Dixon Hunt clarified this important idea in 2000 in a book on landscape theory called provocatively *Greater Perfections: The Practice of Garden Theory*. As he showed, the triple distinction was nature as (1) wilderness, (2) farming and husbandry and (3) the art of gardening. So it was logical to add to these distinctions (0) the laws of nature as zero, at the bottom, because they underlie all else, and industrial waste as (4), at the top, the last to appear in history. Why is waste a form of nature? Because rubbish and leftovers are as 'natural' to economic life today as perspiration is to exercise, by-products with a life of their own.

Such thoughts occurred to me as I contemplated the old red sandstone bridge, another railroad structure in our garden that was failing. Railtrack had plastered an official warning in orange beside one of its arches 'If you see a vehicle strike this bridge ring _____ immediately.' What a funny and ghastly sign: the Surrealism of juxtaposition had become the dirty realism of Health and Safety. Yet this failing four-arched bridge could also be seen differently. Given the right context, it might be reborn as an aqueduct in the Roman Campagna. It only waited to be stripped of its midden and orange sign, to be transformed into a contemporary Poussin. Robert Smithson had a point. Fourth Nature could be reconceived as a potential new kind of art.

After several months of hard bargaining, Railtrack and representatives of the construction company arrived at my door one Saturday morning. 'How can I negotiate with you,' I asked, 'since you don't exist?' The previous few days they had effectively gone bankrupt and had not yet emerged as Network Rail. 'You can trust us,' they countered, 'our future is assured,' and it turned out they were as good as their word. Over several more years of bargaining and designing, the engineers Scot Wilson, the construction company Carillion and the new conglomerate would meet around a table. Together we would somehow come to mutual conclusions.

For them I would provide the land, the assurance of continuity and the assent for construction. I would not demand that they remove the waste products and berms, which by law they were required to carry off. All of their existing leftovers – concrete ties, red ballast, boulders, shards of the old bridge and rails, lots of rusted rails – could be re-used. For this assent and these savings, they would agree to positive constructions, everything I wanted and designed.

The moundettes, following the engine (right), rise towards the end mounds, or Bum, and view of the landscape. The plan (left) shows the idea of 'four natures'.

This list expanded at each meeting: to the building of seventeen moundettes, a new cantilevered transformation of the old viaduct and several other features, even, if they could find it, a disused train engine. They also agreed to collaborate with me on the design of the 90-metre bridge with zigzag trusses overhead and some other visual refinements. Unbelievable: a positive-sum game! Among the visual refinements were an internal zigzag railing, a smoothly curving profile to the outer arch and inner joints. Such details have the elegant precision of Italian product design in the 1960s, the curves of an Olivetti soft-touch Divisumma portable electric typewriter blown up in size. Another shapely innovation was the strong serrated flutes of the heavy concrete piers, which I drew and they cast in huge metal moulds. Colouring the whole of the structure in shades of red was added into the bargain, another welcome surprise. 'Public-private partnership' was a piety, but here it seemed to be coming true.

Enlightenment as a Train

Over the next year, 2003, the new work ran as smoothly as our monthly meetings, and the bridge and garden took shape as designed. As they developed so did another plot in my mind: the idea that the moundettes might signify something akin to the railroad revolution, the conquest of space by machine, the story of technology, or early modernism. It was not far-fetched to think of the emergent rail garden as signifying the narrative of industrial development – what could be more symbolic of this than the train? This progressive account of history was formulated by Enlightenment thinkers in the eighteenth century, in England, Germany, Italy, France and particularly Scotland. One after another, starting with Francis Hutcheson in the 1720s, Scottish moralists, philosophers, economists and historians persuaded themselves that social evolution had a moral and progressive direction crying out to be explained. Why had we developed socially from clans to tribes to townspeople and then citizens who were polite to each other? From savagery to fellow-feeling, from ignorance to enlightenment, from brute competition to reciprocal altruism (as it would be called today)? A book I happened to be reading at the time, Arthur Herman's *The Scottish Enlightenment*, subtitled importantly *The Scot's Invention of the Modern World* (2001), told this progressive story in its amusing and nationalist detail. English critics slated the book as Caledonian exaggeration. Yet it turned out Arthur Herman was not an academic Braveheart, but rather a Jewish-American Professor Emeritus with no axe to grind. He might even be right. If any nation deserves credit then perhaps the Scots did 'invent the Modern World'. So, if the question was 'What should a rail garden be?' or 'What narrative is adequate to the impact of trains on social progress?' then a plausible answer was a Garden of Scottish Worthies.

Since its location was by necessity raised on a plateau above the rest of the garden, particularly the line of poplar trees, the Worthies would become, according to the inherent landscape pun, 'the high road to Scotland'. It was to be a high-minded collection of characters and it was also oriented due north. Furthermore, this meant that the row of poplars downhill could become the 'low road', the site for the more complex and extended history of Scotland. The Bloodline, as it is unfolding, marks the fractious story of clan warfare and bloody death, the theme that you either murdered your enemy or married them (or sometimes both). The Bloodline, under construction, contains much more than this turbulent narrative but should be seen in contrast to the progressive line of Worthies.

That story of the Scottish Enlightenment, which jumps back and forth between Glasgow and Edinburgh, is as unlikely as it is seductive. Emerging from constant strife, economic catastrophe and a repressive Scottish Kirk, in a short time the citizens of these growing cities unearthed the laws of civil life and the political economy. Francis Hutcheson, son of a Presbyterian clergyman and always searching for why God had made man virtuous, was the spiritual father of this Enlightenment project. Thus he became the first Worthy in my progressive train. To put it baldly, he argued that human beings were born to make moral judgments, that benevolent fellow-feeling was deeper than Hobbesian fear, and that everyone's goal in life is love and happiness. His arguments were subtler than this summary implies and acknowledged the selfish instincts. Indeed, by connecting self-interest with altruism, and describing them as natural, built into human nature and its economic condition, he started the discussion that would culminate with his student Adam Smith. By 1776, and the latter's *Inquiry into the Nature and Causes of the Wealth of Nations*, one Scottish writer had followed a predecessor developing the same theme. We use the metaphor of a 'straight-line argument'

to show how ideas follow logically on from each other. The Scottish Enlightenment could be seen as train cars moving along a coherent track pulled by the overriding idea of social and economic progress, the machine.

Adam Smith, in his treatise on wealth, reassembled the successive arguments of Hutcheson, Kames, Robertson and David Hume. He accepted that the moral nature of human beings was deep, but also, as Hume said, that they were driven by self-interest and the passions, not God. He could see that the historical social evolution that Lord Kames had analysed – from hunter-gatherers to nomads to farmers to traders – demands more and more cooperation and competition. William Robertson, Smith's friend, had applied Kames's four-stage theory to the history of Europe since the fall of Rome and come up with the progressive view of the Enlightenment. It culminates in the 'manners . . . which occupy and distinguish polished nations'. 'Polished nations': this was another metaphor of Hutcheson and Smith I particularly liked, especially because I was starting a collection of polished stones. As Arthur Herman wrote of the Enlightenment thinkers, the leading values of 'refinement, manners and polish' came from the world of jewellers and stonemasons. Polishing stones and marbles, making gems shine, was seen like social intercourse, the good dinner parties of intellectual discourse in eighteenth-century Edinburgh, where 'we polish one another, and rub off our Corners and rough sides by a sort of amicable Collision'. The words are Lord Shaftesbury's, but the sentiments

LEFT: Francis Hutcheson (1694–1746) and the train in the background.

BELOW: Adam Smith (1723–1790), the sign and saying on the back of a moundette.

were taken up by successive Scots to help explain the cooperative passions and reconcile them with the selfish ones.

The contradictions lay at the heart of Smith's *Wealth of Nations*. Why should human beings cooperate positively rather than follow their self-interested passions and compete negatively? Or, what makes the sum of individual greed turn ninety degrees to its direction as a social force and result in general benevolence? The cynical French aphorism 'every man for himself, God for us all' no longer explained this hidden hand, this unexpected outcome that non-capitalist people find so counter-intuitive. Adam Smith found the Enlightenment answer and positive equation. It was (1) the specialization of labour that increased productivity, plus (1) the motive of self-betterment: two human forces leading to the progress of civil society. But these also led to monopoly and a conspiracy against the public unless they were deflected by a third force in a new direction – real, small-scale competition, the kind that was going on in Glasgow. (1) plus (1) deflected by (1) = 5. If the synergy worked there would be real progress.

This idea, I began to think, could be well represented by train cars hurtling along a single line and pulled by a mechanism, the engine, which James Watt and other Scottish inventors had perfected. Hence the notion of a train garden of Scottish Worthies leading forward in a procession to the near present, pulled by the engine of progress. Each Worthy was conceived as a train-car-animal, a friendly beast made of industrial and growing material. The Worthies should seem to slouch into the future, up the track. Each would have a boulder for the head, concrete beams and ballast for shoulders, *Mahonia japonica* – with its yellow berries and perfume – for its back and a red bridge-flange surmounted by a sign for the tail. The 10-foot aluminium flash would have the Worthy's name, dates and a fitting epigram laser-cut in the metal. For Adam Smith there was an obvious aphorism: 'Thus without intending it, without knowing it, the rich advance the interests of society . . . They are led by an invisible hand . . .'

As with some other sayings, I had to change the order of Smith's famous words to fit the space. But like so many other aphorisms it worked on a connotative level with the idea of a linear train of progress. Words in stone or metal are dangerous signifiers, tending to dominate all other meaning. They are cannibalistic and imperial, as semioticians argue, swallowing other signs like a voracious slogan. They may be reductive like a one-liner, distracting experience of the whole landscape just as a pedantic insertion does in a text. Hence the gentle art of epigraphy has to weigh meaning so that evocation and description exist in some ambiguity. The cut signs here say more than they appear to and often relate to the overall idea and train of thought. Metaphor is 'a carrying over' of one idea to another, and words carry meaning as train cars carry coal. So there is a line of thought in the actual quotes, but it is an idea to be weighed after the experience of walking the site.

Who is Worthy?

I found Arthur Herman's account of the Scottish Enlightenment convincing and enjoyably informative, but it had one drawback that became more and more obvious. As I started to work out a long list of suitable Worthies from which to choose, before reducing it to the seventeen for which I had moundettes, it became apparent there were no women. Could there be an Enlightenment Project of only one sex? It sounds more like the Dark Ages. There must have been some women who were actively involved in the transformation of Scotland. Beyond this question, there was the definition of worthiness, an eighteenth-century notion that had inspired the Temple of British Worthies at Stowe. Should they always be connected with the political economy or the technical progress of the Enlightenment – be inventors, philosophers and scientists? Only types, who were obvious to choose, like David Hume and James Watt? Would 'good' women be eligible: St Margaret or Mary Queen of Scots?

In the end I settled on the notion of compound worthiness, the idea that it could not be just good works or technical invention or progressive politics, but something more. As I conceived it, the Worthy candidate should be first of all dead (no lobbying wanted) and above all creative, risk-taking and poetic as well as rational. This more expansive definition allowed on to the list the semi-Enlightenment characters such as Robert Burns and Walter Scott, writers whose mix of nostalgia and progress was complex but certainly creative. It also opened the train to women. I consulted friends and acquaintances such as Charlene Spretnak and Tina Louise Fiske; I wrote to Rose Pipes, who was compiling a biography of famous Scottish women; to their suggestions were added lists of Scottish women writers and artists that could be gleaned from the Internet and from conversations with historians. For the final list of Worthies and their quotes, see below, but it did include four and a half women: the poet Joanna Baillie, the scientist Mary Somerville, the healer and suffragette Elsie Maude Inglis and the writer Rebecca West. The 'half' was a split sign shared between husband and wife: Margaret MacDonald, the designer and artist who greatly influenced Charles Rennie Mackintosh. She is usually overlooked for her more famous partner and, put together with a personal quote on a sign, the pair became a compound Worthy:

> Nothing could be more perfect than sitting where I was
> this morning
> Only you did not come to meet me at the end of the tunnel.

Their misspelled 'tunnel' adds to their poignant, long-standing connection.

A bridge is a natural symbol of collective endeavour, since it joins opposite sides of a river, often two communities. The anarchist dilemma 'Where to meet and in whose middle of the river?'

CRANE

To make a 90-metre bridge jump the water in one leap takes a lot of muscle, here the combination of two structural types: the arch and the truss. And to assemble the parts on the site and swing them into place takes what was called 'the biggest crane in the world'. This itself, as it moved in pieces around Europe, had to be assembled from many struts and joists. The process of construction thus became a landscape event, something to observe over the weeks and an excuse for midnight parties when zero hour approached. Individual struts and connecting elements made in Wales were bolted and welded together to form two giant arches. Then, late on successive Sunday nights after the main line was closed to trains, both sides of the River Nith were floodlit. The site resembled an instant city, crawling with men in hard hats, a James Bond fantasy of ant-men, each of whom knew precisely what machine to drive, how they fitted into the superorganism. Then, at 2am, the giant crane lifted, ever so slowly, one arch to just above its supports so that finally two little ant-men could push it into place by hand, exactly. That the equivalent of a skyscraper could be nudged on to its minuscule foundations by twenty fingers beggars belief, until you remember that anything hanging down far enough, from the biggest crane in the world, swings easily.

ABOVE LEFT AND CENTRE: The Cantilevered Zigzag Bridge.

LEFT: Arch truss.

RIGHT: The bridge finished.

BELOW LEFT: The biggest crane in the world lifts a 90-metre truss into place at night, 27 December 2003.

BELOW RIGHT: Aerial construction view of Zigzag Bridge.

has to be faced and overcome. Consensus and teamwork are the deep metaphor of bridge-building, as they have proven in our design, jointly worked through by me with the engineer from Scot Wilson, Mike Hackney, and the representative in charge of the Carillion construction group, Andrew Stocks. Because they and the foremen of the contractor played such an important role in making the bridges and gardens, I had their names laser-cut in another aluminium sign. This now starts the whole sequence of space from the river and it stands in the Rail Garden between the Zigzag and Cantilevered Bridges.

PORTRACK SCOTTI AND GARDEN OF RAILS 2004
For those who have helped
Andrew Stocks Mike Hackney Chris Curley Harry Cain Gary Muir

With all this cooperation, however, the competitive instincts that the Enlightenment thinkers had debated came to the fore. On completion of the Zigzag Bridge, banners were festooned over the top arch of the structure as a series of identity brands: the Welsh flag and its griffin, the Scottish cross of St Andrew, the English red cross and the logo of Scott Wilson. Several nationalities had had a role to play and they were claiming it. Is this counter-claiming the evanescent notion of Britishness, such mutually expressed nationalism?

The Bloodline, which is not yet constructed except for the hanging banners in aluminium, will present the struggle of the Scotti tribe versus the Picts, as well as earlier and later battles. War, as the intermittent human condition, is an idea behind other landscape schemes I have pursued and, as Ian Hamilton Finlay has shown, a fitting subject of garden art. The Scots as a nation have often fought for their independence, obviously, and their history is swimming in blood, for both admirable and unfortunate reasons. That the Scots are good mercenaries and selfless fighters is clear from the record of sacrifice. More men from Scotland were killed in the First World War per capita of population than from any other country except Serbia and Turkey. The Rail Garden will some day convey this sacrifice and ferocity in its elements: the red sandstone, red ballast and blood-red metal. All of this is now countered by the green of the landscape and the wedges of wild strawberries between the rails.

If culture is destiny, and that includes the fierce struggle for identity, then so too is geography, especially Scottish. As the theorist of fractal geometry is fond of asking, 'How long is the coastline of Scotland?' 'Infinite,' comes the answer because, measured down to the smallest details, its fractal dimension shows literally countless ins and outs. This complexity, and fractured landscape, has no doubt isolated the clans and contributed to both the loyalties and the disagreements. But it is also a reason for the rugged beauty of which every Scot feels proud. Walter Scott's aluminium sign carries his well-known words:

LEFT, ABOVE: The Cantilevered Bridge from The Bum, with its forced perspective and map of Scotland. LEFT, BELOW: The Red Bridge, designed by Charles Jencks in conjunction with Scot Wilson and Carillion, won the Saltaire Award for Engineering Excellence 2004. ABOVE: The Scotti Garden of Rails, and those who built it.

> Breathes there a man with soul so dead,
> Who never to himself has said,
> This is my own, my native land.

Thus the landscape is the subject of the Rail Garden too, especially by the Cantilevered Bridge, the remains of the 1845 structure that now lean 60 feet over the water and point north. The ancient myth of Scota was the injunction to her to 'Go north!', a command followed by so many Europeans, Romans, Irish and others. The bridges, happily for the symbolism, point due north at the distant landscape, across the water. When you walk up the legs and bum that grow out of the seventeen Worthies, and climb to the top to survey trains hurtling along the new Zigzag Bridge, the view of the River Nith and distant hills can be taken in, a spectacular sight made more dramatic by the sudden emergence of a train. You may look down and see underfoot angles of a triangle coming together, and then look up to see the convergence of the forced perspective in a small model of the bridge. Then you will note how these, and other angles in the ground, relate to a miniature map of Scotland made from the same red ballast and rusted metal of the Rail Garden. Four red lines divide the map into its geological sections, the four main faults that run through Scotland creating the extraordinary lochs and, now, canals. The rocks, fossils and faults tell a strange story for those who have eyes to see it: Old Scotland, bounced into by England and the Continent, partly bounced off to Nova Scotia and North America. Its ancient rocks are both beautiful and billions of years old, just as much part of the story as the characters who have enjoyed them.

THE HIGH AND LOW ROAD

The Enlightenment is set against the Bloodline as two views of Scottish history. At the top, small mounds carry the signs of Enlightenment thinkers and the seventeen figures are conceived as railway carriages pulled by the engine at the front – the 'train of progress'. The row of poplar trees holds red aluminium signs with important dates and names, events and massacres that punctuated Scottish history. The bridge was designed along with engineers Scot Wilson to relate to the seven red bridges of Portrack, and the Cantilevered Bridge to its right was converted from the remains of the previous one.

THE SCOTTISH ENLIGHTENMENT

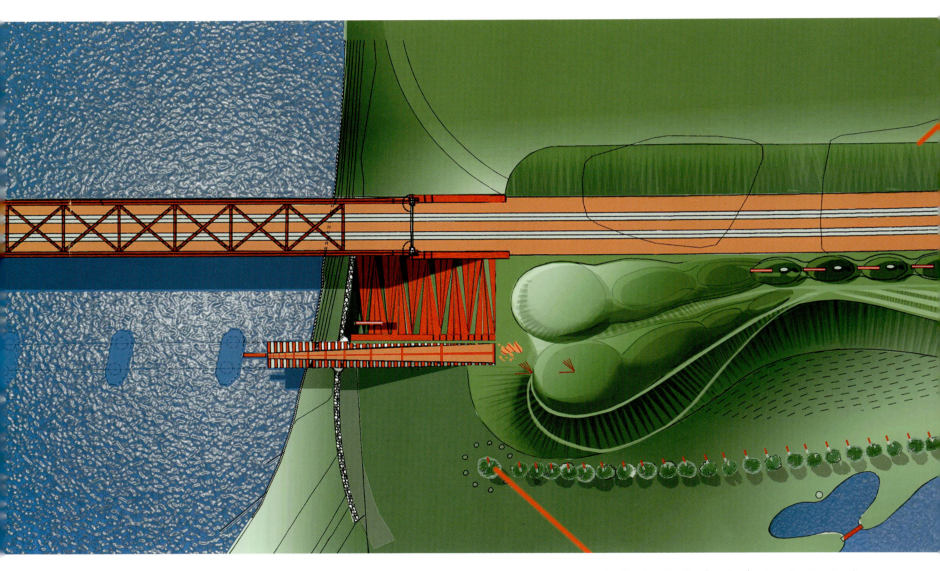

THE BLOODLINE

EDWARD I (1296)
AULD ALLIANCE (1294)
ALEXANDER III (1249)
MACBETH (1032)
KEN CONSTANTIN II (940)
DUNNICHEN (685)
ST EOCHAID (580)
ST COLUMBA (563)
ALBA PENTAGON (500–843)
FERGUS MAC EIRC (500)
ST NINIAN (397)
AGRICOLA (84)

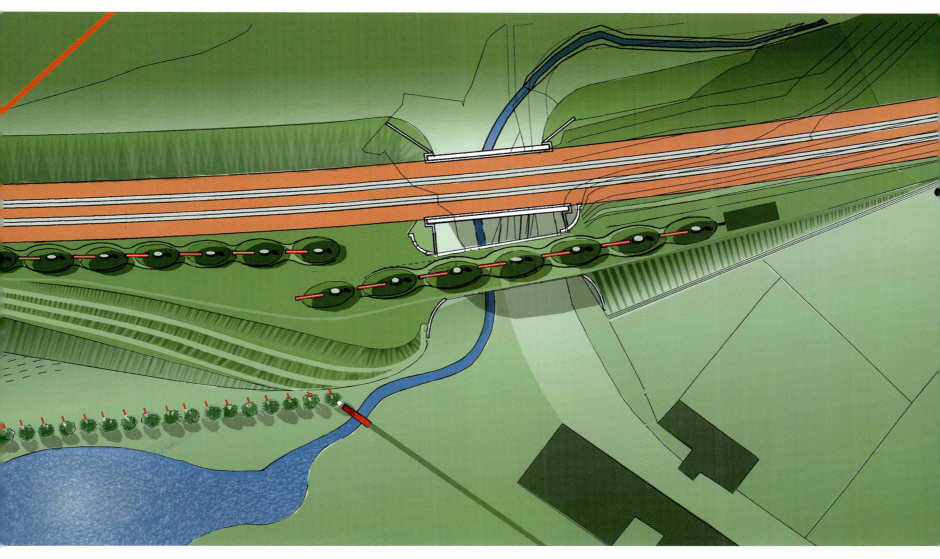

SCOTTISH ENLIGHTENMENT: THE TRAIN OF PROGRESS AND THE PASSIONS

FRANCIS HUTCHESON (1694–1746)

My first Worthy is an attractive figure from the beginning of the Scottish Enlightenment because of the way he questioned the two depressing accounts of human nature dominant at the time. The Presbyterian dogma that we are predestined for good or evil was as grim as it was repressive, and equal in virulence to the other main view, the Hobbesian account of the primeval state of nature, the war of all against all. The former exonerated fundamentalists and witch-hunts, the latter justified the Fascism of the period and the Leviathan. Hutcheson, by contrast, had a passion for freedom expressed in his posthumous *The System of Moral Philosophy*, which, in the words of the time, 'boldly asserts the rights of resisting in the people, when their fundamental privileges are invaded'. It sounds American, but the Scots' love of freedom and their strong resistance to tyranny are also intermittent passions, expressed in the Declaration of Arbroath of 1320. With Hutcheson and the following Worthies, that resistance is as much intellectual as physical. He held tenaciously to the idea that human beings are born with an innate moral sense: 'From the very frame of our nature we are determined to perceive pleasure in the practice of virtue, and to approve of it when practised by ourselves or others.'

His first book, *An Inquiry into the Origin of Our Ideas of Beauty and Virtue* (1725), extended this spontaneous pleasure to aesthetics, but it was the natural affection between people that motivated his theory. If happiness and pleasure are goals in life then the greatest delights come from helping others – not only because we, or the species, want some future payback from altruism, but because the affection is basic, a pleasure in itself. 'There is no mortal without some love towards others and desire in the happiness of some other persons as well as his own.' This 'delight in the Good of others', Arthur Herman shows in his book *The Scottish Enlightenment*, was not held naïvely or without taking into account the 'self-love' that Hobbes said underlay it all. But Hutcheson's point was that fellow-feeling, even if it had a utilitarian component, could not be reduced to a complex equation of future rewards. One of Hutcheson's later publications was *Reflections upon Laughter and Remarks Upon the Fable of Bees* (1750), and anyone who has reflected on a joke knows it is funny not only because it may be good for the future of our species, improves the immune system and exercises the stomach muscles, but because it upsets habitual thought and is enjoyed 'for itself'. The reductivists that Hutcheson was fighting at the time, just like today's 'selfish gene' theorists, could never accept that there were multiple causes of behaviour and that some were by-products of primary causes. Beauty, love, altruism, happiness, laughter and culture in general may serve some utilitarian purpose, but they are also semi-autonomous genres that have their own being. Hutcheson fought gently for this view, one that his students – the next two Worthies, David Hume and Adam Smith – developed and modified. We think of the Enlightenment as the triumph of reason over the other dispositions, but one of the Scottish contributions to this movement was to show the primacy of all the passions. Progress, by acknowledging and redirecting the passions, was their gift to posterity.

Deciding which epigrams summarize each thinker and fit into the available space – the aluminium rectangle set atop a 12-foot section of the old bridge – was a comparative exercise. Each Worthy is constructed from growing nature and industrial waste: the old railway parts, the ballast of small granite rocks, the concrete tie-beams and above all the huge I-beams of the 1840s. I watched these being torn apart by a giant machine, with mammoth pincers for teeth. They could rip through each steel gusset plate in about thirty minutes. Mass de-production, and very progressive it was too. As I observed this spectacle going on over the gently flowing River Nith, I reflected on some of Hutcheson's words, wondering what epitomized his thought, and what was brief enough. 'Wisdom denotes the pursuing of the best ends by the best means. . . . From the very frame of our nature . . . a delight in the Good of others . . . natural impulse . . . freedom . . . New Light . . . fellow feeling?' All the creative destruction leading to progress was going on about me, so I settled on a quote from *Concerning Moral Good and Evil*: 'That action is best, which procures the greatest happiness for the greatest numbers.' Hutcheson believed that goodness was a basic impulse written into human nature but, like a good Scot, he also believed it paid dividends.

THE PHILOSOPHER AND THE FISHWIFE: DAVID HUME (1711–76)

On his way home from Edinburgh one day, Hume fell into a deep bog and shouted for aid. 'Is that David Hume the atheist?' asked a passing fishwife, who refused to be the good Christian and help. 'That may well be,' she replied to Hume, 'but ye shall na get out o' that, till ye become a Christian yourself: and repeat the Lord's Prayer.' This he promptly did, and she pulled him out of his hole. Hume recounted his temporary conversion with humour, the kind of wit that, in spite of his unfashionable atheism, recommended him for sparkling dinner parties. Hume was the first philosopher of the future consumer society and totalitarianism, because he viewed human nature as based on self-gratification and passions, not on reason. Learning from Hutcheson the primary place of desires and affection, he outlined a realist psychology in his *Treatise of Human Nature* (1734), much to Hutcheson's displeasure. For Hume, our naturally depraved passions had to be channelled or canalized in a new direction by society, laws and government: 'There is no passion, therefore, capable of controlling the interested affection but the very affection itself, by an alteration of its direction.' Understanding the passions as a forcefield that had to be redirected was an idea that Adam Smith took up in his idea of the competitive market, and Hume's realism famously awoke Immanuel Kant from 'dogmatic slumber'. But it was Hume's passion for liberty, both social and individual, that puts him in the great line of Enlightenment thinkers.

Each Worthy is laser-cut in an aluminium rectangle 2 feet high by 10 feet long, placed on the train girder of the destroyed bridge. The average height of the name characters is 7 inches and the epigram characters average 3 inches. Thus the progressive Worthies each rolled off the assembly line, blazed and braised in sparkling aluminium.

EMPATHY AND SOCIAL CONSTRUCTION: ADAM SMITH (1723–90)

Adam Smith adapted many ideas from Hutcheson, above all the notion of the way fellow feeling is basic to human beings and society as a whole. Because personality is forged through empathy with others, we feel their feelings, understand their minds and can learn to appreciate such things as virtue and beauty. Such judgments are internalized and soon morality emerges as the inner debate of different opinions: 'When I endeavour to examine my own conduct I divide myself, as it were, into two persons . . . the first is the spectator, whose sentiments with regard to my own conduct I endeavour to enter into to, by placing myself in his situation, and by considering how it would appear to me, when seen from that particular point of view. The second is the agent, the person whom I properly call myself . . . The first is the judge; the second the person judged of.' (*The Theory of the Moral Sentiments*, 1759.) The clash of multiple inner selves, the notion of conscience – even thought – arising from different voices that are learned socially, helped Smith to take the next step. This was his famous formulation of the market system led by an invisible hand. It resulted by deflecting greed or self-interest by another force – competition – in a new direction, that of benign production. As long as there wasn't a monopoly, the invisible hand of the marketplace would tend to produce 'the system of perfect liberty'. Reality may not be that simple, but the notion of redirecting base social forces towards greater freedom remains one of the great Enlightenment ideas of emergence. 'It is not from the benevolence of the butcher, the brewer, or the baker, that we expect our dinner, but from their regard to their own interest . . . a simple system of natural liberty establishes itself of its own accord.'

DEEP TIME ROCKS: JAMES HUTTON (1726–97)

With Adam Smith and other public intellectuals, Hutton convened Edinburgh's convivial Oyster Club, where ideas and food replenished each other. His *Theory of the Earth* (1795) explained the notion of deep time, that the earth's history was millions of years old, not the thousands that had been assumed by philosophers, scientists and the public. Looking into this 'abyss of time' was indeed frightening, but it was also irrefutably evident. The way rocks set above each other in horizontal layers could be dated, and then more layers were found vertically stacked underneath: thus the 'unconformity' proved the earth existed for aeons, not biblical years. Charles Lyell created the science of geology from such insights; and from the same conversations Erasmus Darwin picked up ideas for *Zoonomia, or the Laws of Organic Life* (1794–6).

WILD AND REFINED: ROBERT ADAM (1728–92)

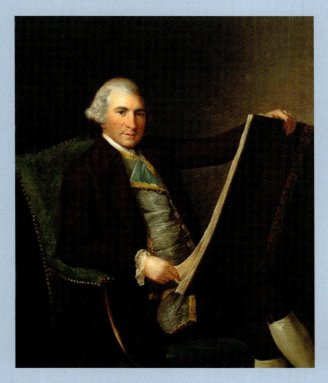

The Adam family of architects were not afraid of speculation, overreaching, political intrigue, risk, beauty, vulgarity, history and contradiction. Robert Adam made the most of contrast and movement in his architecture. The wild Scottish landscape outside could be set off by a daintily cosy interior. He took classical decoration being dug up at Herculaneum and the Dalmatian Coast and 'transfused it, with novelty and variety'. Employing more than 3,000 craftsmen in their English workshops, the Adam brothers mass-produced a quality version of that standby oxymoron, the 'modern ancient'.

PRACTICAL INVENTION: JAMES WATT (1736–1819)

Not the inventor of the steam engine but its philosopher and improver. Self-taught in most things, and an indefatigable optimist when it came to problem solving, Watt epitomized the Glasgow spirit of making things work, hence his goal to outsmart or seduce a difficult mistress: 'Nature has its weak side – if only we can find it.' The weak side for steam power was its potential for constant, rotary action, and once discovered by Watt it led to the engine being applied to ironworks, pottery kilns, dredging canals, steamboats, steam-trains, most factory work and then the entire Industrial Revolution.

SHRINKING SPACETIME: THOMAS TELFORD (1757–1834)

In the early eighteenth century it used to take ten days to travel from London to Edinburgh and a day and a half from Glasgow to Edinburgh. By the time Thomas Telford finished with his bridge, road and canal building, the journey time had shrunk to two days, and four and a half hours. The engineering feats were amazing. The Menai Strait Bridge of 1826 was the longest suspension bridge in the world and the Caledonian Canal, finished in 1822, connected the Atlantic Ocean to Inverness with 60 miles of lochs and locks. His visual refinements were equally impressive. Cast-iron and filigree steel struck one geometrical tone, while dense walls of masonry hit a very welcome counterpoint.

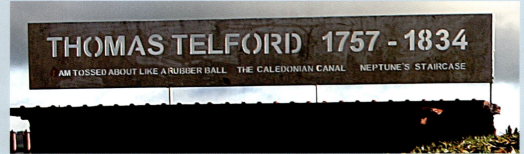

NEW MUSIC: ROBERT BURNS (1759–96)

The young poet worked Ellisland, a farm next to Portrack, that looked across the Nith Valley at the weathered hills and ancient stronghold of the Comyns. From these points he composed new songs, collecting fragments of vernacular and popular music that were disappearing. In the field Burns would hum and whistle away a tune that elaborated the basic idea. Then, when inspiration flagged, he would race to the farmhouse to write up his combination, keeping as close to the previous spirit as the new words and sounds would allow. He saw the construction of this 'Musical Museum' as a patriotic not remunerative service, and so it has proved.

> But sweeter flows the Nith to me,
> Where Comyns ance had high command.
> When shall I see that honour'd land,
> That winding stream I love so dear!

LYRICAL MORALIST: JOANNA BAILLIE (1762–1851)

Poet and playwright, daughter of a Presbyterian minister who was brought up on the site of William Wallace's execution and the struggles of the Covenanters, Baillie responded to both passion and piety. Her aesthetic treatise *Plays on the Passions* (1798), as well as her comedies and tragedies, were praised for their 'masculine' rigour, an index of the stereotypes she had to overcome. Lord Byron wrote: '". . . the composition of a tragedy requires testicles." If this be true, Lord knows what Joanna Baillie does; I suppose she borrows them.' As if Byron himself were missing something important, he modelled his romantic heroes on some of her popular characters. Her lyrical imagination is evident on the lines cut through the aluminium flash:

> Butterfly, butterfly, speed through the air,
> The ring-bird follows thee fast,
> And the monkey looks up with a greedy stare;
> Speed on till the peril is past.

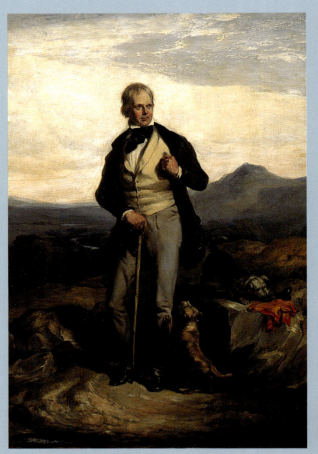

THE ART OF HISTORICAL CONTRADICTION: WALTER SCOTT (1771–1832)

If David Hume made passion the engine of reason, then Walter Scott brought sentiment to the eye of history and dramatized its conflicts. 'All men who have turned out worth anything have had the chief hand in their own education,' he reported, thinking of his own self-invention through folk culture and the art of the historical novel. Dogs and lower animals took a shine to Scott. 'Even a pig,' says a biographer, 'took a sentimental attachment to him.' While his own passion favoured the past and lost causes such as the Jacobites, his art was in seeing that the contemporary sensibility is formed in a dual loyalty, or a tension between progressive and reactionary sentiments.

> Breathes there a man with soul so dead,
> Who never to himself has said,
> This is my own, my native land.

UNITY OF UNIVERSE: MARY SOMERVILLE (1780–1870)

Another auto-didact, Mary Somerville also had to overcome the usual prejudice against women thinkers. She picked up mathematics and Euclidean geometry from the painter Alexander Nasmyth, and then applied them with great purpose to her first love, astronomy. She wrote several standard texts, among them *The Connexion of the Physical Sciences* (1834) and *Physical Geography* (1848), but it was her translation and explanations of Laplace's *Mécanique céleste* (1831) that she valued the most. Widely admired for dedicating her life to the 'noble object' of demonstrating the unity of the sciences, she expressed radical beliefs for the time, feeling that 'the heavens afford the most sublime subject of study . . . and that not only man, but the globe he inhabits, nay the whole system of which it forms so small a part, might be annihilated, and its extinction be unperceived in the immensity of creation'. This feeling for the scientific sublime was also expressed in poetic insights: 'I saw the edge of the moon leave the limb of the sun.' Oxford's Somerville College, where other independent women followed their self-education, was named after her example.

INTELLECT: THOMAS BABINGTON MACAULAY (1800–59)

Good works, good histories, good journalism, good speeches in the House of Commons and too many quotes from which to choose. Macaulay helped form the Anti-Slavery Society in 1823, wrote for *Edinburgh Review* and penned his multi-volume classic *History of England* from 1849. 'Knowledge advances by steps, and not by leaps'; 'The gallery in which the reporters sit has become the fourth estate of the realm'; 'The highest intellects, like the tops of mountains, are the first to catch and reflect the dawn'; 'The history of England is emphatically the history of progress'; 'There is only one cure for the evils which newly acquired freedom produces, and that is freedom'; 'The issue is not whether the constitution was better formerly, but whether we can make it better now'; 'The great cause of revolutions is this, that while nations move onwards, constitutions stand still'; 'In listening to him,' said one spectator, 'you seemed to be like a traveller passing through a rich and picturesque country by railroad.'

THE GOOD DOCTOR: DAVID LIVINGSTONE (1813–73)

A medical missionary and anti-slavery activist, through his long explorations Livingstone redrew the maps of Africa. He ascribed moral and physical energy to exploration: 'The mere animal pleasure of travelling in a wild unexplored country is very great . . . Great exercise imparts elasticity to the muscles, fresh and healthy blood circulates through the brain, the mind works well, the eye is clear, the step is firm.' But the example of Christ inspired him to use medicine and the healing as weapons in the fight for aboriginal cultures: 'We must smile at the heaps of nonsense which have been written about the Negro intellect . . . I do not believe in any incapacity of the African in either mind or heart.' And, against the bigotry of the Boers: 'Africans are not by any means unreasonable . . . I think unreasonableness is more a hereditary disease in Europe.'

GARGANTUAN OPTIMIST: ANDREW CARNEGIE (1835–1919)

Taking a benign view of human nature, opposed to that of David Hume, Carnegie was ever the optimist about society, the end of monarchy, the superiority of democracy and applied altruism. The example before his eyes was his own ascent from poverty and ignorance. Since he amassed the greatest fortune ever made through transport, oil and steel, he was determined to give it all away. Hence his idealism about learning and Shakespeare, self-betterment and literature, pulling oneself up by the bootstraps. He harangued millionaires: 'Man must have an idol and the amassing of wealth is one of the worst species of idolatry! No idol is more debasing than the worship of money!' 'My aspirations take a higher flight. Mine be it to have contributed to the enlightenment and the joys of the mind, to the things of the spirit, to all that tends to bring into the lives of the toilers of Pittsburgh sweetness and light.' 'Free to the People' was his munificent contribution.

SACRIFICE: ELSIE MAUDE INGLIS (1864–1917)

Inglis was raised in Edinburgh and became a fully qualified doctor. Yet when war broke out in 1914 the War Office put her down with the remark: 'My good lady, go home and sit still.' Having been a keen founder of the Scottish Women's Suffrage Federation in 1906 she was hardly one to cave in, and much to the British government's displeasure she went to the battlefields of France and established the first hospital fully staffed by women. Thereafter in 1915 and 1916, fighting adversity and in great personal danger, she set up women's units in Serbia, Salonika, Romania, Malta, Corsica and Russia. As she said: 'It was a great day in my life when I discovered that I did not know what fear was.'

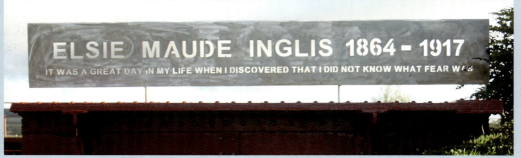

NEW LIGHT: MARGARET MACDONALD (1865–1933)
AND C.R. MACKINTOSH (1868–1928)

Her husband got nearly all the credit in spite of crediting her, but MacDonald probably originated the Mackintosh Style of elongated and symbolic stylization, of geometricized ornament and suggestive veiling. Dismissed in England because of their mysticism as 'the Spook School', the Glasgow Four culminated a hundred years of national romanticism, traceable through Robert Burns and Walter Scott. The Mackintoshes' take on this included nature and the vernacular, as long as they were rendered fresh and particular. Where others tended towards naturalistic swirls and historicism, they aimed towards a spare abstraction punctuated by enigmatic nature symbols. Their opposition between the individual and the generic influenced Europe, particularly Vienna and then the whole Modern Movement: the greatest visual impact of the Scottish Enlightenment. But their joint creation and affection also look prescient today:

> Nothing could be more perfect than sitting where I was this morning –
> Only you did not come to meet me at the end of the tunnell.

CRITICAL WIT: REBECCA WEST (1892–1983)

As a young woman she was a socialist and suffragette and then she developed into a journalist, novelist, broadcaster and political analyst, with strong opinions well expressed over sixty years. She picked her men – H.G. Wells, Charlie Chaplin and Max Beaverbrook – as major protagonists and then shared the stage with them. Ironic about the dark side of motivation and a sceptical humourist, she summarized Enlightenment thought on the unintended consequences of the passions: 'It is always one's virtues and not one's vices that precipitate one's disaster'; 'Life ought to be a struggle of desire toward adventures whose nobility will fertilize the soul'; 'It is the soul's duty to be loyal to its own desires. It must abandon itself to its master passion'; 'Did St Francis preach to the birds? Whatever for? If he really liked birds he would have done better to preach to the cats'; 'For certainly we need rebellion. Unless woman is going to make trouble she had better not seek her emancipation.'

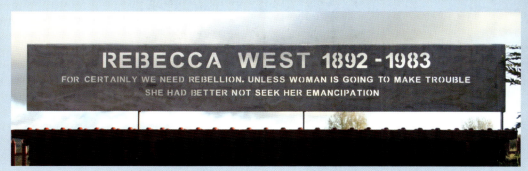

A screen of forty poplars marches to a steady beat. Each one has a metal banner that is laser-cut with the name of one incident or person in the Bloodline. The red line of aluminium names the event or battle or wedding or important creation in Scotland over the last 1,700 years, culminating in the Parliament of 1999. Down the hill from the Worthies, this Bloodline is the Low Road. One either killed one's enemy or married them, or both, making the bloody and gruesome history so often told that is punctuated by remarkable achievements. The Bloodline, still under construction, signifies the old and new genetic uses of the phrase.

ABOVE: The Fife Earth Project. Landforms and lake at St Ninians, Kelty, 2003 initial design, 2009 final design, construction starts (perspective, Madelon Vriesendorp).

RIGHT: Several early projects made over five years, as the requirements changed: from Coal into Landscape to ScotWorld–ScotLoch.

6: SCOTLOCH

The Fife Earth Project

Five miles beyond the historic town of Dunfermline, on the main route going north in Scotland, the M90 mounts the crest of a small hill and then descends into a wide green valley. Ahead to the left are the dark pines of Thornton Wood. They define the side of the hill, and a natural bowl that frames the site of work: an open-cast coal mine. This became an opportunity to restore the land not as is usually done for such jobs – flat and for cows – but with four landforms, a lake 500 metres long and some social facilities. For the community and those travelling north, I also saw it as a chance to explore the idea of Scotland as itself a miniature landscape. The logic of the situation led to this conclusion because of the by-products from digging coal. Two artificial lakes, a lot of rocks, some attractive woods and a precipitous peak from which to view all of this: that is, the four essential features of the Scottish landscape. If national identity was forged by the land, then why not use it to further explore identity? Hence the resultant design, with a lake in the shape of Scotland, an orientation point for travellers and a world within a world. Depicted as a *mappa mundi*, this site maps both the Scottish nation and the way it has dispersed over the earth. The Scottish diaspora, it is sometimes called, is at once both tragedy and exemplary act of transformation. Did the fleeing Scots invent the modern world, as the historian Arthur Herman suggests, and export their version of the Enlightenment? They certainly took their culture with them, and renamed a good part of it.

Four large mounds afford a view over the artificial loch in the shape of Scotland. Pathways allow one to explore the layout of the land, to find the major cities picked out as stone islands and to understand the four major faults. These geological shifts in the land give Scotland its characteristic mountains and valleys running north-east–south-west, the landscape that has done so much to define Scottish identity. While ascending the helical mound nearest the road, one can see how all this fits together and, at the top, view the real Firth of Forth and its relation to the map outlined below by water. For travellers driving north, ScotLoch provides a vivid introduction to the wilderness, settlements and geology. Touring from one art destination to the next has created that contemporary character known as the 'art pilgrim', a traveller not unlike those European explorers of 5,000 ago. Every year they walked, and sailed, the route from Galicia to Norway, stopping at such ritual landscapes as Brodgar and Stonehenge. At that time these destinations were orientated to the salient cosmic points and landscape features. Today the compulsion to define identity and explore is serviced by the machine, but the ritual is no less compelling.

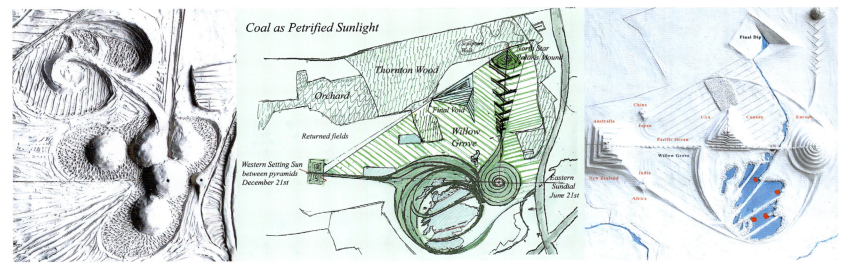

Coal as Petrified Sunlight

The Great Influence of the Rock People

For the last 300 years, Scotland has had a pervasive influence around the world through its culture and unlikely temperament. The effect of the Scottish Enlightenment is well known, the nation's aid to the British Empire is becoming understood and even its nastier virtues, the mercenaries who knew how to fight, are acknowledged. The people are customarily hard-working and stubborn, with the result that this small culture, like the Jewish one, has had more influence on the rest of the globe than other comparable ethnicities.

There are about 5 million people living in Scotland today and, elsewhere, the rubbery figure of 40 million descendants (I had not come across this sociological term, until trying to pin down this number). Most of the population migrated from Europe in pre-historic times, during the early Neolithic period, starting about 10,000 years ago. These roots are reflected in the myths, language and remaining rock art, especially the stone circles and cup and ring marks that dot the coastlines. Surveying this landscape with imagination, Neal Ascherson comes to a conclusion about what it means, listening to the echoes of his ancestral tones in *Stone Voices* (and a book of that name). Geology and stones are destiny. They divide up and unite the clans and create what, from a fractal viewpoint, is said to be the country with an infinite shoreline of rocks (and this is before seeing the infinite profile of the mountains). The tall stone razor blades of Stenness and Brodgar, speaking to each other across a causeway, epitomize an art that will carry on for five millennia.

The Scottish have emigrated in vast numbers, setting up plantations, or colonies, in the seventeenth century on the Vistula River in Poland, and in Ulster in Ireland. Two centuries later millions emigrated to Canada, North America, Australia and New Zealand. These four countries benefited enormously from this influx of creative people. Andrew Carnegie, raised near the Kelty coal site, made the point: 'America would have been a poor show had it not been for the Scotch.' The same could be said of the other three countries and, ironically, has been said of the British Empire.

Some of this unlikely and humorous story is told in Arthur Herman's *The Scottish Enlightenment*. Whether or not they are the most responsible for creating the modern world can be argued, but indisputable is the widespread and deep influence. The globe is, in part, a 'Scot World', and this relatively hidden story deserves to be celebrated with the rocks and landscape that have helped make the people.

In the first instance the most significant influence was geological. Tectonic plates separated from each other over a billion years ago as Europe bumped into England and parts of Scotland ricocheted off to Iceland, then Greenland and Nova Scotia. Admittedly this is a very approximate description, but we know its poetic truth because of living and dead evidence from both sides of the present Atlantic divide. The rocks and fossilized plants of the two continental edges

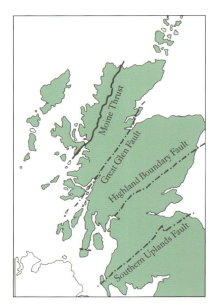

TOP LEFT: The four faults divide Scotland into geological epochs and the oldest, westernmost rocks prove its connections to Canada and America.

TOP RIGHT AND ABOVE: Stenness and Brodgar Stone Circles on Orkney, 3,000 BC, epitomize the Scottish tradition of stone-land art and remain the standard.

RIGHT: Australian, New Zealand and American Scot names.

show these connections. For instance, Scotland and Canada share big trilobites, while England, which did the bumping, has small ones. Reflect on the sequence of movement west. Emigrations follow the tectonic shifts and plants. Then place-names follow the emigrants, with traders and companies preceding or following both. From this global movement comes the idea for a layout of ScotLoch and the icon of the *mappa mundi*: ScotWorld.

Scots Emigration

The following rough figures were gleaned from the Internet, census data and books, with no attempt to resolve the inconsistencies. The 'rubbery' figures are partly the result of varying definitions of ancestry, and lack of records. Four countries receive most of the newcomers: Canada, USA, Australia and New Zealand. In the eighteenth and nineteenth centuries over 2 million left Scotland, mostly to Canada and USA. By 1961 over 2 million had gone to Canada and by the end of the nineteenth century over 1 million had departed for the USA. Between 1918 and 1938 half a million went to Canada and USA. By 1850, 12,000 had gone to Australia; as of 2001 the first generation of Scottish descent stood at 28.2 per cent of population. In New Zealand the number of residents who had been born in Scotland was, in 1858, 7,976; in 1901, 47,858; in 1951, 44,827; in 1976, 47,827; in 2001, 28,680. So New Zealand has accepted a steady stream of Scots. Scottish colonies, plantations or settlements were made in the sixteenth century along the Vistula River in Poland and in Ulster, Northern Ireland. Large numbers of 'Scots' still live in both places, but like the overall head count of 40 million alive around the world today, the figure is largely one of definition. How does one define ancestral identity; how many generations and Scottish customs does it take to make one part of the extended nation? If one is of Chinese descent, one is always Chinese.

Renaming the World

As the Scots adventured abroad they rebuilt the map partly with the place-names of the mother country and partly with its architecture and landscape. Many cities, towns, mountains and islands are marked with a memory of this cultural exodus. In Canada you will find Aberdeen, Alexandria, Banff, the Campbell River, Campbeltown, Campletan, Coldstream, Cochrane, Craigellachie, Dalhousie, East Angus, Elgin County, Fernie, Fort Laird, Fort Mackay, Fort McPherson, Fort McMully, Glengarry, Graham, Hamilton, Lewis, Lewistown, the McLeod Lake, McGill University, Perth, Minto Dalhousie, Murray Harbour, Renfrew, Rothesay, Stewart, Strathmore, Strathnaver. In the USA you will find Aberdeen, Alexandra, Berwick, Brisbane, Cameron, Currie, Crawford, Douglas, Dunmore, Elgin, Glasgow, Glencoe, Glen Ulin, Fergus Falls, Irvine, Kelso, Mackay, McGregor, Melrose, Morton, Montrose, Scotsville. In Australia you will find Adelaide, Albany, Ardrossan, Ayr, Blair Athol, Brisbane, Broome, Campbelltown, Cairns, Charters Towers, Darlington Point, Donald, Drummond Point, Glenelg, Glen Innes, Inverell, Iverloch, Keith, Lismore, Lithgow, Lochnagar, Lorne, Mackay, Melrose, Menzie, Mount Bruce, MacDonnell Ranges, Melbourne, Melrose, Musgrave Ranges, New Caledonia, New Hebrides, Perth, Port Douglas, Port McArthur, Port McQuarie, Scone, Tweed Heads. In New Zealand you will find Blackall, Clyde, Dunedin, Fairlie, Hamilton, Hampden, Invercargill, Mossburn, Napier, Palmerston, Ross, Roxburgh, St Andrews, Stewart Island. In South Africa you will find Caledon, Calvinia, Campbell, Clanwilliam, Dundee, Douglas, Elgin, Grahamstown, Glencoe, Kelso, Maclear.

Scots Trading

Traders, merchants, and then the companies that they formed and funded, had a big influence on foreign countries. Many individuals and families from Scotland thus settled or lived in the following countries: India, especially Bombay, New Delhi, Calcutta; Ceylon; China, especially Shanghai and Hong Kong; Japan, Tokyo; and Africa, especially South Africa and Eastern Africa.

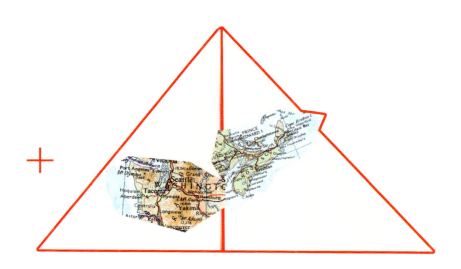

40 million Scots?

A MAPPA MUNDI

Imagine a map of the world, as it used to be drawn before it was navigated and surveyed, a *mappa mundi*, both a cultural idea and theoretical landscape. Such beautiful constructs are not totally realistic but rather idea maps. Like the famous plan of the London Underground, they are diagrams for thinking about relationships that matter, ideological artefacts, charming guides to the cultural universe.

A *mappa mundi* of Scottish identity could be simplified into four basic continents and four basic mounds. Reading this from the right, there is a helical mound, the Old Europe from which peoples emigrated to Scotland from 10,000 years ago. In the centre is a twin-peaked pyramidal mound, the North American continent focused on Canada and the USA (where perhaps 25 million Scottish descendents live). To the far left is a triangular landform with ramps and a twin peak, the Australasian continent (where there are perhaps 10 million people of Scottish blood). Below, to the south, is the curved landform of India, China and Japan, settled sparsely by Scot traders.

OPPOSITE, ABOVE: Watercolour by Madelon Vriesendorp.

Al-Idrisi, Mappa Mundi, 1454

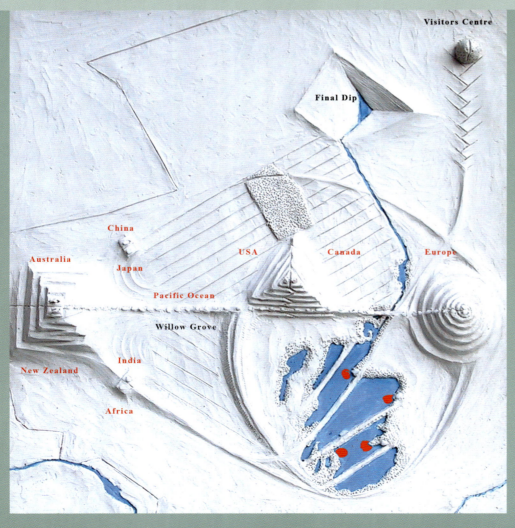

Visitors Centre

Final Dip

China
Australia
Japan
USA
Canada
Europe
Pacific Ocean
Willow Grove
New Zealand
India
Africa

LEGEND

Coniferous woodland	Viewpoint
Mixed Broadleaf Woodland	Existing Track (On Site)
Species Rich Grassland	Existing Track (Outwith Site)
Shingle Area	Proposed Track
Exposed geological feature	Potential Link to Kathellan
Peregrine Nesting Area	Art Fence
Exposed Wooden Raft (Island)	Watercourse \ Pond
Water	Monuments
Car Park Area	Sheep Holding Area
Reed Beds	Site Boundary
Marshy Grassland	Fence Line\Gate
	Fence\Hedge Line

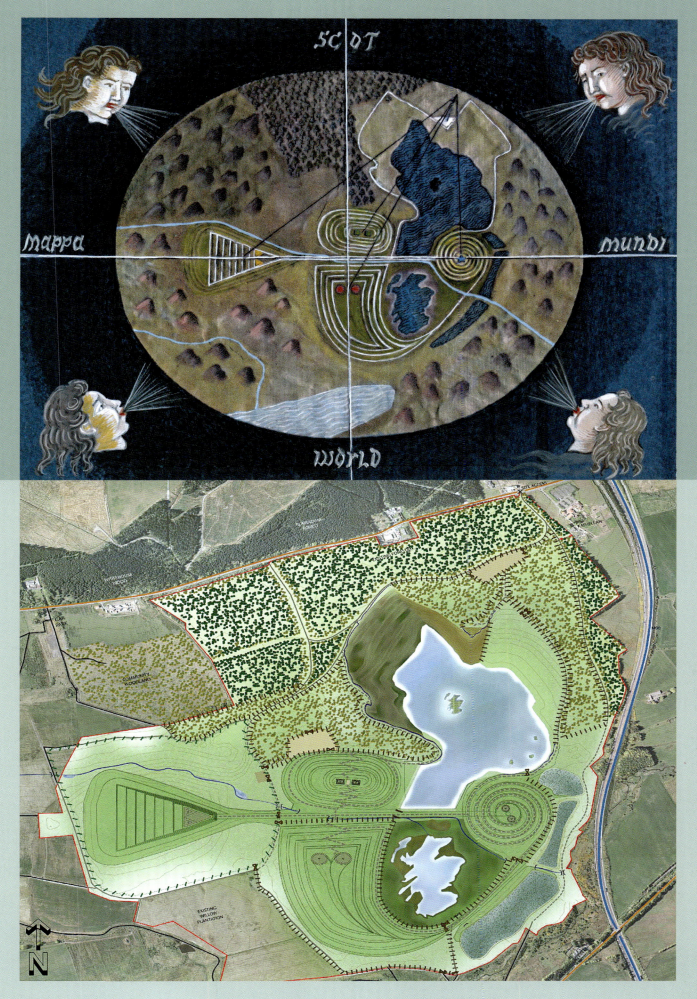

Attracting Visitors to the Top

The public spaces at Versailles and Washington DC are so huge as to be cosmic landscapes, though inhuman ones. These flatlands are scaled to the movements of a helicopter. The Kelty coal site is also extra large and under a big sky, which dwarfs landmarks and topographical features. A work of art placed in this setting disappears into the background, so an artificial ground has to set up its own smaller world that is then self-proportioned. The difficult goal becomes attracting people to take the long walk, to become excited by the pilgrimage. The summits of the mounds therefore must have enigmatic attractors, visible aims to reach: some planting, shade and significant sculpture. Here a type of Fourth Nature, heroic and rusting machinery, keeps the memory of those who have dug the coal and created the landscape. On the top of each mound one set of three poles marks a continent where Scots have settled, another, also using rust art, marks the life and work of the Kelty coal miners.

OPPOSITE, ABOVE AND BELOW: The Avenue of Doubles, under construction: a Fourth Nature. Industrial leftovers will be set as heroic ruins. On the top of windswept mounds an enclosure will be formed by robust shrubs that survive heat, hurricane and drought. To distinguish one continent from another these corrals will be given four distinct geometries: circular, square, triangular and rhomboid. Geological specimens may be left here, and a primitive art formed of the industrial waste set in patterns.

BELOW: Strategy for the tops. A spiral path reaches the last set of mounds with its three telephone poles (in red), past a area of planting that shields the top (in blue) to open on to a small turf berm that holds the rust art (in red).

Nature's Five Levels:
0. Laws 1. Wild 2. Farming 3. Gardens 4. Waste

A theme of my work, shown on other pages, is the idea that nature's different levels should be celebrated in a garden. Here in Kelty it is the romantic oppositions of Scotland – rocks and mountains in contrast with water – that become the most basic symbol. Call this fundamental level Zero Nature after the laws of nature, because it signifies that we know how to exploit them, and it is represented in the bands of black coal and the Final Void (see next page). Then above this lies First Nature, the growing wilderness of Thornton Wood. Second Nature and Third Nature are, respectively, the useful willow plantings to be harvested on the west of the site and the garden art, the design as a whole. But one climbs upwards towards the fourth level, the summit of the mounds. Here hardy shrubs and boulders surround the artificial construction, placing industrial waste in a geometrical layout. A result of the economy, this fourth level of nature is a by-product of our efforts to survive and prosper. Adam Smith was born near the site and there formed his notion of the 'hidden hand of the economy'. It created wealth as a by-product of competition, greed and specialization. The other side of this profit is industrial leftovers, something that can have a moving pathos and beauty. It is a question of context. If one sets up the route as, for instance, it was laid out on an acropolis, then the journey can be made meaningful. The sequence here, as then, is through increasing specificity, towards greater artifice and a culmination. The mount towards the great bowl of the sky is marked by the rusting jewels of hard work.

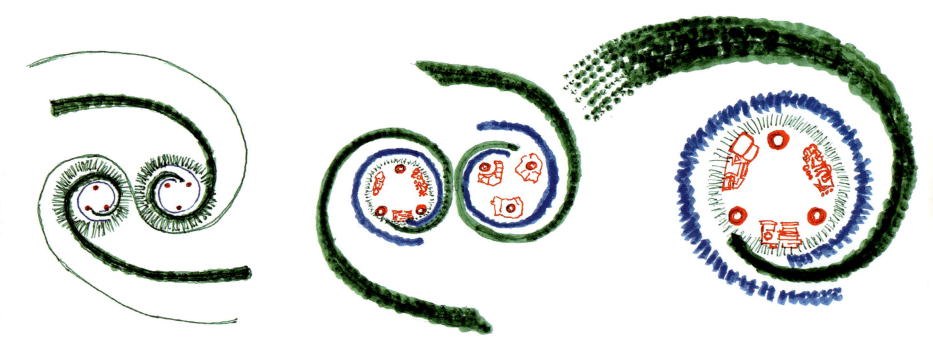

BASIC LANDFORMS OF COAL WORKING

The large scale and heavy equipment used for digging coal mean that any resultant shapes had to be primitive, mostly horizontal and very bold. The grammar and geometry tended towards the centralized pyramid, the classic shape of what are called in the trade 'overburdens'. How coal men came to this exotic parlance is a mystery to me, but it is as poetic as the place they end the digging, which is called the Final Void. The schemes and drawings here wrestle with the implications: how to create a landscape at the scale of a grand canyon, but one that tends towards the open horizontal and big sky.

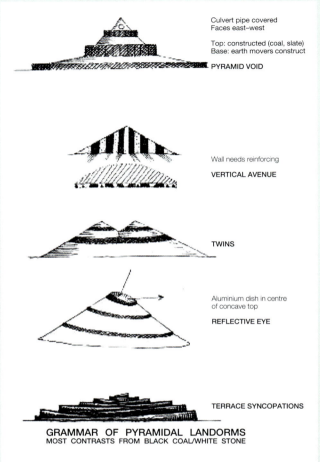

Culvert pipe covered
Faces east–west

Top: constructed (coal, slate)
Base: earth movers construct

PYRAMID VOID

Wall needs reinforcing

VERTICAL AVENUE

TWINS

Aluminium dish in centre of concave top

REFLECTIVE EYE

TERRACE SYNCOPATIONS

GRAMMAR OF PYRAMIDAL LANDORMS
MOST CONTRASTS FROM BLACK COAL/WHITE STONE

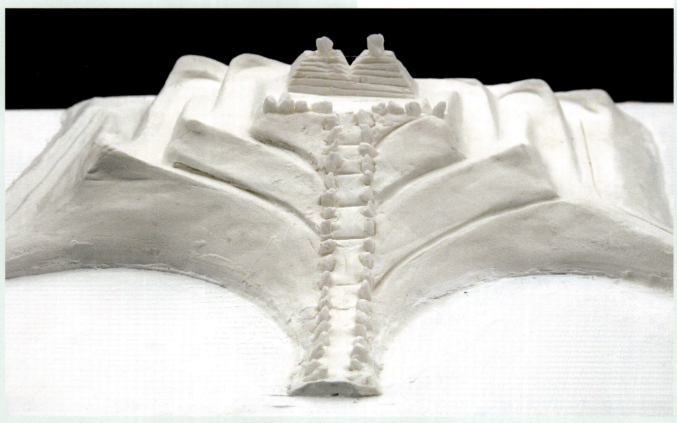

ROCKS AND THE FINAL VOID

The boulders excavated during coal extraction are used to bring out the ruggedness of the landscape and define pathways of Scottish identity. People from different parts of the world will be invited to bring their local stones and add a sign of their visit, in the past a custom while visiting graves and cairns. Each stone marked the memory of a visit. Perhaps major geological specimens of the country can be placed on the water map of Scotland as an analogue of their actual location. Thus the whole site could grow as a rock analogy, and memory could grow a sculpture of stones. The largest boulders now mark the cardinal axes, the causeway beside the lakes and the walkways from one 'continent' to another. The four main nations where the Scots settled are also accented by twin peaks, remnants of telephone poles on the site. Where possible the old coal machines and detritus are recycled as industrial sculpture. Thus the fundamental levels of nature are celebrated. To the north, the black coal beds, tilting out of the water signify petrified sunlight, the energy to be exploited as black gold. The Final Void was the last area to be excavated. A Taoist gardener could not have named it better.

CONSTRUCTING IDENTITIES

The landforms under construction on OB4 pull together traces of the people and their equipment that have dug the coal and built this work as well as the lands to which the Scots travelled and sometimes settled. Fragments and scrap from the past are pulled together as the imagination walks the site looking for connections. We enlisted the help and scholarship of Billy Kay, the writer and broadcaster who has travelled the world collecting the stories and anecdotes of this invisible web. His book, *The Scottish World: A Journey into the Scottish Diaspora* (2006), came out after I had started the project, but is by far the most inclusive and engaging on the subject, and his willingness to consult on the project is most helpful. He will be a continuous inspiration for stitching together this elusive fabric. The story is dispersed in a thousand places; the shards have to be collected, the connections found or created.

7: MEMORIES OF THE FUTURE

German Jujitsu

In East Germany, after the 1950s and for the next thirty years, some of the largest moving machines in the world were created and, because of the Cold War, it is natural to see them as a Communist answer to the travelling molochs of capitalism. Comparable mechanisms in the West were medium-size. For instance, in America, harvesters were as big as a house, or at Cape Kennedy the travelling gantry cranes that moved rockets into place were ten or more storeys. Their competitors here in the East were even larger in volume, the size of a moving village, a quarter of a mile long. Today some of them still inch along on railroad tracks, gently digging up one level of earth after another, creating as they go beautiful terraces of dead sand. They search for the lignite below, the brown coal, the cheap energy that helps run life above ground. Nothing stands in their way – forests, castles, sentiment – as they eat up one village after another, devouring all memory and landscape, creating a void of unstable sand, an artificial moonscape on earth. Slowly water fills these holes and a few pioneer weeds come

back. Desolation on this heroic scale can capture the imagination, at least appeal to those with an eighteenth-century taste for the sublime. It results in the beauty of landscape diagrams, or in the simplicity of a single pattern resulting from a single motive. The driving force of modernism is written here: Go forth and prosper. Dig the earth as cheaply as possible. Open-cast its riches with a pure instrument of engineering. Devise a mechanism with a fearsome set of coordinated engines and run by only four technicians – a movable factory – the apogee of progress. The Eiffel Tower is doubled in size, turned into the Ford Motor Company and put sideways on rollers.

As they contemplate the trade-off, and spectacle, Germans might recall Goethe's Doctor Faust and his pact with the devil, just as the English might think of Shelley's Frankenstein, and indeed mining for lignite has been going on here since the early 1800s, when both books were bestsellers. It is an epochal struggle so well known as to be almost invisible, but nowhere else so dramatically manifest as here. Pure, Platonic exploitation, catastrophe and beauty. Surprisingly, this area by the Polish border, called Lausitz, adds another twist to Goethe's morality tale. For the government, in partnership with the semi-utopian group called IBA, is trying to rewrite the ending. With deft Germanic jujitsu they are attempting to invert the exploitation and turn it into the biggest landscape project in Europe, with new land art and thirty or so new lakes.

Abstraction of water and landform depicted in a limestone relief, left, and the machines and lost buildings of Lausitz, below. IBA, led by Rolf Kuhn, and LMBV (Lausitz and Central German Mining Association) have overseen the opportunity of turning earth voids into new lakes, recreation and art.

sites of cars

4 terraces constructed at once

level of brown coal

ALTDÖBERN

gives

takes

IBA, the International Building Exhibition, reconstructed Berlin urbanism in the 1970s and 1980s and now, led by Rolf Kuhn's vision, they might just create the largest artificial lake district in the world. This will only happen, however, if the vision remains in the front of public consciousness. Having started work in 2000, it will take thirty years for the giant holes to be stabilized and filled with water, for the nine main areas of Lausitz to grow their plans and artworks. Some of the lakes and schemes are finished, but the visionary project as a whole depends on will-power and focus. Since the imperative of progress destroyed thirty towns, and the social and transport connections to thirty more, my design is based on the question of lost identity and is called Memories of the Future. For unless these memories are kept strong they will not work. Jujitsu, after all, is the martial art of using the attacker's energy against him: energy out, energy in.

PRITZEN

Disconnect – Reconnect

The town of Altdöbern used to be a twenty-minute walk from its smaller twin, Pritzen, and part of a larger community of four other villages. The latter have disappeared, their traces long since erased by digging and water, but they remain as hazy recollections, old photographs and melancholic thoughts of community. Melancholy can radicalize creativity. The memory of the ruined past played a catalysing role in the Roman Renaissance as the former glories were re-imagined; *sic transit gloria mundi* inspired a sweet pathos. So, east of Altdöbern and its old castle and central church, I have envisioned a gesturing hand reaching out to Pritzen. In the words of Nietzsche and Le Corbusier it is a sign of 'man's grip upon nature' (as noted with Northumberlandia), one 'that gives and receives', a gesture of welcome, embrace and other anthropomorphic meanings. The forearm here is a gently sloping landform that protects the swimming area with its bracelet of changing rooms and a kiosk. Further up the hill walkways lead to spiralling highpoints and then down to a landing area for boats, and the pier of the thumb where ferries from Pritzen might dock.

Andreas Kipar asked me to work on this project and I in turn asked the help of Margherita Brianza, at that time a designer working on Parco Portello. Once again she was instrumental in translating design intentions into fine landscape drawings, while the office of KLA carried out much of the detailed work. After looking at the logic of the situation we realized why the landscape designer Prince Hermann von Pükler-Muskau (1785–1871) called the area a 'flat pancake'. Whatever is put into this wide expanse of 5,000 square kilometres disappears, making no impact. Furthermore, there are no orientation points, no hills, indeed nothing much to visit by way of high culture except Pükler-Muskau's eighteenth-century park and landforms, a library by Herzog & de Meuron in Cottbus and the massive industrial ruins that have resulted from digging for lignite. Pine forests, cows and a big sky dominate consciousness, and the sadness of a landscape destroyed by war. The flat pancake needs contrast and something memorable. Thus the basic idea, the hand surrounding a map-garden of the region, cupping it on three sides to cut down the wind, and beckoning towards Pritzen. This giant landform also relates to the nine smaller ones in the oval garden, those that embrace the towns and the art projects: hands within hands.

A MAP-GARDEN
OF THE REGION

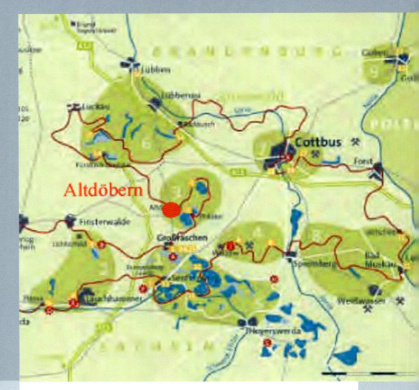

From the loss of land and towns, the destruction can be turned into a new identity, into the nine main areas of Lausitz and their many new lakes. If realized it would be comparable to the Italian and English lake districts, places of poetry and landscape loved around the world. How to keep this bold vision alive, to work for the long term? Already ten years of projects and reclamation have resulted in a few identifiable icons among the fifteen IBA schemes under way. As the water slowly rises over the next twenty years and the landscape is reformed, these projects will become part of the new memories. Our garden is a stylized map of the region, of Lausitz 9 and its building projects. Placed at the centre of a protective hand, from where it can be viewed from above, the model shows the major roadways and three rivers, the big towns and the artificial lakes. The architectural and land art projects are to be silk-screened on the sides of concrete seats, or built as miniature sculpture. They act as orientation points on the map, and animate the walk. Near the centre is a viewing point and a well-known icon, a small version of the Altdöbern steeple above a seat. It looks over the miniaturized version of the new lake, and then the real thing. The sculpture and images of the fifteen IBA projects are meant to be enjoyed as garden artefacts *and* keep development on track: Memories of the Future.

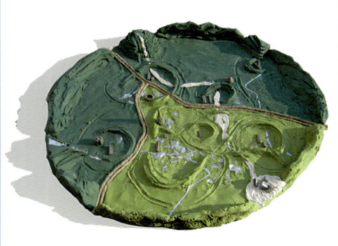

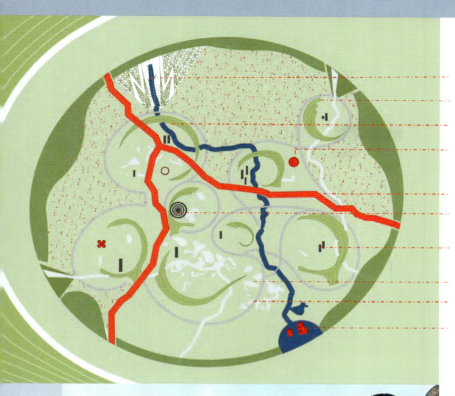

Cistern

8 Hands - Hearth Crescent

Spree River - Real Water

Icons (Biotowers Lauchhammer, Slavonic Stronghold Raddusch, Furst Puckler Pyramid)

Highways - Main Path

Altdobern

Cities - Concrete Seats with 15 Projects printed on the surface. (Memories of the Future)

Lake district + Rivers

Labyrinth - Secondary Path

Cubes into the water - Lost Cities

Map of the nine IBA areas and the major city, Cottbus, the highways and train lines and the three main rivers (including the River Spree which runs through Berlin). This 5,000 square-kilometre project generates the oval garden, its planting, landforms and details. Several of the projects under way include some renovated industrial icons, some land art and the IBA Terraces.

PART THREE
DEATH AND WAR

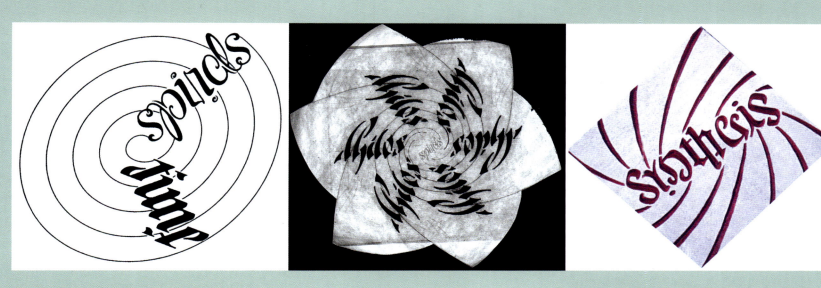

LAND WAR GARDEN: LINEARISM

Land war gardens stand either side of the entrance path. You pass through tilted planes of grass and rock that rise and fall to either side of an implicit trench, a memory of the conditions under which much of the First World War was fought. This 'trench' is lined with stainless-steel retaining walls that hold back the green grass and AstroTurf pressing in from both sides. Where necessary, these walls rise as protective rails to keep people from falling. The experience contrasts nature and man-made elements, following the geometry of the time lines that run from north to south. One larger red and cut signifies a mass extinction; other shifts in the parallel lines represent the geodesic lines of the globe. An aesthetic of Linearism unites these patterns of parallel lines and like the weave in a complex fabric leads to harmonies and breaks. Created from rocks, grass and different coloured green AstroTurf, the lines can be read as geological strata, the unifying theme of all four gardens. Rock fields, made from rocks that originate in the north of Britain, are also positioned to keep people from falling off the tilted planes.

One can mount these shapes from either side. They culminate in eight seats carved from rock sent from various parts of the Commonwealth and they are located, roughly, in their global positions on the time line. Reading clockwise from the left they are: Malta, Nigeria, Mozambique, Zimbabwe, Botswana, South Africa, Namibia, Barbados and St Vincent. The central entrance axis is Britain, and Greenwich Mean Time. The seats are inscribed with the country's name, and with reversible words, ambigrammi, that can be read backwards, such as 'synthesis', 'philosophy' and 'spirals time'. On these seats one can sit and get a view of other war machines and gardens. The idea is clear: nature and conflict are in conflict and one has to think about the paradox. Machinery, warfare and progress march together but suppress a deeper truth: the ecology on which we depend. It may seem strange to mix philosophy, nature and war, yet many people, such as Darwin and Churchill, have philosophized on nature and come to the conclusion war is a permanent condition of nature.

THE AESTHETICS OF WAR

A theme throughout the gardens is the aesthetics of war. Camouflage and the language of aggressive display and armour were first evolved in nature. There are several obvious signs we have adopted from its example, such as heavy armour and the display of an aggressively large mass. From such things as this comes the spiky nature of knives and projectiles or killing instruments. The dazzling optical repetitions of mimicry have led to our versions of camouflage.

The origin of the language of warfare is evident in the Cambrian explosion, that is, the period 530 million years ago when countless types of multicellular animals exploded on to the scene. Why did evolution suddenly produce so many new types in such a short period? One theory is that sight developed and with it the aesthetics of war, an arms race of display and camouflage. Thus we have imprinted some types from the Cambrian explosion on to the flat concrete area where people drive. These evolve into the reptilian arms race we know: armadillos, turtles, snakes, beetles, spiders and scorpions. All develop a distinctive aesthetic of war.

Young men who come to the Imperial War Museum are often attracted by armaments and this is undoubtedly related to a universal appeal of the aesthetics of fighting. This language was extended in the 1920s by the machine aesthetic of the Futurists and Le Corbusier: their love of speed, precise and pure shapes that glisten, complicated machined parts and warships. Children's toys, especially Japanese robots and video games based on them, have further developed the genre. From the Cambrian explosion to the symbolic arms race of the Cold War is a history that is abstracted and diagrammed in the gardens.

8: METAPHORS OF DEATH AND WAR

Gardens without Nature

The Imperial War Museum North was a millennium project in Salford, Manchester, that grew from its parent in London. Warfare flourished in the twentieth century along with other high-growth industries, and the concept of Total War – aimed at civilians – became a common policy of governments, even if denied. Against this dismal background the IWM-N, designed by Daniel Libeskind, was born and given the general aim to stimulate debate on armed conflict and its eternal victims: the population and environment.

When Libeskind asked me to design a series of gardens to surround his building, the Earth Shard, I faced some ironic problems. The polluted site was itself a result of economic conflict, Darwinian competition, and the museum could not afford any planting or maintenance of living things. How to design gardens without nature? That is quite a challenge, but in an important sense it is the typical urban situation. Designers such as Martha Schwartz have created an interesting hardscape from the challenge. Here I have followed this new tradition, developing aesthetics and thematics of warfare. Further ironies, that the museum ran out of money and built only a version of my fencing, mean that these hard landscapes were born dead: a great deal of effort and design lost. Nonetheless, the exercise led to some realizations, both physical, as seen in the next chapters, and conceptual. Fundamental is the idea that death and life are intimately interwoven and suitably combined in a garden. 'Et in Arcadia ego' (I, Death, am even in Arcadia) is a theme that my friend Ian Hamilton Finlay dramatized in his Scottish garden, sometimes using the modern instruments of war: the battleship, missiles and howitzer. To say that conflict can produce beauty and symbolism is not of course to glorify war, but rather to admit its place in a poetics of art and landscape. Can misery and destruction not be turned to other ends? Can we not transform missiles into trees, shell casings into bollards, and the history of mass extinctions, nature's killing, into a landscape? Transformation is the basic strategy of these designs.

NATURE VERSUS CONFLICT

The goal of the gardens was to be a place of tranquillity, pleasure and reflection and also to present a major truth: nature moves in after conflict and shows its robust healing powers. This is clear in the way it has transformed First World War battlefields, the Chernobyl meltdown, or the fenced-in area between North and South Korea. This strip has more biodiversity than much of inhabited Korea, and the Chernobyl disaster, in spite of the radioactivity, has generated a nature reserve. Nature moves in where warriors fear to tread. Since the design of IWM-N by Studio Libeskind has developed the metaphor of the globe broken into shards, a symbol of conflict, it is only proper that gardens present the robust force of nature fighting back. This is shown in different ways, by nature transforming vehicles of war – indicated by a green cut of grass or glass – or by strong contrasts between nature and machinery.

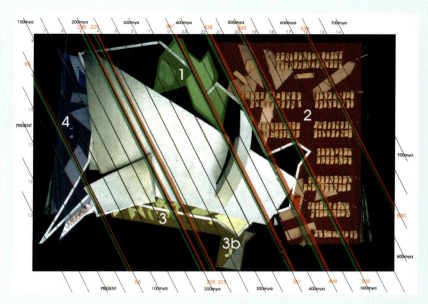

Secondly, the history of the earth shows that conflict is an essential part of nature, indeed always changes the face of nature. Over the last 4 billion years there have been at least five mass extinctions, the last one 65 million years ago, which allowed mammals and us to emerge. Nature has three kinds of violence: the familiar competition and arms race of one species versus another, the competition that takes place between members of a single species, and the external impact of asteroids and volcanoes on life. Hence the overall garden site is divided into a linear timeline showing the history of mass extinctions over the last 700 million years. These are represented as coloured linear cuts and geological strata running from east to west on the cardinal axis. Red cuts signify a mass extinction, such as the big one 225 million years ago. These deaths are quickly followed by black cuts – the carbon traces found in geological layers – and then green lines, representing the fact that after calamity nature bounces back. Fossils, real and simulated, are embedded in the hardscape.

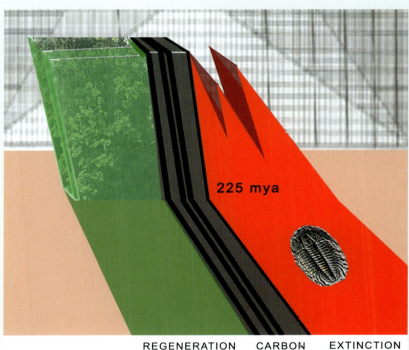

REGENERATION   CARBON   EXTINCTION

As the site plan also shows, there are four main gardens, based on the fundamental kinds of war, and they circle around the building: war on land, sea, in the air, and often resulting in fire. These four elements relate to Libeskind's museum, shards of aluminium based on the same

Circular Time 06.00 hrs		05.00 hrs		04.00 hrs
700 Million Year Linear Time - Line		208 mya		225 mya

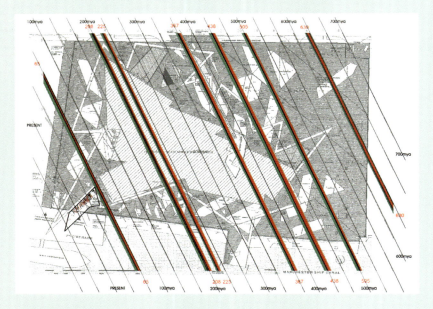

Nature moves in after conflict: a slash of resurgent life, the contrast between a robust nature and machinery, healing and warfare, natural and artificial, real grass and AstroTurf. Throughout the gardens this theme is transformed. Its sign is a cut of grass or glass or grasscrete running through the concrete and asphalt that seals the toxicity of the site.

The several mass extinctions, indicated in red, leave their trace in geological strata, usually as levels of black earth, or carbon. Then regeneration occurs, indicated in green. A unifying naturalistic code is thus adopted on the site, of red, black and green. The five major mass extinctions, which wiped out 70 to 92 per cent of all species, raise a question about the inevitable progress in species and biomass. The last extinction, 65 million years ago, probably the result of an asteroid impact, destroyed the ammonids and dinosaurs and allowed mammals, including us, to flourish. We are at the start of the sixth mass extinction, when one-tenth of all species has been cut back. Our economic progress has, in effect, made undeclared war on the natural habitats of other species. We, like asteroids and super-volcanoes, are part of nature but the only part that is semi-conscious of causing extinction. The gardens thus show both the healing and destructive powers of nature.

idea. This layout immediately presented a question – Where to place the entrance path in the sequence of time? – and a solution. The entrance should signify Britain, and Greenwich Mean Time, and the other time zones of the globe should relate to places in the Commonwealth. This layout thus suggested a mixture of the two basic types of time: linear across the site, and circular around it. The earth, and its cosmic axis, pull together on a north–south line all the garden themes in a common visual language of cuts and strata.

The site plan shows the conflict in nature, depicted in the time-line. This runs on a north–south axis over the entire site, starting from the vehicular entrance (above right in plan), and 700 million years ago (mya), and ending near the bridge entrance (lower left in plan), the present. The larger extinction events – death caused by extra-species events, such as asteroid impacts, super-volcanoes, Ice Ages, and the shift of continents – are still a part of 'nature', and they lead to shifts in ecological history. Human war is nature's war by other means.

Since Libeskind's Earth Shard was the largest covered space, we have placed, by the entrance (1) a corresponding Land War Garden (2). Next to it is the entrance used by most people arriving in cars and buses, a car park turned into garden which, through its planting and instruments of war – tanks, personnel carriers and missiles – shows the visitors where to park and how to enter the building. This, the Fire Garden, creates a focus for driving around with an explosive shape at its centre (see page 146) and green cuts in the paving. (3) Beyond this, near the Air Shard, is the Air Water Garden, which presents an aesthetic of war, a children's playground and, on the existing jetty (3b), the Garden of Reflection, where one can relax, reflect on warfare and be in close contact with water, the canal and growth. (4) From this you reach, not too far from the Water Shard, the Sea War Garden, where there are two further subdivisions: the Total War Garden, showing that, in the twentieth century, civilians were slaughtered as an instrument of warfare, and a sculpture by Anthony Caro, presenting some realities of war (like the garden as a whole, alas unexecuted).

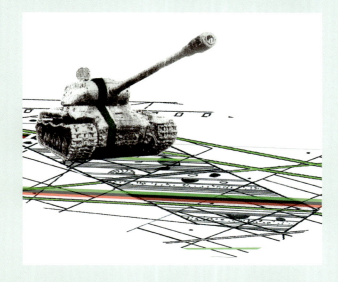

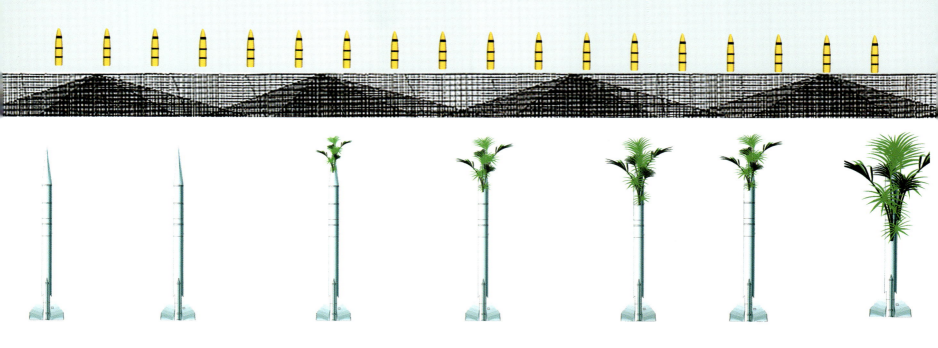

UNIFYING THEMES

Conflict fragments the globe; nature reunifies it according to the logic of biomes. We designed several themes that also unite the variety elements. For instance, the Water Path leads to the entrance and around the site; the Syncopated Fence rhythms define three sides of the site. A row of shell casings is transformed as bollards. The missile row and the buried tank remind you where, in a large parking lot, you have left your car. Sometimes we show the military hardware in its beautiful dignity, the way the machine aesthetic celebrates precise form and marvellous detail. A tank or vehicle is cut away in section to show its wonderful internal workings, or seen emerging from the ground, partly covered by earth and paving. Other times we grow nature through it to reiterate the basic theme, nature versus conflict.

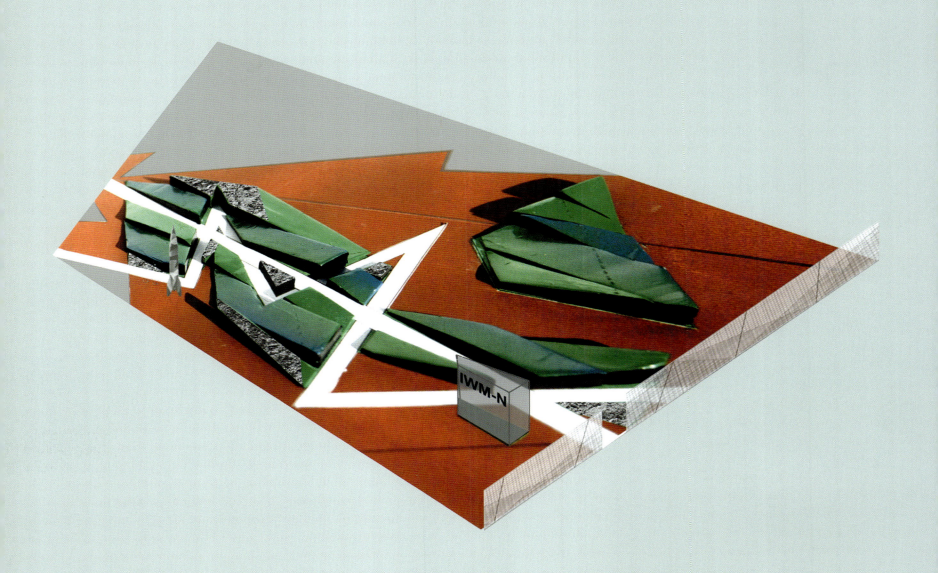

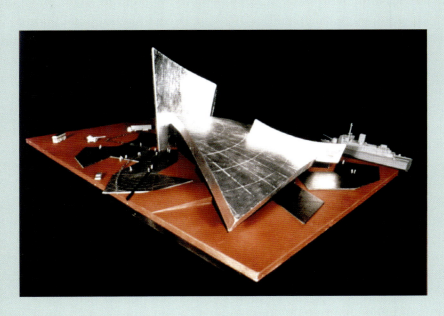

ABOVE: Land War Garden by the entrance. LEFT AND RIGHT: Daniel Libeskind, Imperial War Museum North, 1998-2001 represents, with large aluminium volumes, the shards of the globe shattered by conflict.

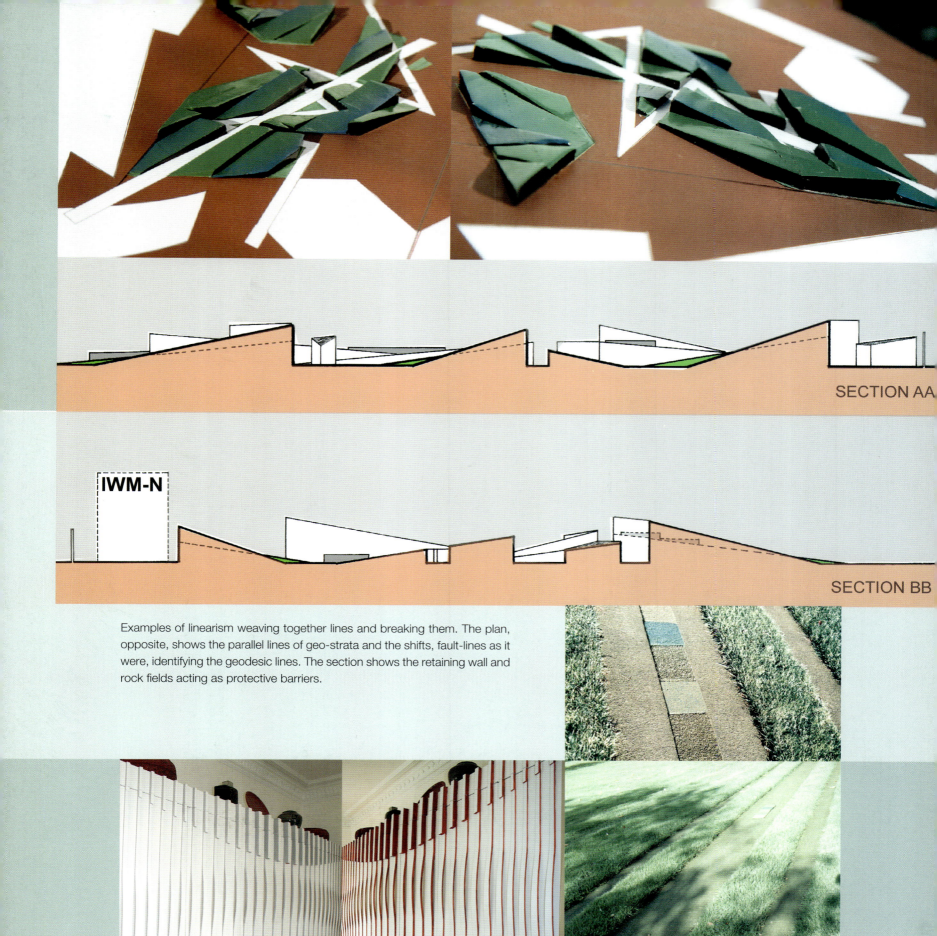

SECTION AA

IWM-N

SECTION BB

Examples of linearism weaving together lines and breaking them. The plan, opposite, shows the parallel lines of geo-strata and the shifts, fault-lines as it were, identifying the geodesic lines. The section shows the retaining wall and rock fields acting as protective barriers.

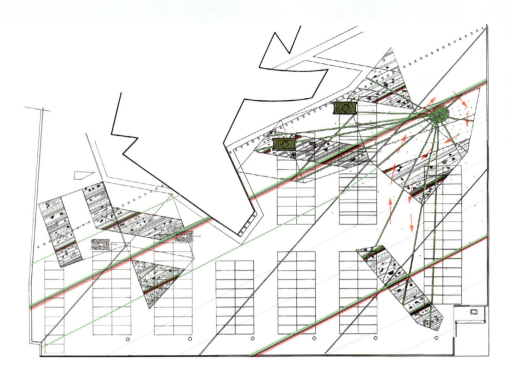

All of the gardens are conceived as geological sites, but this one, because it is flat, presents the most different strata, showing the passage of time. Layered elements are set in the concrete depicting the different periods and types of warfare. Geological strata have revealed the long duration of time, 'Deep Time', long before biology and evolutionary theory confirmed this new dating. What better method than to show some of the major themes of natural warfare with elements of rock layers and the types of aggressive display and defence animals evolved before humans?

THE FIRE WAR GARDEN

Most people arrive in cars and buses, so the large car park is turned into garden, which, through its planting, paving and instruments of war – tanks, personnel carriers and missiles – shows the visitors where to park and how to enter the building. Because cars and buses must turn around after they drop off passengers, a very clear roundabout is necessary. Thus we foresee a mysterious explosive structure made by an artist such as Cornelia Parker – one of her hanging explosions. This sculpture would tilt to reinforce the lines of vehicular movement. We have shown a solution based on the context. Through it grow climbing plants, and cutting through it are two shards of green glass. Their axes point to the two main north points, true north and the north point of the building, a contrast between the cosmic and the human, nature and conflict.

The ovoid explosion is also marked by landmines laid in the asphalt and concrete in a series of shock waves. This, the Landmine Garden, is possibly dedicated to Princess Diana because of her efforts in stopping this new instrument of Total War. Landmines are directed mostly against civilians, and are used to keep them confined to a small area and destroy a local economy.

The 'green glass mountain', a consequence of our inability to recycle enough bottles, is used as a resource for constructing the cuts of green glass that radiate out as explosive lines into the parking lot. These come from the ovoid and might cut through one tank while deflecting off the armour of the pristine tank. Parking bays are marked by tanks and armoured vehicles as a memory aid to where one has parked. An avenue of missiles marks the vehicular edge of the parking area while an avenue of shells as bollards defines the pedestrian area. Thus instruments of war, transforming from pristine to violated, show the basic truth of nature versus conflict. The second theme of Conflict in Nature is again presented by the time line of evolutionary events – the Cambrian explosion and several mass extinctions are marked in the recurring cuts of red, black and green.

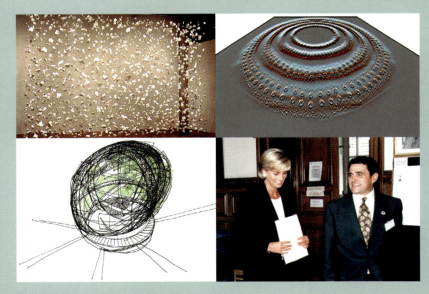

THE GARDEN OF REFLECTION

A pre-existing jetty overlooks the canal. This became the Garden of Reflection, the quietest and most protected part of the site, a place where, after visiting the museum, people can reflect on war and remember the consequences. It is also a place to memorialize these thoughts. Contemplation is underscored in the shiny materials, the dark growth and a reflecting pool. It is a tranquil garden protected on one side by a small hedge and on the other by a slide of water.

You enter under this wedge of sliding water, walking on the water path (which is solid at this point). You look up through the clear glass and see the names of those events in the Manchester area that relate directly to two world wars (the bombing of this city, the factories of war, etc.). Sliding water gives extraordinary illusions. When you see the sky and words from below, through fast-moving water, they take on a hallucinatory aspect, they pulsate. Names from the locale, in black, flutter against the cosmic backdrop.

Then you move into the garden, perhaps pausing to sit under a topiary (and AstroTurf) shelter. From there one can move to the flat reflecting pool, a wedge of water that spills gently over two sides and thereby visually unites the pool with the canal just beyond. (The water is recycled here up to the top of the slide.) Just as the words on the slide are made part of the sky, a wall of words (cast through concrete) is seen against the water beyond in the canal. These words memorialize the dead. Thus, with planting, water, canal and sky, you take your pain back to nature and reflect.

SALFORDMANCHESTERTR
TRAFFORDMANCHESTERSA
TRAFFORDSALFORDMANCH
MANCHESTERTRAFFORDSALFORD
SALFORDTRAFFORDMANCHESTER
MANCHESTERTRAFFORD SALFORD
MANCHESTERTRAFFORDSALFO
MANCHESTERTRAFFORDS
MANCHESTERTRAFFORDSA
SALFORDMANCHESTER
TRAFFORDSALFORD
MANCHESTERSA
TRAFFORDM
SALFORD
MANC
TR
S

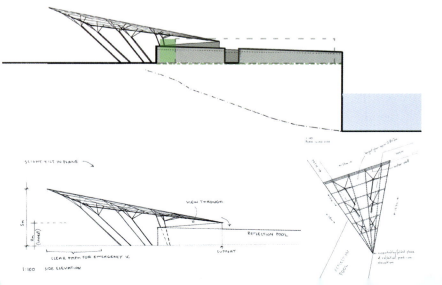

THE SEA WAR GARDEN

The great advantage of the site of the IWM-N is that it is adjacent to a wide canal. Where the rest of nature is diminished because the site had to be sealed, water is plentiful and becomes the major theme of the garden. We have thus proposed a dramatic waterwalk that takes one across causeways and up and down water performing in different ways. Not far from Libeskind's Water Shard, you reach the Sea War Garden. Here a double cascade shows the matrix for life, water, cascading down one side to a spiral whirlpool or vortex, and the other side to a waterfall.

A kinetic sculpture animates the approach from the bridge. Two catapults throwing water at each other are, at once, a playful game and a fascinating object lesson in the physics of chaos – a new invention called a 'waterpult'. Watch as the spouts slowly load the waterpults, and they bend under the growing weight of the water. Then suddenly they reach a critical moment and let loose their spray over the opposition. Because of slight imbalances in their starting positions no one can predict which will fire first – a delightful illustration of the hair trigger that starts the oldest battle of tit-for-tat. Some wars start by accident, but they do not end as engaging water fights.

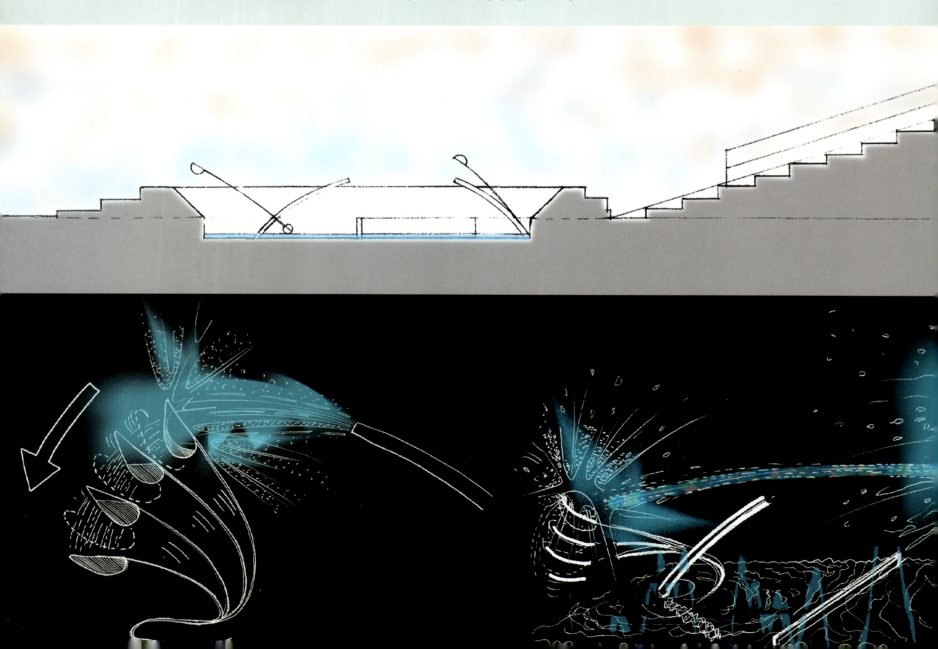

The waterpult battle empties through a half-parabolic channel into a small circular pool and tiny vortex. Then you mount steps to one side of a skewed waterslide cascade and reach a causeway. From here you have a view back to the canal and mine-sweeper, and down to a large extraordinary vortex encased in an acrylic cylinder, 1 metre in diameter and 3 metres high. At ground level this can be seen up close on all sides. From the top you proceed on the causeway down the steps next to a cascade which, because it is pinched in plan, picks up speed, forcing the water to spout and splash into a circular vortex at the base. This is also fed by another parabolic form, a large stainless-steel spout in which water completes the parabola.

Throughout this area the major theme of nature versus conflict is emphasized by the duality of elements: seats in pairs, two waterpults, two cascades, two parabolas and so on. The colouring and materials, at a detailed stage, will also carry through this duality.

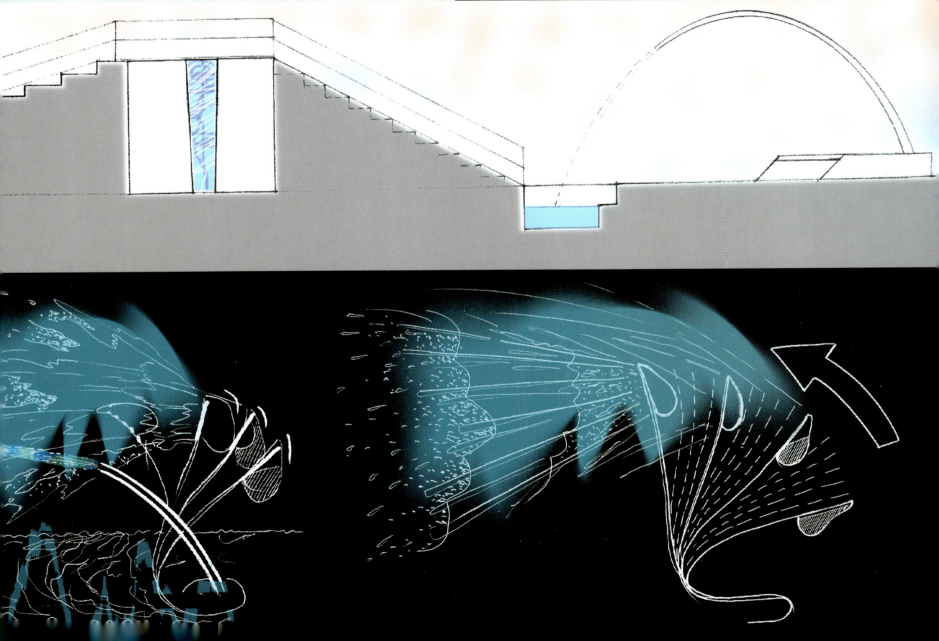

THE GARDEN OF TOTAL WAR

When approaching the site from the bridge entrance, you pass a flat parterre in concrete and stone. This wedge shows the truth of our era: the period, as military historians have called it, of Total War. The twentieth century was the time when war was made not just between combatants but on civilians. Ordinary people who have no interest in fighting are killed as a direct consequence of decisions made by politicians and military leaders, to bomb the opposition into submission. This policy shift is a mutation in warfare, a fact underlined here by the black and red stones. These are laid in shafts cast in the white concrete base. The depth of the black (and grey) signifies the number of military dead (leaders, officers and common soldiers), while the red signifies the number of civilians killed. Thus statistics are translated into an arresting architectural form that makes you reflect on common experience. The major battle names are cast in black concrete rectangles (e.g. Somme, Verdun) and also slotted into the linear grid. Down the centre are the dates of battle, and a typical weapon of destruction, such a machine gun, cast into the white background. Two sets of explanatory pillars, one black, one red, are set at either end of the Garden of Total War, describing this shift in warfare.

The numbers of mass-produced dead in two world wars were far beyond anything previously known in war – something like 37 and 50 million – and civilian deaths increased proportionally as the century progressed, a fact made vividly clear by the increasing ratio of red stones. Since the IWM-N intends to educate the public and engender debate, this garden by the bridge entrance will bring up the fundamental shift of our time, and pose a very difficult question.

REALITY

Because the canal site has for a long time had an industrial use, even including some toxic substances, it has had to be sealed and this has created a flatscape. Realities dictate a fairly hard, flat landscape with low maintenance requirements. Thus where planting is possible we have chosen hardy wildflowers (by the canal) and used grass sparingly and in a way that is easy to cut. Minimum watering systems such as drip feeds are presumed for certain areas, and in artefacts such as the tanks holding shrubs, and these will need intermittent maintenance depending on the rainfall. Artificial materials such as AstroTurf will contrast with living plants in a way that brings out the main theme, nature versus conflict. Two other realities have impinged on the design: speed of construction and the high volume of pedestrian and vehicular traffic. Again these lead to a hard flatscape; but within these constraints, rather like war itself, we have tried to bring out moments of humour, reflection and delight.

TREE WEDGES

Because of the toxicity of the site, sealed in by the asphalt and concrete, very little green is allowed. To compensate for this hard surface a wedge of trees is planted at various key points. These aim towards the entrance and end in a definite shape defined by a small wedge that also acts as a seat. Benches are formed by stretching Astroturf over a frame. Thus again the theme of contrast, the man-made versus the organic, or nature versus conflict.

Posssible trees: 1. Conifers: gorse or yew, which vary from gold to deep green, cypresses or perhaps leylandii for quick growing and to keep a vertical shape; 2. Crab: *Malus tschonoskii*, grows to 40 feet; *M. trilobata*, 22 feet; 3. Thorn: *Crataegus monogyna* 'Stricta', 30 feet but slow to grow; 4. Elder.

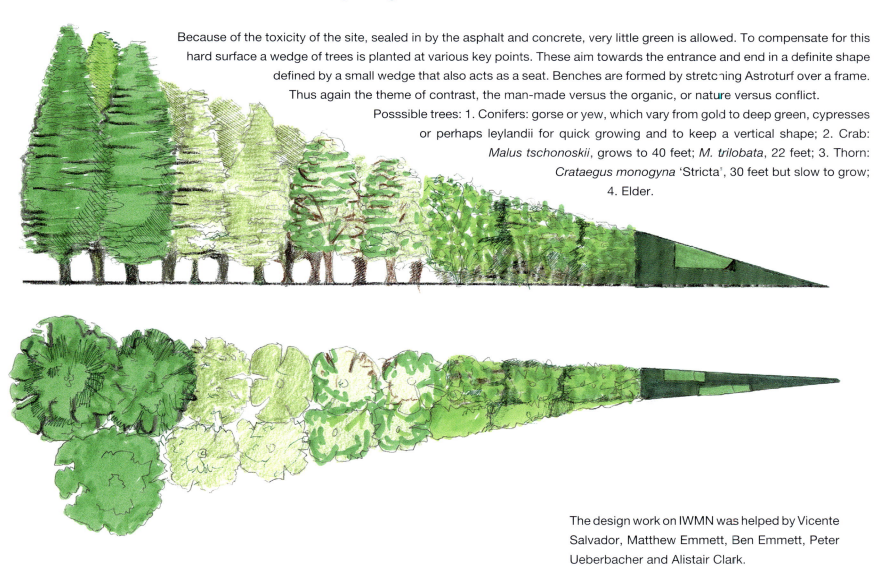

The design work on IWMN was helped by Vicente Salvador, Matthew Emmett, Ben Emmett, Peter Ueberbacher and Alistair Clark.

GARDENING AND WAR

As I was designing several gardens and landscapes in 2003, the political scene darkened and the Bush–Blair axis began to launch their 'War on Terror', as they defined it. Aware that this action would kill many innocent people and become the precedent for other nations to justify intervention wherever they wished, I curtailed other work and, with the President of RIBA Paul Hyett, organized a pressure group called Architects Against War. By January 2003 the Iraq invasion was becoming likely, and we hoped that Blair might listen to the professions, if they could unite against unilateral action. British architects, lawyers, the Church, doctors – most professionals with an institutional charter to work for the good of society – looked as if they might coalesce into a unified coalition against invasion: a reverse domino effect. If their collective voice were heard then Britain would not support Blair and then Bush (in spite of his boasting) might not go to war.

Eighteen international architects (including such luminaries as Frank Gehry, Zaha Hadid and Rem Koolhaas and three Presidents of RIBA) signed the following letter (published in the *Independent* on 20 January 2003),which correctly predicted the results of invasion:

> The case for a Just War cannot be convincingly made; the link
> of Saddam Hussein with Al-Qaeda has not been established;
> a war against Iraq is likely to kill large numbers of civilians and
> intensify the great suffering there; and unilateral action by the US
> (with Britain's support) will undermine international law and set
> a precedent of pre-emption by other nations in places such as
> Chechnya, Palestine, Kashmir and Tibet. . . . A consequence of
> invasion by the USA and Britain is likely to be the very clash of
> civilizations sought by terrorist groups such as Al-Qaeda . . .

The letter starts with the forecast that invasion 'will very likely lead to an increase in international terrorism', later ironically confirmed in 2006 by CIA reports. By the end of January the anti-war movement was international and driven by popular sentiment, and the question was whether Blair would respond to public opinion or disregard it (my theme in further letters to newspapers and magazines):

> Tony Blair listens to the public mood: if the demonstration on
> 15 February is large enough and the opinion polls show a large
> majority against unilateral action, it could make him drop his
> support. Without Britain on board, 80 per cent of Americans are
> against war and this dangerous precedent of flouting international law would not be set. (*Independent on Sunday*, 2 February
> 2003)

One or two million citizens turned up in London on 15 February, the figures varied according to political slant. Whatever the number was it was the largest political demonstration in British history, but not enough to budge Blair from his secret agreement with Bush. The invasion went

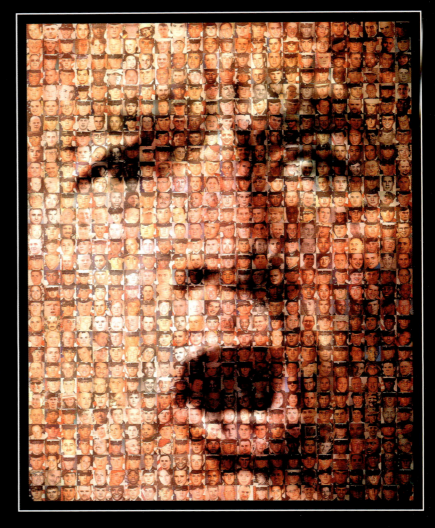

ahead in March 2003 with the consequences we had foreseen. The CIA reported that the unlikely number of 11,111 terrorist incidents had occurred in the three years after the invasion, many of them 'caused' by it.

Other forecasts came true, a fact of some interest, since architects are neither politically trained nor any more perspicacious than other professionals. It also did not take a political specialist to see that an invasion would kill many innocent Iraqis. The British *Lancet*, and other responsible publications, put the number at about 100,000, climbing by 2006 to 655,000. As these architects also forecast, several nation-states looked to this US precedent to justify their illegal repression, especially in such places as Chechnya and Palestine.

In the event, our professional protests and the mass rallies had little effect on what Gore Vidal and others called the Bush–Blair Junta. Their war in the name of freedom and democracy treated both with contempt.

OPPOSITE: Architects against War Letters, January 2003–2004.
ABOVE: Bush portrait by the US war dead (2004). After the first 1,000 American deaths, anonymous portraits of the President were created from photos of the servicemen killed in Iraq, and posted on the Internet. The US and UK governments did not ever tally the Iraqi dead, but by 2006 estimates varied from a conservative 50,000 'excess' deaths to 655,000 extra dead, or 2.5 per cent of the Iraq population.

LETTERS TO THE EDITOR

Letters to the Editor, The Independent, 191 Marsh Wall, London E14 9RS. Fax: 020-7005 2056. Please include a daytime telep
pendent.co.uk; e-mail correspondents are asked to give a postal address and to send no attachments. Letters may be edited for

Jan 20, 2003, P. 13

Why we must speak out against an immoral war

Sir: We believe that the case for war against Iraq has not been made, that it is immoral, and that it will very likely lead to an increase in international terrorism. As with other professions and bodies directly concerned with the wellbeing of people and the environment, we feel that taking a moral stand at this moment is necessary. The American and British public have already declared its distaste for coercive pre-emption and unilateral action. Not to take a stand, as a profession, amounts to silent complicity, while speaking up now in the present uncertainty may persuade leaders to pull back from the brink or, at the very least, oblige the Prime Minister to put the choice of war where it belongs: to the people and Parliament.

Our position rests on four main foundations. The case for a just war cannot be convincingly made; the link of Saddam Hussein with al-Qa'ida has not been established; a war against Iraq is likely to kill large numbers of civilians and intensify the great suffering there; and unilateral action by the US (with Britain's support) will undermine international law and set a precedent for pre-emption by other nations in places such as Chechnya, Palestine, Kashmir and Tibet.

It is possible to imagine circumstances where pre-emptive war could be justifiable in this age of mega-terrorism. But these must be exceptional and based on concrete evidence of an immediate and severe threat. Such a showing has not been made in relation to Iraq.

A consequence of invasion by the USA and Britain is likely to be the very clash of civilisations sought by terrorist groups such as al-Qa'ida. Arab statesmen from all Muslim countries have said an invasion would be seen either in terms of a Christian crusade (President Bush's initial reaction to terrorism) or Western imperialism and the grab for oil. The goal of the terrorist is to make the nation-state itself adopt terrorist tactics, and thereby lose legitimacy in the eyes of the people. In the eyes of the Arab world, the USA and UK are perilously close to being regarded as rogue states who do not respect international law and, if they invade Iraq without just cause, many of their own citizens will so regard them. Terrorism will have won the War on Terrorism.

CHARLES JENCKS *Architectural Historian and Designer;* PAUL HYETT *President, RIBA;* Lord ROGERS OF RIVERSIDE *Architect;* Sir TERRY FARRELL *Architect;* Professor WILLIAM ALSOP *Architect;* RICK MATHER *Architect;* PAUL FINCH *Writer;* EVA JIRICNA *Architect;* MOHSEN MOSTAFAVI *Chairman, Architectural Association;* ZAHA HADID *Architect;* REM KOOLHAAS *Architect;* Sir RICHARD MacCORMAC *Architect, Past President RIBA;* KEN POWELL *Architectural Critic;* RICHARD MURPHY *Architect;* FRANK GEHRY *Architect;* GEORGE FERGUSON *Architect;* TED CULLINAN *Architect Royal Institute of British Architects* London W1

Nov 2, 2003

Write to the Editor at The Independent on Sunday, 191 Marsh Wall, London E14 9RS, or fax to 020-7005 2628, or email to sundayletters@independent.co.uk. Letters should arrive by Thursday noon and include a postal address and daytime telephone number.

THE INDEPENDENT
ON SUNDAY

World against the war

War would be costly, its aftermath worse

As an American who has lived in Britain for 38 years and as someone who loves both places, I see a risk that perhaps has been underrated. For more than a billion Muslims, the attack on Iraq looks like an old Western gambit: might makes right, there is one law for the West, another one for the rest. However evil and wily Saddam may be, Muslims do not believe there is a "clear and present danger" that he could attack foreign countries. He is too crippled and isolated, and will be, as long as the UN is taere. Terrorism feeds on obvious injustices, both felt and known to be wrong. It follows that if the West goes ahead with its policy the likely outcome will be to create the very thing it purports to be fighting: more terrorism, and aimed at the very centre of the Anglo-Saxon world where it is most vulnerable, London. However, we can avoid this catastrophe. Tony Blair listens to the public mood: if the demonstration on 15 February is large enough and the opinion polls show a large majority against unilateral action, it could make him drop his support. Without Britain on board, 80 per cent of Americans are against war and this dangerous precedent of flouting international law would not be set.

Charles Jencks
London W11

March 2004

Terror warning

Charles Jencks, London

After the Madrid bombings and a year since the invasion of Iraq, it is a good time to reflect on how terrorism is working. We should consider what a national response should be, and, as a profession responsible for the environment, we should start a more open and balanced debate.

We tried to do this before the war, when a group of architects wrote to the national press to protest the proposed invasion. Our major points have, unfortunately, all been vindicated: fictitious weapons of mass destruction, fictitious links between Iraq and Al-Qaeda, huge civilian casualties, a blow to international law and the impression of western imperialism to muslims.

Through their actions, Blair and Bush have recruited new terrorists. They have forged an Iraqi nationalism of Sunnis and Shias against Anglo-Saxons. With their hope of creating a client state, with 100,000 occupiers kept in the background, and the fact that the official policy is not democracy, it is no wonder Blair predicts terrorism on these shores.

Architects are complicit in the situation if they don't stand up as a profession. We are a profession that cares about the environment, we are a utopian profession and we are morally obliged to anticipate the future. Take away that, and we are just plumbers.

I believe Blair and Bush will respond to pressure from professionals. It is Israeli architects who are leading the assault against the construction of new settlements in the occupied territories.

Staying silent is not an option

Charles Jencks, London

Architects, like the 50 diplomats in the UK and US, must stand up as a profession and take on the politicians, who, as usual, are not able to admit their policies have failed, and thereby change them. If not we will all be complicit with an amoral policy that, in the name of freedom and democracy, is bringing quite the reverse to Iraq.

Mission Creep is racing at a gallop and all the clichés are coming home to roost — Shock and Awe is becoming Hit and Run, Liberation has become Occupation, and the War on Terror is now the increase in the Terror of War. We might reconsider at least one goal in light of these realities: the safety and autonomy of minorities. If a tripartition of Iraq seems most likely, and is covertly under way already, surely a new coalition under the UN should be empowered to oversee that this happens with the minimum of bloodshed and maximum of civil order. The real victors in this will be the long-suffering Kurds. Their border with Turkey will present a most difficult job, and only Nato (under a UN umbrella) could face up to it. Minorities in the Shia and Sunni sectors must be protected where possible, and moved where not.

When troops do finally leave,

Taking on the politicians: Richard Rogers at one of last year's anti-war demos

the spectre of ethnic cleansing becomes likely, and not to prepare for it would be to commit yet another crime. To stand back in silence is to implicitly condone a tragedy. If, through pressure from the media and other professions, politicians were to admit what is happening and take effective action, something positive could still emerge: the secure borders of three would-be nations having the freedom and democracy we promised in the first place.

9: THE CURSE OF AGAMEMNON

A Water War Garden

In 2004 the Chaumont Garden Festival, a leader in the genre of international garden design, came up with an unlikely theme for its annual event: disorder in the garden. Twenty-four designers were asked to create their idea of nature's bedlam; each one enclosed his or her notion of landscape anarchy behind a petal-shaped hedge. They called the exhibit *Vive le Chaos* (long live pandemonium). By that time 'chaos' had become the fashionable word for the highly unmemorable science of 'non-linear dynamics'. But this label was something of a misnomer because the real subject of scientific chaos is the opposite of disorder. Its proper study is the way organization actually grows out of apparently random activity.

By the late 1980s scientists began to understand that organization grows, in their words, 'on the edge between order and chaos', that edge where nature self-organizes at its greatest complexity. Thus the choice of theme was particularly apt for a garden festival because one could use nature to show this important edge, just the point where gardens flourish. Perhaps since so much of my design had been involved with complexity theory, the organizers asked me to do a keynote garden mostly made out of water. In any case, since at the same time the American and British governments were misleading their publics into war, with the spectre of a 45-minute chemical or nuclear attack, I put the two ideas together: a Water War Garden.

Instead of fighting over oil, water could be the medium of dispute; instead of firing guns, liquid catapults or 'waterpults' could throw it; hoses could shoot it; water-canons could reflect its drumbeats.

In the nineteenth century Charles Darwin saw what he called the 'war of nature' as a fundamental truth that drives natural selection forward, the decimation of nine in ten species so that the tenth might prosper. A similar notion has engaged political theorists and statesmen from Hobbes to Churchill, who saw human war as eternal. The hypothesis common to both is that nature and culture are perpetually struggling with themselves, or its corollary, that competition can lead to mass killing. Whether this is an everlasting truth or not, it is quite obvious that war does cause chaos, particularly today among civilian populations. The phrase 'Total War' is now used by historians to signal that war against civilians has become the norm in the last hundred years. It is our dismal contribution to the history of strife.

At Chaumont the visitor approaches the garden up a ramp or steps and enters through a large red barrel. This circle might recall a Chinese moon gate or classical arch, except that where a keystone might have been it is marked with a tiny gunsight. Blood red sets the war theme and the organizational layout: the wooden walkway in the form of a circular loop is designed as a 'chaotic attractor'. On this are stencilled orange letters that cue the planting and how it relates to the garden elements of war. For instance, to the left and next to the broad leaves of living gunnera is the phrase 'La Vie – Le Grand Ordonnateur' (life, the greatest of organizers).

LEFT: Final plan.

RIGHT ABOVE : Developmental sketches. These plans show the three basic chaotic attractors: the blood-red walkway, the green channels of pondweed etc. and the blue metal reflectors (final drawing, Matthew Emmett).

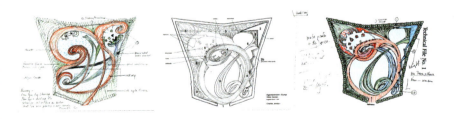

RIGHT BELOW: Entrance through a gun barrel. Stencilled letters cue the themes and planting: Malediction d'Agamemnon – Jardin de la Guerre, La Guerre du Jardin.

CHAOTIC WATERWHEEL AND DRUMS OF WAR

To the right, and across the shallow basin, one sees the high point, the symbolic source of wealth and dispute in the Middle East: water in the V-shaped cistern with exit spouts to either side. The one to the left spills on to a waterwheel. The spinning wheel is set acentrically, so that it moves in chaotic motion. It pulsates first slowly then quickly, creating optical illusions because of the overlapping black and white curves. White flashes, blades of light, explode at the viewer. Water, the source of life and power, is seen to cause sudden bursts and flares, visual reactions that portend the role of water in war.

On the other side of the V-cistern water drops on to a sequence of six metal spouts. They pivot chaotically up and down, giving off an aperiodic drumbeat, banging on top of reverberant cylinders of different shapes and sounds. The syncopated music of the machine gun: ratta-tat-tat.

The V-cistern gives a constant stream on to the chaotic waterwheel. As it turns acentrically, interference patterns, in black and white curves, create explosive pulsations. Stencilled opposite: 'La Roue Chaotic'.

The Drums of War rise and fall chaotically on top of cylinders. Stencilled opposite: 'L'eau source du puissance', 'L'eau connait la musique', 'The Noise of War'.

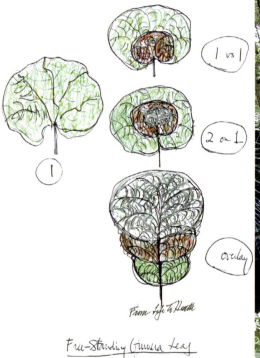

From Life to Death

Free-Standing Gunnera Leaf

GUNNERA FLARES AND WATERPULTS

In the background one sees several different kinds of 'gunnera flares', cones of chicken wire holding foliage that varies from small to large. Gunnera, a water plant whose elephant-ear leaves can grow to 8 feet across, is a dramatic way to visualize life turning into death. The lifecycle flares from green at the base to brown and silver at the top. As the garden ages and is tended, dead and rotting elements are placed on top of the curved metal mesh, a reminder of the constant garden theme 'Et in Arcadia ego' (I, Death, am even in Arcadia). Usually decomposition is banished from the artificial landscape and gardeners are paid to clean up the evidence of entropy and put it out of sight or turn it into compost. But the idea here was to freeze death at various stages of decomposition and turn it into a recurrent pattern of undulations, curves that relate to the grammar of the garden, the three large chaotic attractors.

The red attractor leads to the central basin and two waterpults. Two catapults can be cranked at the base, throwing water at each other that then spills on to the rocks below. An unintentional side effect of war is to stimulate invention and grow the economy. Here the water fight (very popular among children at Chaumont) had its by-product, turning the limestone rocks into a luscious living sculpture.

The way the waterpults fill with water and suddenly release it is both determined by the constant input and made random by the initial conditions and the unpredictable interactions. Scientists call such action 'deterministic chaos', and it has a counterpart in the tit-for-tat response of war, the curse of Israel and Palestine today.

LEFT: Gunnera flares from green to brown to silver. Stencilled opposite the dead cones: 'La Mort – Le Grand Désordre', 'Order out of Chaos', 'Creative Destruction'.

RIGHT: Waterpults. Stencilled in front: 'Moyen Orient', 'Coup pour Coup', 'Tit-for-Tat', and (near the growing moss on the rocks): 'Life from Death', 'Water is Life'.

THE SUPERPOWER SETTLEMENT AND STRANGE ATTRACTOR

Competitive games, such as croquet and badminton, take place in a garden, elegant forms of ritualized aggression. The interactive Water War Garden at Chaumont proved so popular that it was often tested to destruction by children, and from time to time it had to be repaired. Most damage took place at the head of the red walkway, where the visitor was invited to take part in the Superpower Settlement. Here five hoses were placed with their names stencilled behind the nozzles: 'La France' and 'Allemagne' to the left, 'Grande Bretagne' and 'Espagne' to the right, and 'USA' in the centre. They pivoted to shoot at three black boats that bobbed about, small floating vessels with water shields and the words 'Iraq', 'Iran', 'Satellite'. The game of superpower control consists in aiming a stream of water at these boats. Two superpower-hoses, the Bush–Blair Axis, work in conjunction to force the satellite back in its place ('A Vos Places! – A Vos Places!' the words demand). Their place or pigeonhole was two black harbours, of similar species, colour and shape. But once pushed into their harbour by force, and then left alone, because of the turbulence elsewhere they would drift out, towards freedom.

As mentioned, the overall organization of the garden is based on layering three different chaotic attractors: walkway, metal reflectors and channels holding water plants. The latter start under the V-cistern with the gunnera, large plants that are transformed into lower-growing water weeds. Floating on the top is a mixture of duckweed, algae, cape pondweed and water lily. Their metal flares follow the self-similar curves that sometimes reveal water between the channels. The third chaotic attractor, made from coloured metal channels placed deeper in the water, visually connects elements and it ends in a small curved dish under the canons.

Nearby orange lettering identifies the bloodline of imperial presidents: 'Les Bushs – Voodoo Bush Père, et bush tres petit' (a dangerous, prickly bush).

Harmonious and self-similar curves are woven through each other, the destructive-creation that can result in regeneration, beauty and humour, partial consolation for the curse of war. As my friend the Scottish gardener Ian Hamilton Finlay put it: 'A garden is not just a retreat, but an attack.'

The Superpower Settlement. Growing species – *Candelabra primulus*, *Dicentra spectabilis* 'Alba', *Salvia patens* – and plastic flowers are laid out like white corpses on a black bier. The force of the water hose guides the boats into their harbours. Stencilled on one free boat: 'Satellite-semi-libre'; on trapped boat: 'Satellite Coincé'.

RIGHT: Three chaotic attractors weave through each other: warfare, plants and water on metal.

ABOVE: A friend, Marcia Blakenham.

10: THE BIRCHBONE GARDEN

'It might make one in love with death,' declared Shelley, 'to be buried in so sweet a place.'

Veiled Centre

They say the human is the only species that can laugh at death, that can play games and joke about it or, as Shelley implies, fall in love with a beautiful cemetery. Moreover, when one looks hard at the most natural and permanent sign of death – that is, bones – they often turn out to be amusing-looking structures with an aesthetic dimension. Or, in the hands of a Hamlet contemplating a skull, or a

At the core of circle of birch trees are two metal spirals. One holds dark coal, the other a silver helichrysum, which topples over the edge and grows up the bones. Coal is really dead life, a fossil fuel that remains as a petrified reminder of its former self, while life is virtually unsuppressible, eternal, and will grow and prosper wherever possible. Early drawings show life (in red) and death (in black) wrapping and confronting each other in various ways against green turf circles, while later drawings show the conceptual layout of three circles of trees and a central spiral (and green here signifies life and red death). The final scheme adopts a black and white symbolism for death and life, with small variations.

Henry Moore playing with a large hip joint, they can be both striking and sculptural. Indeed, since bones are white and birch trees are white, a black and white garden of death and life is an inevitability waiting to happen.

Here, such a design occupies the centre of a ring of trees that is veiled by a grove of brilliant white birch, the slender stalks of *Betula utilis* 'Jacquemontii' that grow straight up like thin steel rods. These both hide and reveal an indistinct figure. At the heart of the circle, the shape can be made out as two little towers. These screw upwards at an angle, small Towers of Babel as it were, made from bent metal. The forms lean forward past each other but hold together in tension. Connecting them is a twisted coil of bones, an ascending loop. This is made from cow vertebrae flying up into the air as a Möbius strip. What are they? Ex-T-bone steaks that spin above the head; they curve into the blue of the sky, a miraculous structural form that never comes to an end (according to geometricians).

Here also is food magic, for bones are very airy structures that nature knows how to grow even lighter than most engineering works. And then the Möbius strip is one surface with two sides, something of an interesting paradox. So, the mathematics of death is turned into life in a never-ending loop, a riddle.

CIRCLE ONE: THE LIFE AND DEATH PARADOX

The way death leads to new life is the oldest theme of gardens, celebrated and debated since the time of the Egyptians. This paradox was summarized in the god Osiris and one of his incarnations, the Djed-Column, a beautiful-looking bundle of corn sheaves wrapped together like a present. It symbolized agricultural regeneration, the annual flooding of the Nile and the predictable rebirth of corn on which Egypt depended. In Christianity, and in the Muslim Paradise Garden, the resurrection of nature and the strength of life – virility, humour, pleasure and triumph over death – became *the* cosmic theme. It carries an unwelcome truth. Every gardener, like a hard-working god, struggles to keep alive those plants he wants, while banishing those sinners who do not fit into the plot. But a stupendous change has occurred since the nineteenth century, as the average lifespan has more than doubled in the West and the medical revolution has opened up new vistas. Attitudes towards life and death have become more utilitarian and even more paradoxical than they were in Egypt.

With such conceptual breakthroughs as apoptosis, programmed cell death, we now know the body is formed through the systematic culling of unwanted cells. For instance, as a child grows within the womb the web between the fingers has to be edited out. Indeed, a growing baby's thought is unthinkable without the killing off of unneeded brain cells. As agriculturalists have known for more than 7,000 years, life depends very intimately on the compost of decaying matter, on death; but now we know it literally grows amid such slaughter within an individual. Perhaps understandably, this dawning truth was discovered and then repressed three times in the twentieth century, because it was thought to be too depressing and paradoxical. Life, in part, *is* programmed death. Culturally, a related truth also started to be acknowledged about the same time, after 1900. For instance, the physicist Max Planck opined ruefully how hard it was to get the old guard to accept his new theories. Professorial tenure and dogma saw off his new ideas. You cannot convince the opposition by reason alone, but you can hope to outlive them: 'Physics proceeds death by death.' Cardinals in the Vatican, it is said, sick of the old Pope and looking forward to the new, express the same idea of progress through death and then add, as punchline, 'where there's death there's hope'.

The entrance of the first circle in the Birchbone Garden expresses this basic idea. You walk to either side of a white birch tree, and step on to a white Corian plaque with the inscription:

THOUGHT
STEPS FORWARD
DEATH BY DEATH

Put another way, progressive thought moves forward when nature harvests culture. If one is in an ironic state of mind, like Max Planck or the cardinals, this thought can be itself an amusing liberation. If one then moves to the right, the next plaque underfoot has an inscription with a similar idea. This sentence can be read in either a forward or backwards direction:

HOPE
THERE'S
DEATH
THERE'S
WHERE

Read upwards, it is Vatican hopefulness again; downwards, a question: 'Where is death's hope?' The next plaque you come to is a pun private to the garden, a place where moles continually dug and are culled. But its deeper and second meaning is the way DNA molecules and lifeless chemistry turn into life. The way this happens is still a mystery, but it's a basic one of the death/life paradox. Again the major meaning has to be read from the bottom up, in the direction of movement (and the spelling 'cull' changed in the mind to 'cule').

LIFE
INTO
TURN
CULLS
MOLE-
DEAD

Some people will find that a positive conjecture. Turning left at the entrance produces another sequence of positive thoughts on death: the idea that life is so strong in the universe it is virtually eternal, or in constant remission.

remission
eternal
is in
life

This line of thinking ends in a curved plaque that compares the power of death, as symbolized by bones in the Birchbone Garden, to both beauty and thought. Again the phrase should be read from the bottom up, in the line of movement, starting with 'beauty.' It is the old idea expressed by a number of Shakepearean sonnets on the immortality of beauty and its superiority to thought; but of course it can be read the other way too.

thoughts

outlasting

bones

bones

outlasting

beauty

From here you then step into the second circle and quite a different take on the theme.

CIRCLE TWO: EXTERMINISMS

The second circle features non-natural death, that is, various types of murder that have occurred and been engineered by a careful orchestration of language. In effect, euphemisms are manufactured by the state to make the killing easier for soldiers and police, or those operatives who do most of the murdering. But these slippery words also oil the gears of an extended machine throughout society, particularly the media that must encourage the mass-production of death over time, and make it smooth. Because this non-natural death has been an integral part of modern systems from 1500 to the Holocaust and the War on Terror, I have, in the second circle, modulated the linear pipes and turned them into turbulent swirls. Thus black and white 'fish' are wrapped in a viscous and tilted manner, and confronted. The circle starts with a plaque set at right angles to movement on to which you step from the first circle. This sets the theme of the euphemisms we have used in the West. American euphemisms are in black on a white fish; European ones are in white on black. The 'truth', in so far as it can be reduced to a one-liner, is in red.

EXTERMINISMS
WORDS THAT KILL

One then turns right to the next Corian plaques, which start a sequence. These refer to the time of the 'discovery of America' and the first 'acts of faith' of the Spanish Inquisition, the *auto de fé*. Because the European words are not always familiar, their literal translation into English is made first, before this euphemism is translated. Of course, the first one in the New World, its so-called discovery by Columbus, was not a direct euphemism for 'extermination of the natives'. But seen by the indigenous population it was not a discovery either, since they had been there for thousands of years. The general narrative of discovering a virgin land very cleverly masked what was happening: the natives of that land were being displaced. This has been clarified in many books such as David E. Stannard's *American Holocaust: Columbus and the Conquest of the New World* (1992). Stannard puts the reduction of the population in the first half-century of contact to at least 60 to 80 million, a contentious figure. Most of this was caused by the spread of inadvertent and planned disease. Although perhaps only 40 million were killed, in North and South America over a hundred years, and a much smaller number were murdered, it is pointless to deny that genocide wasn't an implicit policy. It was encouraged, or positively allowed, by the State. The narrative 'Discovery of the New World' played a big role in hiding this truth to the population. At the same time in Europe, the Spanish Inquisition started its implicit form of anti-Semitism in urban spectacles with the 'act of faith', the *auto de fé* or *auto público*. For instance, in Madrid in 1680, heretics who would not proclaim the faith were taunted and led through the streets to a square where they were very publicly burned. In effect, the euphemism of faith, for some, meant burning for others.

DISCOVERY OF THE NEW WORLD
EXTERMINATION OF NATIVES
AUTO DE FE
'ACT OF FAITH'
PROCESSION TO BURN

'Relocation' has often been a euphemism for tacit killing and in the New World it was discovered that usually about 15 per cent of the native population would die under this state directive. When President Andrew Jackson had 17,000 Cherokees forcibly marched to a New Land in 1833, 8,000 men, women and children died. The Spanish Church used the word for 'relaxation' as a euphemism when they turned over heretics to the authorities for death by burning.

Relajar
RELOCATION
CHEROKEE DEATH MARCH
RELAJACIÓN
'Relaxation'
STATE KILLING

In Iraq, after the American invasion of 2003, the occupying authorities fashioned a large lexicon to hide from the home country, and Britain, what they were up to. This story has become partly known through film and photographs, but I was particularly moved by David Bromwich's article 'Euphemism and American Violence' in *The New York Review of Books* (3 April 2008). In addition to those euphemisms that follow, and the well known 'shock and awe' and 'liberate Iraq', I was struck by the way Bush could pronounce a 'sharp, short war' or 'taking out Saddam' and then declare 'mission accomplished', as if words were facts, created by uttering them. This is usually a role reserved for God, or the nomothete of several creation myths, who speaks things into existence. Condoleezza Rice was equally divine when she declared the war 'the birth pangs of a New Middle East'. To manufacture confessions through near-torture became 'standard operating procedure'; to protect American operatives were a group of 'contractors' and hired professionals, among whom one of the most murderous was 'Blackwater'. Under the National Socialists in Germany the *Einsatzgruppen* were the most efficient and feared contractors, the 'task forces' who were really killing squads. There is no equation of the war machines of different countries, but there is a similarity of evasive language, designed to be anodyne yet understood by those who count.

BLACKWATER INC.
MURDER CORP.
Einsatzgruppen
'Task Forces'
DEATH SQUADS

A standard speaking procedure for those whose unhappy job it is to report the accidental death of civilians caused when more than a target is taken out is 'collateral damage'. Death can be rather damaging to individuals and is even predictable with 'surgical strikes' and 'guided missiles'. *Sonderbehandlung* literally means special treatment or special handling, but Eichmann and Himmler said those who count knew what it really meant.

COLLATERAL DAMAGE

KILLING INNOCENTS

Sonderbehandlung

'Special Treatment'

EXTERMINATION

A provocative but predictable aspect of euphemisms is the way they can grow around pleasant associations. These subtract horror and add the promise of pleasure. Thus waterboarding sounds enjoyable, like surfboarding, except the danger is not that you fall off. It was carefully designed to simulate drowning, so closely, indeed, that those waterboarded for a confession could be taken right to the edge of death and believe they were suffocating. There was also another euphemism handy for such torture that didn't sound so nice: 'compromised respiration'. *Badeanstalten* is still used positively in Germany and Denmark to mean a public bath or bathhouse, but at Auschwitz it was used for the erection of two giant ovens, and became a synonym for gas chambers.

WATERBOARDING

VIRTUAL DROWNING

Badeanstalten

'Bathhouses'

GAS CHAMBERS

The Global War on Terror was declared several times by George W. Bush, and the number of Iraq dead, as a consequence of the invasion and occupation, was conveniently never tallied by the US and UK governments. Responsible journalists and investigations by the *Lancet* put the number killed at 100,000 and, by 2006, the 'excess' deaths were put between 50,000 and 655,000. Terrorism, as a CIA report showed, actually had increased as a consequence of the war and, in three years, reached 11,111 incidents. So Bush's War on Terrorism turned out to be a euphemism for creating state terrorism and an excuse for killing Iraqis. *Die Endlösung*, 'The Final Solution', became the most notorious of the Nazi euphemisms, which today has become a symbol of governmental double-speak around the world. It is a truth now generally acknowledged that before you can kill and torture large numbers you have to invent a series of well-crafted exterminisms, words that oil the way. A garden of death and life can not shy away from this fact.

WAR ON TERROR

EXCUSE FOR KILLING

Die Endlösung

'The Final Solution'

EXTERMINATING JEWS

CIRCLE THREE: BLACK AND WHITE LYRICAL

As one approaches the centre of the Birchbone Garden, and sees the swirling bones close by, the mood changes again to something lighter and more rhythmical. You step across to the third circle and on to a plaque with gently undulating words:

> life flows sweetly
> in birchbone curves
> of a white wood

Then as you walk to the left there are some simple repeats of form and colour leading to the white entrance of the inner circle where helichrysum and white Corian alternate in a spiral shape:

> **Bones White**
> **Birch White**
> **Night Light**

And continuing on, in this clockwise direction, one reaches the final inscription, with its mixture of suggestion and description. It leads to the black coal entrance to the inner circle, a sign of dead life:

> **In Britain Mourning**
> **Is black**
> **In China**
> **White**

The bones at the centre circle up overhead. They morph in size like a continuously changing backbone and are graded in colour, from silver to white at the top to black. The form is a twisted curve, something of an incomplete Möbius strip. This implies the continuous loop of life and death and life. The looping form rises up into the blue or grey sky framed by a circle of white birch trees. It is an old Roman idea, which I saw carried out very successfully in a secret garden outside Verona: an illusionist 'dome of the sky' can be created by a surrounding circle of trees, a growing architecture.

COMPUTER EPIGRAPHY

Written inscriptions were a staple of Chinese gardens and they operated in different ways. Some were writ large in beautiful calligraphic flourishes and placed above a garden vista, or at the entrance to a pavilion. These classified the view and its feeling with a poetic conceit, or a verbal or visual metaphor. More extensive messages were written on slates or carved into stone and, like the colophons written on the side of a painting, they were to deepen perception. Thus words could accrue to scrolls or gardens like barnacles to a rock. Time was the author. Today new possibilities have been opened up by computer epigraphy, the laser-cut writing on aluminium, or the cutting of synthetic material by a digital router. Here Corian plaques of white and black have been cut and painted. In several ways the hand carving of stone, the traditional approach, provides a superior and more flexible outcome for lettering, because it encourages last-minute inspiration and artistry. But with computer production one can achieve other kinds of perfection, and choices that were not possible with handcrafted stone. Digital fabrication allows one to modify the shape of words – to wave, bend and angle them – with an extraordinary geometric precision. It also enhances sequential production, the ability to think about many plaques in a row or a relationship, and modify them together. This would be laborious by hand. Furthermore, different typefaces, colours and shapes can be mocked up and compared very quickly. The quality of computer epigraphy, its cool impersonality, is sometimes even desirable.

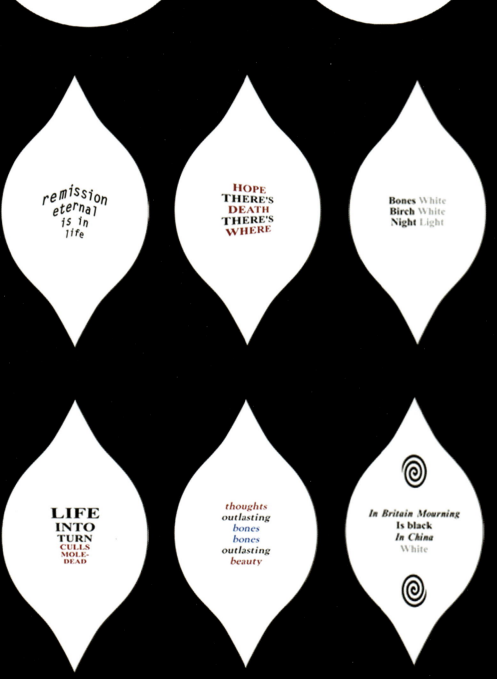

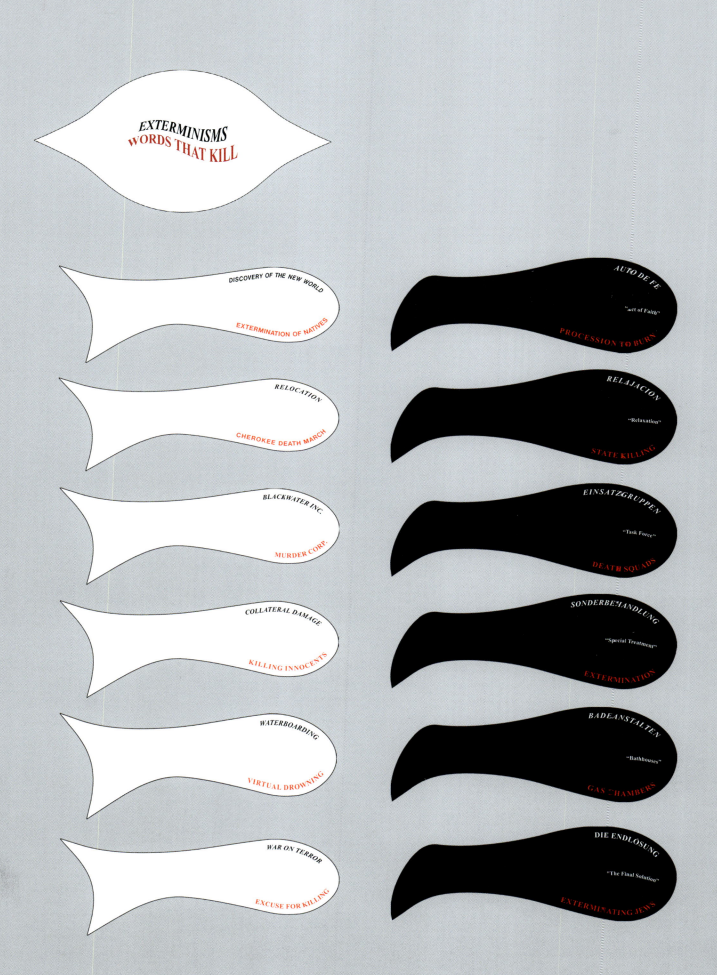

EXTERMINISMS
WORDS THAT KILL

DISCOVERY OF THE NEW WORLD
EXTERMINATION OF NATIVES

RELOCATION
CHEROKEE DEATH MARCH

BLACKWATER INC.
MURDER CORP.

COLLATERAL DAMAGE
KILLING INNOCENTS

WATERBOARDING
VIRTUAL DROWNING

WAR ON TERROR
EXCUSE FOR KILLING

AUTO DE FE
"act of Faith"
PROCESSION TO BURN

RELAJACION
"Relaxation"
STATE KILLING

EINSATZGRUPPEN
"Task Force"
DEATH SQUADS

SONDERBEHANDLUNG
"Special Treatment"
EXTERMINATION

BADEANSTALTEN
"Bathhouses"
GAS CHAMBERS

DIE ENDLOSUNG
"The Final Solution"
EXTERMINATING JEWS

PART FOUR
LIFE'S REINVENTION

11: SPREADING LIFE

Comets Bring Life?

'What is life?' is a perennial question for gardeners, as it was for the physicist Erwin Schrödinger, who wrote an epochal book with that title in 1944. He hoped for an answer and saw that it might come with discoveries in nuclear physics and chemistry. The query is also a philosophical issue based on whether such minimal things as a virus can be considered living. Even when looked at broadly life's multiple definitions do not command universal assent. Indeed, its origin has become more enigmatic the more we know. Life appears too complex to have evolved according to the standard theory of the 1950s and the experiments by the American chemists Miller and Urey. Several competing ideas seem just as implausible and, in any case, the ancient origins, whatever they were, are likely to have been swept away by subsequent life. Our position is like that of an innocent traveller who has found himself at the scene of a captivating drama, a murder where the body is all too clear but the clues are perfectly erased. There cannot be a smoking gun. Or rather, the many guns are impossible to choose between. They include black smokers, those forms of life called extremophiles that occur at volcanic vents deep under the sea. Coming in during the second act of a long play, all we can do is speculate and pick the most plausible scenarios.

One such explanation is panspermia, a theory that goes back to Ancient Greece and Anaxagoras, a philosopher who influenced Socrates. Literally it means 'everywhere seeds', particularly the dust and nebulae in interstellar space that can be analysed today for its chemical make-up. Panspermia has a long history developing through the French chemist Louis Pasteur, taking hold of the Swedish chemist Svante Arrhenius and more recently the British astronomers Fred Hoyle and Chandra Wickramasinghe. It is an idea that captivates the mind because it is so logical and, like the others, so unprovable.

If bacteria can survive interstellar travel for 25 million years, as two scientists from Cal Poly showed in 1995, it makes sense to believe they may also take a ride on what are called dirty snowballs with ice and water: that is, comets. More recently microfossils have been found on meteorites and they are highly suspected on Mars, among other planets. Bacteria 250 million years old have been revived. Since 1999, even such a conservative body as NASA has accepted that life may come from outer space. Today panspermia is almost a respectable hypothesis, moving from Dan Brown and science fiction to becoming a contender for the smoking gun – that cannot be a proof. Perhaps we are stuck in the Second Act for a long time, doomed not to know life's beginnings.

In landscape and garden design, where the origins of nature are

Comet Bridge from above, left, and the comet Hale-Bopp (Free Software Foundation)

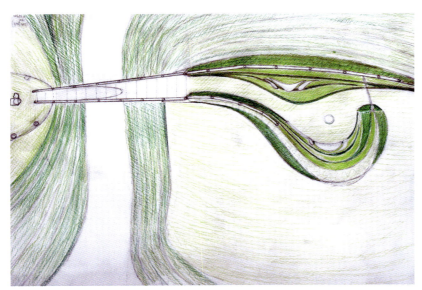

ABOVE: Comet iconography. Comet orbits and flares are one of the few moving systems in nature that have a clear dramatic form. As they orbit a star system, their dust tail always points away from the sun's radiation and sometimes shows two streams, one of ionized particles (shown in blue).

BELOW: The extreme elliptical orbits differ from the near-circular ones of the planets (Halley in red; Swift-Tuttle in green, Encke in light blue, etc.). Hence these long, thin ellipticals become the language for the aluminium seats and all the aspects of the landforms.

BOTTOM: Bridge offcuts are used to hold a geode 'eye' in the midst of wildflowers, nature's similar cometary shapes.

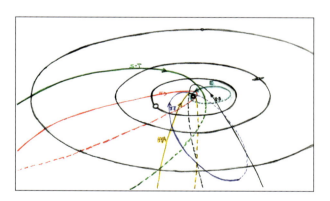

pondered, it makes sense to entertain panspermia as a deep insight into the way life may move around the universe. These theories take nothing away from its meaning, and they merely push questions of beginning elsewhere, on to a cosmic dimension. Moreover, they entail the very important implication that the universe has a predisposition to create life wherever and whenever it can, a spiritual conjecture. If life is normally created by the unfolding of laws and found throughout our galaxy; if it gets a foothold on any habitable planet and flourishes; if it is found under ice sheets on the polar caps of Mars; if all these ifs are true then we could say that the universe has a tendency to produce life, even an animating imperative. How it may then get from one solar system to another adds to the chain of cosmic speculation, and charm of contemplation.

Comets are freezing messengers, ideally suited for preserving organic material over vast amounts of time. They come in billions and their chemistry shows a surprising parallel with the four most common elements making up living material: hydrogen, carbon, nitrogen and oxygen. These are all hard frozen into the ice and water, the very things on which life thrives. Professor A.H. Delsemme at the University of Toledo, who has analysed the spectrograph of comets, has found even more unlikely aspects of the four shared elements. Their proportions in comets and in life are uncannily similar, more similar than they both are to the earth's biosphere. Since they travel in huge, eccentric oval orbits that bridge one solar system to another it means they could be the smoking gun — that cannot be proved.

Cosmic Aesthetic System

Compared to planets, the typical comet has an orbit that is extremely elliptical. Comets' geometric beauty is quite different from the more circular paths of planets and, with their tails of trailing ice and dust that always point away from the sunlight, they constitute one of nature's great aesthetic systems. This has been apparent to the naked eye for a long time and it has led to contrary readings. Because it resembles a flaming projectile, the sudden presence of a streaming white tail in the sky foretells a grim future. The Roman saying epitomizes this omen: 'In coelo nunquam spectatum impune cometam' (In the heavens a comet is not seen without foretelling disaster). Such were the forecasts accompanying comets in Europe in 1531, 1607 and 1682. The Bayeux Tapestry, which depicts the recurrence of Halley's Comet, shows it to be a sign of the English King Harold's defeat in 1066 and it is woven as a splendid flaming star just above his head. The French point at this while the words trail from its rocket exhaust: 'Isti mirant stella' (They wondered at the star). So, depending on which side of the Channel you were, the same cosmic event could have opposite implications. Today, with the interest in panspermia, the meanings of a comet are usually positive although they carry disturbing overtones, with the knowledge that an asteroid probably wiped out the dinosaurs. Whichever the case they are primary cosmic actors: the bringers of life, the possible killers and the astral event with the most striking form.

For the Comet Bridge such images, words and flaming orbits have become both the formal system and the iconography. They are found in the aluminium seats, the overall structure and the landform that wraps a tree. The time-lapse image of a comet, with its occasional double tail, makes for a twisting shape set against a green background. Hence the long thin lines, the stretched curves with a head, and the feeling that there is a centre of attraction around which the twist occurs (the sun). These forces pull the metal and the handrails into gentle swoops. The eye of fertility, the star-flower, the explosive impregnation of planets.

Also engraved in the aluminium are historical images and words from the Bayeux Tapestry. Below, depicting the return of Halley's Comet, is 'Isti mirant stella' (They wondered at the star). Left is the Roman warning repeated for generations: 'In coelo nunquam spectatum impune cometam' (In the heavens a comet is not seen without foretelling disaster).

BRIDGING

The Comet Bridge at Portrack joins two different types of garden: a wilderness to the left, and a pasture or meadow to the right. Underneath run farm vehicles and the occasional sheep or cow. The tail of the comet is designed as aluminium fencing that wraps the low turf mound at various angles to keep out animals. Inside the fence is a protected place for picnics, under the proverbial shady chestnut tree.

Horizontal rails of the bridge follow the swoop of the comet as it lands to the left and spreads a tail to the right. Various functional problems result, including the way those crossing the bridge pick up speed as they reach the steeper side; also there is the possibility that sheep will enter between the spreading rails. Each of these difficulties becomes the excuse for more cometary details, elliptical metal elements that aim towards the focus. This is foreshortened in a forced pespective. Ready-made steel I-beams with punched circular holes resemble the coma, the body of the asteroid, seen in freeze-frame flight.

To the left, the wilderness garden, with its 1,000 nesting crows and its Nonsense Pavilion, has been conceived as the Garden of Taking Leave of Your Senses. Hence the unusual planting scheme, the strange juxtaposition of species and the tilt of the landing point.

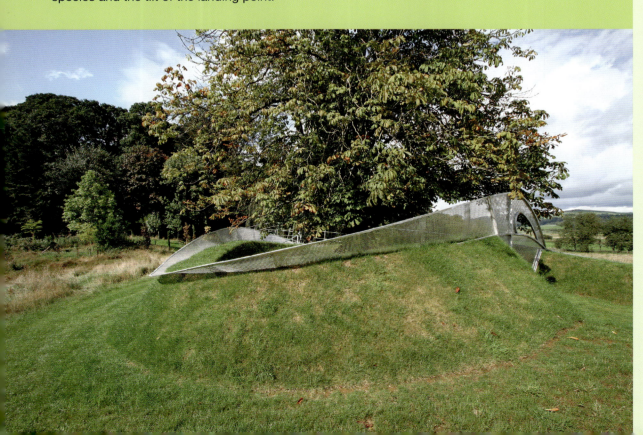

The plan, below, drawn with Matthew Emmett, shows the hill context and where the comet lands – two rocks – both the focus of perspective and a seat for viewing.

SHADE

Two different landforms snake around the chestnut tree, creating a place for seats with a canopy of leaves overhead and tables for food. A swing gate pulls the comet tail down over the window-hole and the tail ties into the rail that keeps out the animals from the picnic.

PARADOX

Comets are paradoxical in their motion, shape, orbits and above all in their unlikely chemical compositions. Hence, left and below, two seats carry the provocative aphorisms of recent scientists. First is that of the cosmologist who had many inspired insights into the hidden workings of the universe, Fred Hoyle. In his book *The Intelligent Universe*, he wrote the tantalizing proposition about the coincidence between the dirty snowball that is a comet and living matter – 'Cometary material *is* life, I would say, not simply its precursor': something to ponder as you sit on the words. A friend and eminent writer on many aspects of contemporary science, Paul Davies, takes a more tempered view of the probabilities – 'Comet impacts blast microbes into space, perhaps to inoculate nearby planets.' This seems highly likely, though we await detailed proof.

The quote, left, from the great eighteenth-century classifier Linnaeus – 'Nature does not proceed by leaps . . .' – concerns the obvious continuities that evolution shows, yet it is followed by my answer – '. . . but by cometary jumps.' The universe evolves both through gradual processes and cataclysmic disruptions, especially those caused by cometary impacts. Comets are the ultimate earthly credit crunch, as the dinosaurs found out, and this led to a quote that I didn't cut in aluminium: 'Comet's crash causes quixotic cataclysm creating curious craters bringing beauty.'

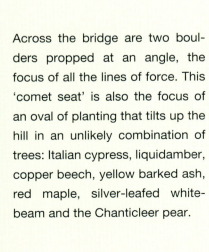

FOLLOWING PAGES: Seats, tables and shelves streak through the green turf.

Across the bridge are two boulders propped at an angle, the focus of all the lines of force. This 'comet seat' is also the focus of an oval of planting that tilts up the hill in an unlikely combination of trees: Italian cypress, liquidamber, copper beech, yellow barked ash, red maple, silver-leafed whitebeam and the Chanticleer pear.

12: METAPHORS OF LIFE

The Cell and DNA

The Comet Bridge was one step in an exploration, the attempt to find suitable metaphors of life, that is, visual forms that celebrate its dynamism and great significance. On this journey I had followed the idea of my friend the biologist Steven Rose, a writer on memory who had questioned the paradigm of genetic determinism. This is the notion that a single gene codes 'for' complex behaviour. Rose argued in several books that life is an irreducible concatenation between at least three different areas: the environment of the cell (or cells), the messages of information that flow through the DNA and the history of the organism (and organisms). In the following

projects I explored these three areas and drew parallels, where I could, between the very small units of life and the world we inhabit. In the past this was part of a religious quest. It used to be normal to relate through art and thought with the ultimate stuff of the universe, especially in sacred art. Today in a secular age it means drawing parallels between the microcosm, the basic atoms of life (the cell and its DNA), the mesocosm (the middle-sized area which makes up the place of human activity) and the macrocosm (the universe as a whole).

After I had worked on the DNA garden at Portrack, the next opportunity I had for exploring these themes was in the small garden for a cancer caring centre in Glasgow, one of several named after my late wife Maggie, which she and I had founded. These we have built along the lines laid out in her *Blueprint for a Cancer Caring Centre*, finished before she died of cancer in 1995. The centre in Glasgow is housed in a nineteenth-century gatehouse to the university, converted by the architects Page and Park into a friendly spiral of space. The pre-existing structure has a romantic tower that surmounts an

LEFT: DNA, left, uncoils one arm into an RNA seat.

BELOW: Maggie's Centre Glasgow, 2001–3, conversion of the Glasgow University Gatehouse by Page and Park Architects. This was an old entry to the campus with mannerist contrasts: big gables versus small walls.

eclectic pile of red sandstone. Its charm lies in the contrast of scale and motif. The crow-step gable belongs on a building twice its size and this pushes down on dwarf corbels to each side. Then a too-big archway sets off a too-little doorway. Edwin Lutyens would have admired the jokes frequently found in the Scottish Baronial style, often more exuberant than historically accurate. Page and Park have knitted a complex plan, a spiral labyrinth, into this old structure and created a series of semi-open rooms leading through to the garden. The relaxation room, for group meetings, opens directly on to this green space. Because the garden area is so small and oddly shaped, I treated it as a single outdoor room. A wall of yew hedge, in two colours, is meant to grow high enough over the years to shut out the urban noise, a red portacabin and the large hospital that looms just to the north.

As you enter the garden your eye is pulled to the left by a large double helix in braised aluminium. The DNA explodes from the nucleus of the cell, a smaller turf circle, and leans towards another little turf mound where a seat for two zips out of its left coil. This horizontal shelf, in effect the messenger RNA, spells out the usual code in its engraved metal slats – ATCG, as well as the donor's gift – 'In recognition of The Evening Times Appeal for Maggie's Centre'. Thus a descriptive legend showing the basic molecules is mixed

ABOVE: Small garden, big DNA (12 feet wide, 18 feet high). The aluminium coils unfold from a nucleus, a small moundette, and lean towards the seat.

OPPOSITE: Lines of planting and stones, in shades of purple, pick up the spiral theme and curve around the mound as RNA which then turns into protein (the pestle-and-mortar-shaped rocks, lower right). The protein built up is also represented by the stacked river rocks, above centre. The plan shows these purple elements and the aluminium seats with their twisted waveforms.

with what could be called cultural DNA. Writing necessarily suffuses everything we do, the tissue of signs, symbols and language is imperialistic, as Umberto Eco has observed, and it is often imposed artlessly on sculpture as an afterthought. In this case I have preempted the necessity and incorporated the dedication to the *Evening Times* so that it runs from the twist to the DNA. The newspaper appeal focused on a walk and a run for the centre. Amazingly for a populist run in the country it raised half a million pounds, a gratifying amount especially since it came in such small denominations.

As far as life is concerned the language of DNA and the communication between cells are the two most important codes – that is, if we exclude the usual cultural channels and the work of the immune system. The point is that languages permeate all levels so that life

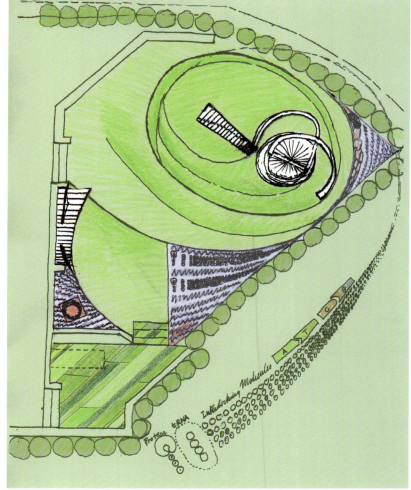

can prosper, a point worth stressing in a garden. The first level of DNA is expressed in the individual letters, as these are turned into words that are repeated exactly. This replication is expressed by the DNA sculpture in its central twist. The rising helix is focused on the hydrogen bonds as they spiral up the middle and unite the molecules, A to T, C to G. For those who care to follow the mapping, the shrubs and stones continue this theme of information spiralling out from a linear source. Parallel waves of planting – sedum and berberis – fan out in brown-red and purple lines. Between them rows of a similarly coloured rock also expand outwards. Even the aluminium seats pick up the theme as the twist flows through them.

The fun of the garden game is to see how far one can continue the symbolism with actual growing cells – the flowers and shrubs – for these too are made through a process of replicating information. The lines of purple plants and stones, to point up some parallels, represent the messenger RNA codons. Once involved in the game of symbolism, you cannot cheat and you have to continue the logic. The codons end in three large rocks, the transfer RNA, and then the pestle-and-mortar-shaped rocks, the protein chains that are built by genes. In the adjacent wedge of planting, purple heuchera contrasts with light red sandstone. Again rocks symbolize the RNA, as it is transformed into protein. These tiny towers are formed from river-worn rocks that have a soft curvilinear surface. Roughly circular in shape, they stack on top of each other like the amino acids that make up our bodies. Not everyone will get it. But because of the clear transformation of themes one does perceive that something more than aesthetics is at stake, and then feels that symbolism may inform the spirals and the purple lines. An intention uniting aesthetics and meaning is felt, if not precisely decoded.

On the other side of the garden is a table for picnics and outdoor meetings. Informal sessions, with a coffee in hand, are essential to these cancer caring centres. Next to the picnic table is another wedge of purple planting, a relic from the old building – again with writing on it – and another string of messenger RNA that emerges out of the ground and transforms itself into an aluminium seat.

Twists and waves flow through the small garden, sometimes symbolizing 'cultural DNA,' such as the dedication, below. The diagram to the right shows the messenger RNA coming through the cell nucleus and being read by a ribosome. It transfers the message into an amino acid which is then assembled into a protein chain: the red and purple rocks in this garden thus symbolize the protein assembly.

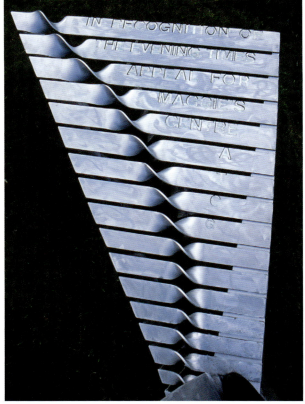

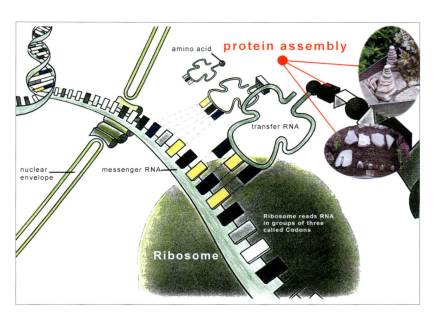

When the green walls have grown to maturity and the purple planting forms a simple background, the next set of moves should be made by those using the centre. More exotic planting and rock placing will give greater life to this big-small room. For me it was an opportunity to test ideas basic to life but at a large scale, the amplified languages of the cell and its replicator. The idea that cancer patients and carers might want to get a perspective on the delicate balances that take place in our 3 trillion cells was in the back of my mind. There has been a long 'war on cancer', since Nixon declared it in 1971, and any sufferer is bound to be aware today of both unchecked cell growth and the heroic attempts of our time to get to the bottom of why this happens. Every week we read of possible breakthroughs in genetics that may make a difference, and this global project often inspires a life-affirming hope in patients. A garden is a place to reflect on these truths.

LIFE BOOTSTRAPS
ITSELF INTO EXISTENCE

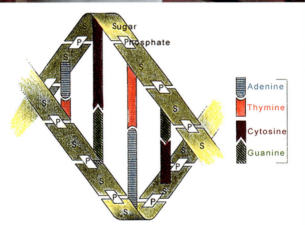

An old conundrum that perplexed the sphinx and many generations of thinkers was which came first, the chicken or the egg? The same mystery surrounds the origins of life and the beginning of the first replicator, DNA. What came before them? The only conceivable answer is a more primitive form of life: chemical compounds, chains of molecules that stuck together and could repeat in some way to send forward messages. They probably would not have left a trace of their creativity, because more complex life would have wiped it clean away. Graham Cairns-Smith, a Glasgow biologist, does some clever sleuthing in his *Seven Clues to the Origin of Life* (1985) and comes up with the idea that the primitive form may have arisen from minerals of clay. His detective work is eminently logical. DNA and cells are already highly evolved 'high-tech solutions' that look specially designed for their job, whereas self-assembling crystals are common and 'low-tech'. Plentiful types of clay found in riverbeds, with crystals much too small to be seen, are a kind of 'zero-tech' solution for the origin of life (a version of the idea is constantly mentioned in the Bible), and so the process may have started evolving from small pieces of dust, in loops. 'For dust thou art, and unto dust shalt thou return'; 'thou hast made me as the clay'; 'Behold . . . I also am formed out of the clay,' etc. However hard to perceive, it's attractive visually: the idea that our ancient mother was a beautiful crystal growing up in a supersaturated solution of water and minerals.

Whatever proto-life may have been, the deep idea is that it would have pulled itself up by the proverbial bootstraps, as life does today all the time. In a way the magic of DNA and life is auto-catalysis, self-creation through feedback in a series of loops that are self-sustaining as they feed off the energy gathered from elsewhere. Once life gets started the loops go round and round in loops of metabolism, growth and reproduction. Loops within loops, in a slowly developing system – such is the symbol of auto-poiesis and life (as I will endeavour to show in designs).

When I was asked by Kew Gardens in 2003 to design a DNA sculpture to celebrate the fiftieth anniversary of its discovery it was this auto-catalysis I sought to depict, as well as the way it interacts with the other loops of life. Hence the sculpture *Bootstrap DNA* sits on an S-curve of planting, the cell of life as it were, a moundette with a dark ground cover in the middle of the plot and two swirls of lighter planting that curve towards its coils. The coils are the structure that visually captures other parts of Kew and then, at either end, turns into a loop of molecules. The letter T keys into A, C locks with G, with the hydrogen twist being the lock and key between them. Again the letters are cut into the brushed aluminium to underscore perfect replication – except when they make a spelling mistake, as in the case of cancer.

Bootstrap DNA celebrates the continuous loop in its balanced form and the way coil and molecule morph through small gradations into each other so that one cannot tell where the chemical chains start and stop – a process I call bootstrapping. But DNA only works inside a cell, inside life, and has to be supported by its membranes and a host of other processes. So here at Kew the planting and the S-curve of the earth-berm are given importance equal to that of the molecule. Some say that the discovery of DNA was the most fundamental insight of the twentieth century, more important than Quantum and Relativity Theories. For all we know the same molecules may underlie life on other planets.

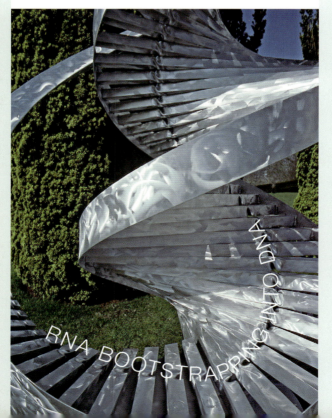

LEFT, ABOVE: The Mother of All Things. Crystals replicate, self-organize and select stable patterns. A strong suspicion is growing that minerals such as clay, calcite or mica, above, may have been the first structures which later were taken over by DNA.

Bootstrap DNA, for fiftieth anniversary of DNA's discovery, Royal Botanic Gardens, Kew, 2003 (aluminium 10 feet wide, 12 feet high). The dark ground cover *Pachysandra terminalis* defines the body of the nucleus, while the lighter growth on the spiral berms, *Liriope muscari* 'Variegata', is symbolic of the active uncoiling of the transfer RNA.

OPPOSITE, MIDDLE AND BOTTOM: The four base-pairs, like letter of the alphabet – A, T and C, G – lock into each other and thus entail exact replication. These letters then construct words and paragraphs that are code for particular proteins that construct the whole book of life. The continuous looping of RNA into DNA into RNA is one of the many loops of life.

RIGHT: Note the strange visual illusions: depending on the viewpoint, the coiling arms always vary in shape and relative height – and the voids capture the background trees.

MUTUAL WRAP

Life uses DNA and DNA uses life; the two are fused inseparably. It is a common mistake to assume that one or the other is in charge, either a 'selfish gene', according to the infamous metaphor of Richard Dawkins, or the 'robot vehicle', his equally degraded figure of speech for you and me. Selfishness is a very 1980s trope and not very apt for unconscious molecules, especially since the genes that survive the arms race have to favour the whole organism and therefore, from this viewpoint, end up being more altruistic than Thatcherite. Yet Dawkins would not have sold so many replicants of his 1976 book to a public hardened by competition and war if he had adopted an equally apt title such as *The Altruistic Gene*. His framing of the evidence inadvertently tells us more about himself than the so-called motives of DNA.

Whatever the case with Dawkins, here at Cambridge the idea was to show the interdependence of life and DNA and depict the two as wrapped together in a dynamic swirl. Hence the DNA sculpture erupts out of actual growing life (two holes in the turf moundette) and embraces life (or at least the many bottoms that sit on the grass and seats). The two voids in the ground also visually pick up the theme of Barbara Hepworth's double-hole sculpture. But instead of surrounding them in muted bronze, it uses a light, sparkling aluminium brushed by a sander. The bright structure is meant to be an eye-catcher for the main walk from old Clare College, and a visual pun on the weeping pear near by.

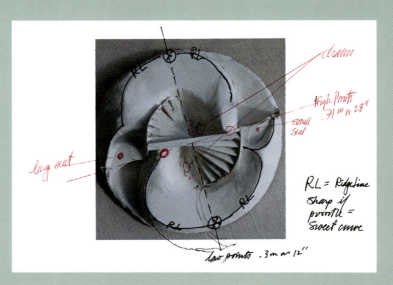

Mutual Wrap, Cambridge DNA, Clare College, 2005 (aluminium 12 feet wide, 18 feet high, on turf mound). The light-tone structure is one focus on the walkway from the older Clare College to the newer buildings and Memorial Court, above. It sits on a route of other curvilinear sculptures, opposite the Barbara Hepworth, above right, and before a reclining work by Henry Moore. The way the DNA erupts out of the two holes in the ground and the wrapping turf was carefully calculated as a continuous loop—to show the parity between cell life and DNA.

SELFISH GENE OR SELFISH ATOM? A PARABLE

DNA is 'an atom of life' and so, as *one* of the several important things that makes us who we are, it deserves proper respect and love. For this reason, it features prominently in this book and my design.

Richard Dawkins' 1976 bestseller *The Selfish Gene* puts a dramatic case for genetic selfishness determining the rest of behaviour. In the first chapter, 'Why are people?' he summarizes the position: 'The argument of this book is that we, and all animals, are machines created by our genes. Like successful Chicago gangsters, our genes have survived, in some cases for millions of years, in a highly competitive world. This entitles us to expect certain qualities in our genes. I shall argue that a predominant quality to be expected in a successful gene is ruthless selfishness . . .' His preface puts this with another robotic metaphor: 'We are survival machines – robot vehicles blindly programmed to preserve the selfish molecules known as genes. This is a truth which still fills me with astonishment. . . . One of my hopes is that I may have some success in astonishing others.'

Dawkins did have an astonishing success with this book and subsequent ones, promoting the idea that Darwin supposedly had answered: 'deep problems: Is there a meaning to life? What are we for?'. The success was also based on a conscious attempt to use metaphor in a popular but, as he admits, 'sloppy' way: 'If we allow ourselves the licence of talking about genes as if they had conscious aims, always reassuring ourselves that we could translate our sloppy language back into respectable terms if we wanted to . . .'. Thus, no surprise to the sleight of hand that dominates his book. Dawkins is perfectly aware that

genes are *not* conscious and do *not* have any foresight or motives. So, in effect, they cannot be 'selfish': as he writes, 'the replicators are no more conscious or purposeful than they ever were . . . Genes have no foresight.' He quickly grants, at this point in his argument, that genes are actually 'cooperative' and 'interacting'. They are involved in creating 'The manufacture of a body [as] a cooperative venture . . . [and] the effect of any one gene depends on interaction with many others'. In short, that 'selection has favoured genes which cooperate with others'. Contradiction compounded? He finally hopes in the last chapter, reversing the previous 200 pages of genetic determinism, that we may be the one great 'exception' to genetic programming and may be able to overcome this spectre with 'memes' of foresight.

So, are genes really 'selfish' or 'altruistic', or is Dawkins just confused? Or is he using metaphor in a sloppy way, selfishly kicking up dust in order to write a potboiler? Clearly if genes don't have consciousness they cannot be selfish, and just as clearly, if they did, their outcomes seen from the point of view of life's victors would be altruistic, because they favour cooperative ventures that help the whole organism. But Dawkins writes exclusively from the individual gene's point of view (even though it doesn't have one) and this metaphor is remorselessly followed, reinterpreting all examples of altruistic outcomes backwardly caused by the individual gene. In other words, Dawkins has made his choice of a figure of speech, where the metaphorical evidence can be construed either way. Perhaps he did this to discredit the notions of 'group selection' favoured by E.O. Wilson and other biologists; or perhaps he did it

The sculpture was opened by James Watson, above, at Clare in November 2005. Tilts and leans and surprising relationships show up when all forms are curving.

to write a bestseller. As he avers in the preface, he has shown the book in 'countless drafts' to 'real readers and critics. I am addicted to revising.' So the metaphors are consciously honed and intended, where they do, to shock and sell books. Moreover, he has tried to make 'the book as entertaining and gripping as it subject matter deserves', and admits that the scientist, 'the expert will still not be totally happy with the way I put things'. Judged this way, what he calls his book – 'almost science fiction' – is an 'astonishing' success, for it managed to convince large sections of the public (selling over a million copies), a great many influential writers such as Martin Amis and a considerable number of biological experts that they were indeed robot vehicles for selfish genes. It seems quite a feat to get paid for telling people they are slaves to an unconscious process but then, as Dawkins has more recently observed about religion, there is a buoyant market for fire and brimstone determinism. As any Gordon Gecko knows, there is money to be made in programmed trading, and convincing robotic traders to deny their freedom.

But hold! Dawkins's metaphor is funnier than it looks. Consider the lowly atom, billions and billions of which make up any DNA molecule; consider particularly the hydrogen atom. Whereas Dawkins's genes may be little Al Capones, ruthlessly machine-gunning their robotic vehicles, the hydrogen atom is a veritable Pol Pot, with millions of dead machines to its credit, telling all molecules what to do. Note how it engineered the big bang for its mass reproduction. (Don't worry, dear reader, I know. When we want to, we can translate this sloppy metaphor back into respectable science.) Talk about replication – it's a stubborn fact that 75 per cent of all matter in the universe is made up of hydrogen atoms. And that isn't the end of it. These little buggers evolve and spread themselves everywhere using the most vicious means: exploding stars, red giants, supernovae – and, yes, hydrogen bombs. They all spew out hydrogen atoms to populate the heavens. The experts, the scientists, mark such

material evolution with the long-winded moniker 'stellar nucleosynthesis', and they show how the ingredients of the Periodic Table – that is, all the elements in the universe – are built up by cooking hydrogen atoms inside stars (big nuclear bombs if that excites you). But permit me to use more common language about these jiggling, sexy, procreative atoms, because their truth still fills me with astonishment and I hope I may have some success in astonishing others. They are egotistical, avaricious little atoms – call them 'greedoms' – that have their way with brainless bigger things like animals or stars or galaxies, in which they multiply. That is the astonishing news. Every time our robot star cooks hydrogen into helium (a billion trillion times every second) – every time a supernovae explodes into a trillion billion bits of heavier elements – the lowly hydrogen atom reproduces itself. It turns into a more complex being like water, H_2O (70 per cent of the earth's surface), and flies around the cosmos. That's real evolution. Selfish DNA? Give me a break. Which atoms really built up this mindless molecule? And every time DNA zips and unzips itself to pass on information, guess who is involved? The hydrogen bond. Who tells the molecules how to join – A to go with T, C with G – atoms built up from hydrogen. Who tells DNA to undergo radioactive decay, to mutate? Who is behind every single act of every single piece of replicating RNA forcing its behaviour? If Dawkins's genes are selfish, then the hydrogen atom, and its gangster family of larger cousins, is a bloody dictator.

The astute reader will follow my metaphor to the point of its truth – that it's a ridiculous untruth to give the atom motives – and its limits: they do not replicate in the same way as DNA. I go to such lengths of ridicule only because the selfish metaphor pervades our society, and a million editions of Dawkins's book continue to infect minds, exemplifying his 'memes' (replicant ideas and usages). The dubious metaphor also cuts us off from appreciating some of the beauties and subtleties of DNA. This is why, when James Watson opened *Mutual Wrap* in 2005, I mentioned the meaning of the sculpture in my remarks during the ceremony and how it was meant as a critique of the selfish gene. To reiterate the aphorism of Ian Hamilton Finlay, 'Certain gardens are described as retreats when they are really attacks.'

CAMBRIDGE

The DNA sculpture was commissioned by Clare College at Cambridge, where James Watson was a student in the early 1950s at the time he was trying to decode the molecule with Francis Crick and others. It was a race to be first, to beat Linus Pauling and the global rush to figure out how life could use chemistry to pass on its codes of innovation. These solution-types, such things as the codes for an eye, were known to be shared throughout much – perhaps all – of life's kingdoms. The replicant molecules – A, T, C, G – were known, but their structural joining and repetition were not entirely clear. The race finally culminated, as

Watson has recounted in *The Double Helix*, when he was given a sneak preview of Rosalind Franklin's detective work by Maurice Wilkins. Her original X-ray photographs may look ambiguous to the untutored eye, but when Watson had a quick glance he realized they related to one of the helical models that Crick and he had developed.

Instead of life being dominated by replicant molecules, the two are part of the same form like two sides of a coin, two protagonists spiralling out of the earth as a joined force. The curved arms differ slightly and this makes the sculpture lean dramatically and set up unexpected

Two wrapped seats, below, cut into the grass moundette (or the nucleus of the cell), each with phrases etched in the same curve. These are part of a continuous sentence, worked out with biologists at Cambridge, that honour both the DNA molecule and its multiple discoverers. The seat backs differ, as do the sharp contour lines of each side. In that sense they parallel the variation of DNA within a shared genome and, like all the aluminium sculptures shown in this section, are generic structures with individual differences. Every living person shares a common genome yet is a unique expression of the code.

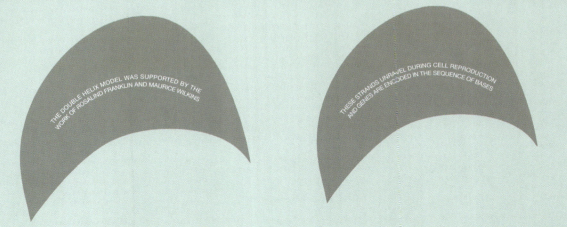

THE DOUBLE HELIX MODEL WAS SUPPORTED BY THE WORK OF ROSALIND FRANKLIN AND MAURICE WILKINS

THESE STRANDS UNRAVEL DURING CELL REPRODUCTION AND GENES ARE ENCODED IN THE SEQUENCE OF BASES

figures. From some angles the metal embraces the earth and a space to sit in a continuous sweep, but then it leaves a tilted void of space overhead. As one circles around the small world, without right angles where relationships can be scaled more exactly, hybrid figures emerge: the grass-metal boomerang shape, a sign of mutuality.

It is interesting to reflect, from an architectural or aesthetic viewpoint, that the helix (or spiral) is one of nature's universal patents for things that grow and change. Thus spiral galaxies or helical hurricanes. In this sense, structural universals come first and life learns to exploit them. In the beginning there was cosmic architecture and then, much later, there was matter and then life.

Four weeks before the opening, just as the sculpture was being installed and the final weld was being made, the fabricator put his blowtorch to the left arm. There was a terrific explosion. A section of the structure shot up 60 feet in the air, creating a boom heard all over Cambridge. The police quickly swarmed to the site, thinking it was a terrorist attack. Luckily neither of the fabricators, John Gibson and his son Greg, was hurt. The villain? Perhaps the aluminium and concrete had interacted overnight, leading to the emergence of hydrogen, which had been trapped and built up. In any case, one headline the next day had it 'DNA in Big Bang', as mistaken a metaphor as Bush's War on Terror or the 'selfish gene'.

Sculpture explodes

What the helix was that?

Blast drama: Workmen examine the sculpture after the accident. The double helix design celebrates the work of Frances Crick and Jim Watson, inset.

Exclusive
By Alex Mott

WORKMEN installing a sculpture at a Cambridge college had a lucky escape when it exploded, causing panic in the city.

The *News* received numerous calls from concerned readers who were worried there may have been a terrorist attack in the Queen's Road area of the city at 10.10am yesterday.

But the explosion happened as workmen carried out final work to a 10ft sculpture at Thirkill Court, near Memorial Court, Clare College.

The blast was caused after gas, thought to have formed naturally from the concrete base, gathered inside the tubular aluminium structure.

It was ignited by a CO_2 welder being used to seal the hole. The structure was badly damaged.

No one was hurt in the incident but two men installing the object were left shocked.

The double helix, commemorating the discovery of the structure of DNA by Frances Crick and Jim Watson, has not yet been unveiled to the public.

Funding for the structure came from Watson – a former student at Clare College.

David Hartley, a steward at Clare College said: "I heard the bang and thought – 'what was that?'

"A member of my staff came and told me what had happened.

"It is quite a spectacular structure.

"It has been quite badly damaged."

He said it was very fortunate no one had been injured.

"We think it was because it blew upwards rather than sidewards, then came down," he added.

"Two people were working on the structure. They were badly shocked but not injured.

"Health and safety procedures were followed correctly."

A workman doing work on parking bollards at the college said: "We just heard this massive bang.

"We thought it was a bomb. We looked for smoke and fire but there wasn't any.

"Lots of metal went flying everywhere."

*alexmott
@cambridge-news.co.uk*

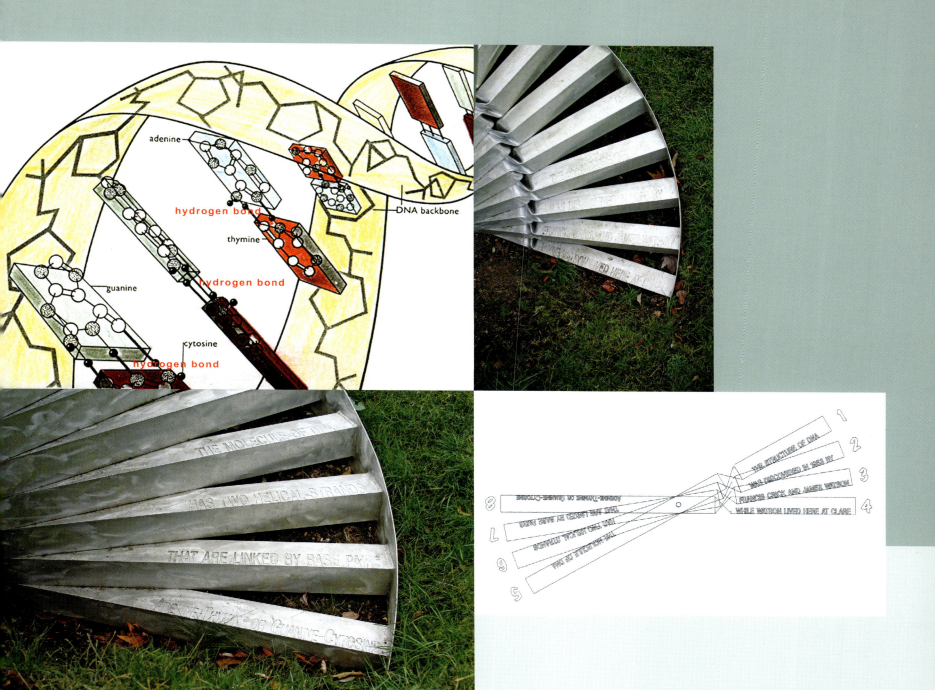

Cambridge dons worked out a lengthy dedication that had to be squeezed into minimalist epigraphy. In a sense, with computer production the mechanical engraving of aluminium is similar to the replication of DNA. Here the letters, and spaces between them, were fixed by the available space and had to vary between 20 and 35 characters. Each phrase has to make a certain sense and look right on its own, while still leading to the next one (an analogue of life's codes, which always have to make sense as short messages fitting into large ones). In the metal bars subsequent phrases also have to be wider as they descend into the ground.

Thus, on bars facing the entrance to Memorial Court, the phrases are:

THE STRUCTURE OF DNA
WAS DISCOVERED IN 1953 BY
FRANCIS CRICK AND JAMES WATSON
WHILE WATSON LIVED HERE AT CLARE

On the adjacent seat is the boomerang curve:

The double helix model was supported by the
work of Rosalind Franklin and Maurice Wilkins

On bars facing the street entrance the epigraph reads:

THE MOLECULE OF DNA
HAS TWO HELICAL STRANDS
THAT ARE LINKED BY BASE PAIRS
ADENINE-THYMINE OR GUANINE-CYTOSINE

And on the adjacent seat:

These strands unravel during cell reproduction
and genes are encoded in the sequence of bases

MOUNDS OF LIFE

In the past, gardens and architecture were unified around a controlling idea, or *concetto*, as it was called during the Renaissance. The underlying concept was the key for persuading different professions to work together, for relating divergent requirements. A prime example is the theatre and sanctuary at Epidaurus, which mixed a most perfect Greek amphitheatre with the most famous healing centre of the classical world. The mixture included the striking architecture of white limestone set in a semi-circle, plus a good play or concert, accompanied by a fine view over a lush landscape. All this was connected to purification in the mineral springs near by and the medical work of Asklepios. In the fourth century BC one couldn't find a more attractive conjunction of opposites. Yet throughout history special sites of landscape beauty have been set apart for such mixed functions, and for purification. One thinks of the ritual bathing places on the Ganges. These cosmic sites were, and are, wonderful places for celebrating the body in nature, places of spontaneous performance and settings for self-transformation.

Such notions occurred to me when working on another Maggie's Centre in the Highlands of Scotland, on the outskirts of Inverness. The cancer caring centres are based on the idea of transformation, of patients taking an active role in their own therapy and then of converting the omnipresent fear in their mind, 'Will I live?', into 'The will to live'. For some patients, and it was true in Maggie's case, the decision to fight for life is not spontaneous, but a troubled choice needing time and help. A cancer caring centre has to assist sufferers facing many such choices. When successful, the transformation can be from confusion and despair into hope and action. It is also one in which nature – epitomized by the garden – plays a part, both physically and conceptually.

Hence in conceiving the Inverness Maggie's Centre, designed by the architects Page and Park, we organized the scheme around the basic idea of life, the theme of healthy cell division and growth. The cell is the unit of life and, when the body renews cells in a healthy individual, they communicate with each other through many signals. These signals finely balance the death of some (apoptosis) to enhance the life of others. Cancer is of course runaway cell growth. Good cell division (the usual mitosis) is a carefully controlled sequence of stages. It is one more loop in a hierarchy of loops, as circular as the many other cycles of life – of metabolism, of sleeping, or even of thinking. Throughout these loops-within-loops signals are always being sent between the cells, just as the brain is always chattering to itself. So, as can be seen in the diagrams here, our unifying concept became the unit of life, the cell, its division and regulating signals. The vesica shape, an oval with points at either end, signifies the cell as it divides across the site, from right to left. The hope is that those using the centre will experience this theme both implicitly and explicitly: unconsciously in the areas of social activity and overtly as they sit in the garden.

Maggie's Centre, Inverness, 2001–5. The theme of cells dividing, mitosis, organizes the site from right to left as the building splits into two mounds. The centre, designed by Page and Park architects, is to the south of the Raigmore Hospital.

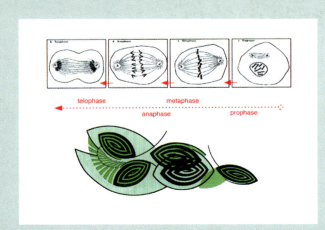

FLASH AND SIGNAL

Communication works only when forms are partly related, and the similarity here came from a risky idea. As we discussed the notion of a unifying *concetto*, and as the building was being laid out, we hit on the idea that the structure could actually work as an upside-down mound. Its vesica-shape could flare up and outwards gently, and function quite well. On the inside, the concept could lead to a spiral of space ending on the top floor, a spiral like the mounds. To underline the pun between building and mound, the former would be clad in green copper. And so it has turned out to be a rare case today where building and landscape are tightly interrelated — in scale, shape, colour and movement.

An upside-down mound in green copper, the centre has a spiral of space that leads to the top floor and lookout. The merging of mounds into the landscape and building was conceived to create ambiguous continuity between usually separate areas. The way the cells communicate with each other through signals, shown as flashes in the grass, keeps the healthy balance. The long endocrine signals (hormones, insulin, adrenaline) can be seen cutting into the turf banks as they mount toward the nucleus of the cell, the seat.

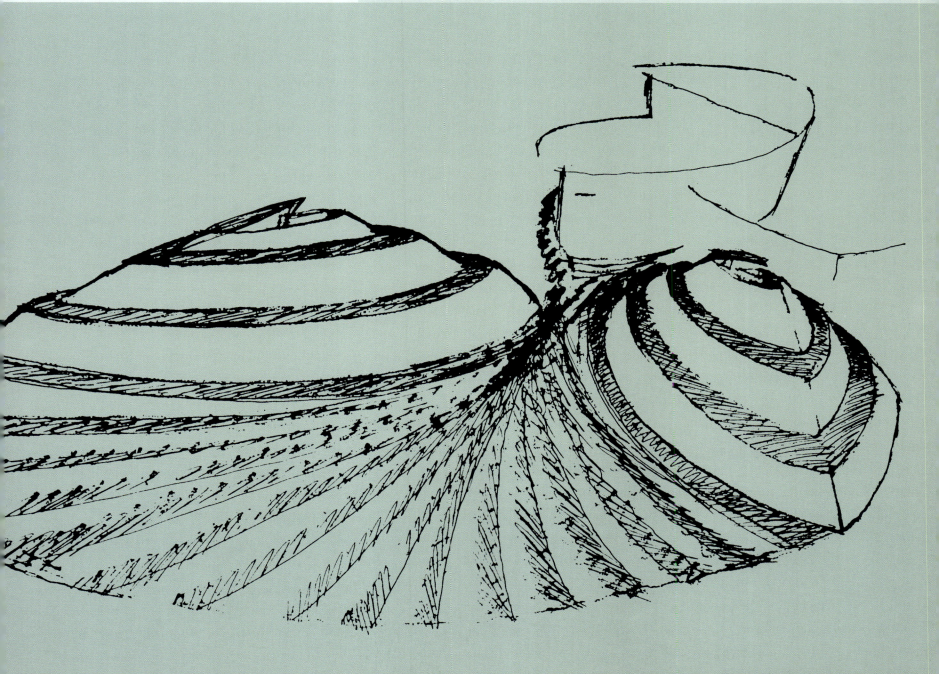

As one traverses the site, the dynamic balance between these forms is immediately felt, an analogue of the continuous balance between cells in the body as they send messages to each other. Looking down from either mound one sees a visual illusion created by white and green stripes alternating as figure and ground. They vibrate and zoom about, creating a dazzling contrast. Most pronounced is a zigzag flash, and a cut in the grass, which travels from one mound (and 'nucleus of the cell') to the other. Why is the zigzag so insistent? And what does it mean, travelling up the mounds to the nucleus? It signifies those imperatives that are hard to disregard, the long, *endocrine* signals, the sex hormones and adrenaline that shout at our body to act, now! If we do manage to overcome these signals, it is done with counter-signs such as the characteristic *paracrine* signals, the short ones, the neurotransmitters that operate between nerve cells, which tell our hormones to calm down. These paracrine signals are marked in the garden by the flash tips, which are closer to both mounds. Finally there is the third type of sign, known as the *autocrine*, where the cell sends a signal to itself. Immune cells called T-cells use it to fight off cancers. This helps them divide when faced with a foreign protein, to multiply the defence system.

In this battle cancers also use autocrine signals to proliferate and dominate the host. Some breast cancers create oestrogen to increase division. This is why the cancer drug tamoxifen is used to block the receptors and slow the cancer down. When Maggie first had cancer we used to discuss the internal battle waged by T-cells, and the positive role of tamoxifen. In the initial fight it certainly gave her time, perhaps several extra years of life. So such issues that sound abstruse at first are likely to exercise the mind of those who decide to fight and try to understand the subtle creativity of their adversary.

In the struggle with cancer, the frame of mind plays an important role. Thousands of physical and social problems come to the fore all at once. How do I cope with pain? Where do I buy a wig? How do I tell the boss? Where do I get a loan? Which therapies should I try out? Who should I believe? Such questions are inescapable, well beyond the capacity of a health service to answer. Quite apart from anything else, the doctors do not have the time. Thus, in addition to the services they offer, Maggie's Centres need a place set apart from the bustle, a protected area in the landscape where one can get a distance from the thousand furies and turn them over in the mind, perhaps even play with them. There in nature one is bound to reflect, not only on the vicious subtlety of the disease but also on the amazing research being mustered around the world to combat it. The genome project, the array of drugs that target every aspect of the enemy, the ingenious attempt to fool the cancer into committing suicide – a thousand potential cures on the horizon – demand respect and admiration. The grandeur of the human struggle, very much between the ingenuity of cancer and the creativity of scientists, is even elating, a monument of our time.

LEFT: The initial sketch shows the basic modes of cell communication: the long endocrine signals are the major zigzags and cuts connecting the two mounds; the short-distance paracrine signals are at the endpoints of the flash; and the autocrine signals are the white forms and paths within the mounds.

On the summit of the mounds is a place for one or two to sit, from where they can get away from people and find a certain perspective on illness. Inscribed there on each white seat are red words forming an ambigrammo, ambiguous because it can be read from two angles. Just as the building inverts the shape of the mounds, these seats can be read the right way up and upside-down. The double reading sets the mind off on a chase, a game of decoding messages, of reflecting on the flashes in the landscape, on the war of signals that is always going on in our minds and, thankfully, very much below consciousness in our cells. The underground chatter, like a benevolent secret service, may never be known to the individual and all the better for that. Yet for many the struggle with cancer engages the mind today, and thus a healing garden might present deeper ideas for those who wish to explore them. The idea of those genetic investigations, key to the war on cancer, could provoke those afflicted to take an active interest in their own therapy, one of the several goals of these centres. Maggie herself was inspired to fight for extra time because of the multiple therapies on the horizon: hope is a provocateur, and the intellect searching out knowledge is its chief agent.

AMBIGUOUS SEATS

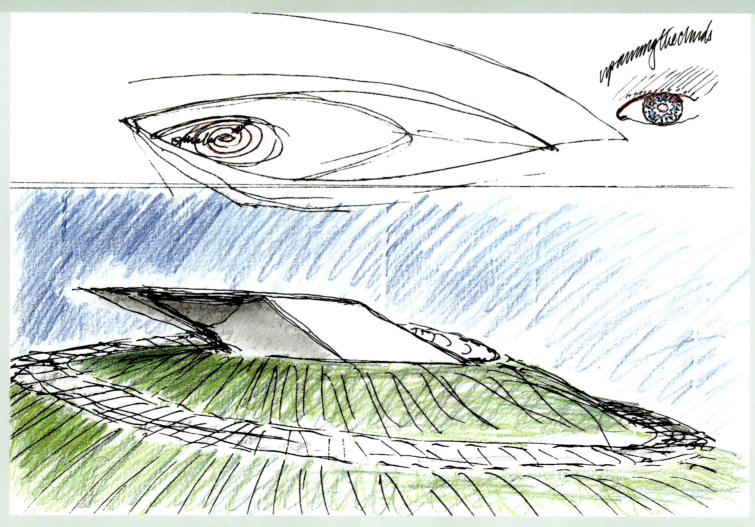

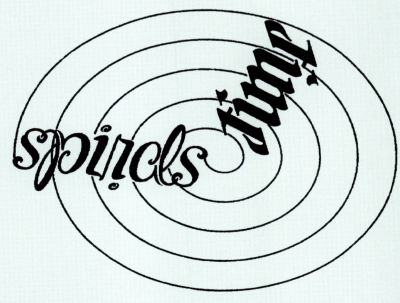

Seats, the nucleus of each cell from where the DNA codes roll out, are inscribed with words that can be read upside-down. Andrew Bateman of Page and Park helped develop the layout and the landscape firm Gross Max helped supervise the construction of the garden, while the ambigrammi have been created from work done by John Langdon.

13: CELLS OF LIFE

Searching for Appropriate Metaphors

What, as the perennial question goes, is life? Sooner or later when pondering this enigma you will hit on the idea that it can be summarized by the cell. This conclusion may be premature, because life appears much greater than its minuscule building block, but it is still one that can reveal necessary properties behind the big question. For a landform project near Edinburgh airport I had the opportunity to explore this metaphor – the cell as the unit of life – on a very large scale, a prospect that Nicky and Robert Wilson were kind enough to offer me. Several parts of my design explore the cell, its nucleus and its division, called mitosis, but the search for the essential character of life remained elusive. It turned out, as we shall see, that life cannot even be defined by a complete list of its properties. Perhaps more important for grasping the enigma than listing its features are a series of pertinent metaphors. This chapter continues the theme of the previous ones with the notion of the cell as the essence of life writ small, its microcosm. Indeed, when magnified in scale and seen alive under a microscope the cell appears like a mini-city bustling with activity.

This metaphor can be grasped in simulations, some of which can be found on YouTube, for instance in as an eight-minute film called *The Inner Life of a Cell*. Actions here are personified by a set of pulsating characters who seem to know what they are doing. Proteins are dragged along superhighways by bug-eyed transporters arriving where they need to be just on time. When watching this purposeful behaviour one is grateful that it continues along in the body's 3 trillion cells without a moment's thought. Although it appears as an alien world, inhabited by exotics called spectrin tetramers and chemokines, the complex action can be appreciated before it is fully understood. After repeated viewings I came to realize it was not just the individual parts that were important but the harmonious complexity. This was the main feature, indeed miracle, of life: self-organizing complexity, the endless feedback loops of action finely orchestrated, loops within loops within loops. Then an example bore it out, close to home. While I was typing up these ideas, one finger with a wound near the tip became infected, and swelled up with puss. It was quickly overlaid by scar tissue. And what did the film show? The very action of healing a sore. Leukocytes, white blood cells, roll along at the start of the film until they come to the inflammation and efficiently devour the infection, the organelles signalling like firemen when to bring in the right equipment and carry away the rubbish. Anyone who watches this film several times will be touched; it opens up some of the mysteries beneath the skin.

In effect, the cell can be seen as a city of sublime coordination and so, for this landform, I took four of them undergoing division as a visual metaphor of life. In photos and drawings they are seen flat as if from above, as they might appear under an electron microscope with their cell membranes and fluid; seen in the landscape, as if from a cerebral helicopter, they become causeways, lakes and islands. In a few cases, the details of the water rill and the seats show what I take to be some basic patterns of life. The semi-transparent microworld is today opening up to our imagination a field of metaphorical possibility.

LEFT: The *Two in One Arch*, and the *Mitosis Rill* in the distance. From the installation *Cells of Life*, Jupiter Artland, Kirknewton, outside Edinburgh (2005–9).

RIGHT: Idea sketch of overlapping four cells and plans.

FAR RIGHT: A still from *The Inner Life of a Cell*, directed by David Bolinsky of Xvivo, shows a transporter hauling a big blue protein behind as it walks up a microtubule. Other webs of the cell are seen here, a three-dimensional lacework of structures and highways.

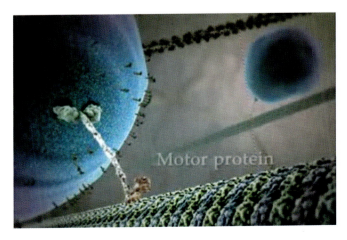

Motor protein

OVERLAPPING CELLS: THE PLAN

The plan, in effect, is generated by the overlapping of cell membranes, as if you could see them transparently superimposed. A causeway sweeps in from the east and crosses four ponds to end with Mound One and a small vesica-shaped island. There, you spiral up to a white seat with an inscription, a model of the animal cell and Liesegang rocks. Mound Two, to the south, is surmounted by another white seat, also with these rocks, but now, because it is up among the leaves, the model with its green chloroplasts represents the plant cell. Photosynthesis is another gift of nature and, along with the origin of life and DNA, an extraordinary jump in organization. Bisecting the water is the Mitosis Rill, a gentle cascade with five tiny waterfalls that spill into basins. To the east of the site, Mounds Three and Four have further signs of life and transformation on their summits. Landforms at the scale of a twenty-minute walk need a visible goal on each peak to pull people around the site, and mix the celebration of landscape with the tiny cells that organize it.

ABOVE: Micrographs of four and eight cells dividing. An interesting discovery is that cells keep a kind of morphological memory of how they are dividing that influences their future growth, as if they could conceptualize a grid. Thus, in the top left photo, the two mouse cells have longitudinal axes that will usually turn into a body, while the lateral-shaped ones, which divide later, usually will make the placenta. Embryonic development is purposeful, directional, but flexible. Conceptual drawings based on these photos show the grammar of transparency and overlapping curves that formed the basis of the plan. BELOW RIGHT: Model (with the help of Madelon Vriesendorp). Mound One, to the north-west, is to the north of the causeway and Mound Two. Mound Three is to the south-west, and Mound Four is furthest west. BELOW LEFT: View from Mound One towards an island, with Mound Two in the distance.

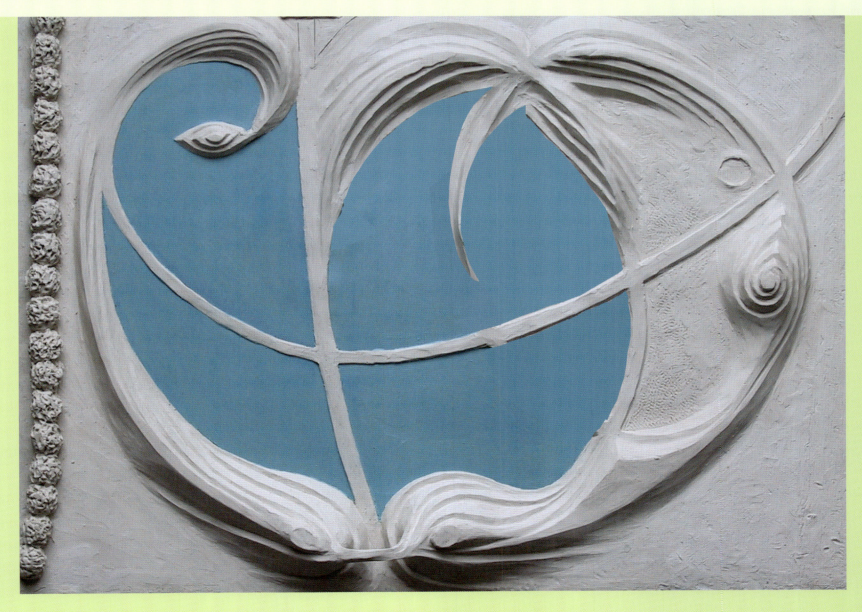

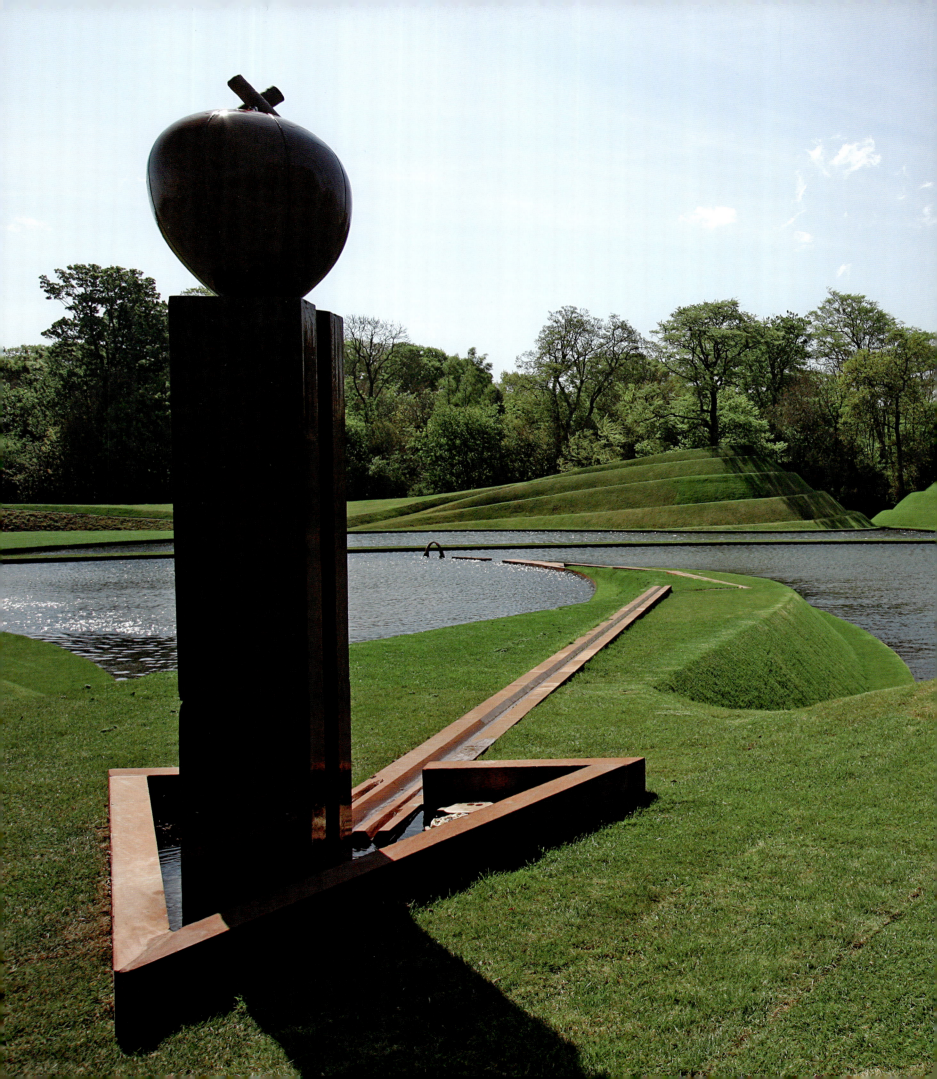

ONE INTO TWO, TWO INTO ONE: THE MITOSIS RILL

Among all the activities that a cell performs, mitosis is the most theatrical, or it would be if we had the opportunity to shrink in size and watch the ballet. Although it is a continuous process lasting one or two hours, it has five or six distinct stages depending on what you want to distinguish. These stages are given highly unmemorable names such as prophase, prometaphase, metaphase, etc. In one way, films dramatizing these splits are a better guide to what is happening than a series of stills, or the stages depicted in a textbook. Videos can show the way the action *unfolds continuously* without interruptions, and is controlled by the centrioles. Most striking in this whole dance is the moment when all the chromosomes of the cell are lined up like rows of partners in a Scottish reel, and are then suddenly pulled in opposite directions. From this point (technically called the anaphase) one cell becomes two. The chromosomes are exactly copied and they rush away from each other, attracted towards the opposite poles. I cannot think of a more magical moment in the orchestration of nature by cosmic laws. It is as fundamental a moment as the origin of the universe and, for me, a moment worth translating into landscape.

The metaphase and anaphase are guided by a pair of strange-looking centrioles at either end of the splitting cell, two bundles of tubes, at right angles to each other. When placed over their globular structure they look like a topknot on the head, or perhaps a Chinese hat. Since this topknot and its spindles guide the whole performance, I have made it the focus of the landform. All visual lines of force sweep up toward a red globe and the pathways and mounds dance to its tune, because, as far as I understand it, the centriole and spindles (spreading down from the globe) control the process. When one strips away the technicalities, these structures push and pull the chromosomes along the highways, or microtubules. Suddenly the complex cell becomes the simplified jewel of architecture. Nature's art, at these rare moments, becomes expressive, which is why I have shaped the landform to undulate towards this point. The length of the rill is designed so that each small waterfall marks one of the five phases. The waterfalls are presented in models and Liesegang rocks. Each waterfall equals a shift in organization – a change in a geometric dance, that is, the splitting of one into two. When sex and fertilisation occur, the reverse miracle unfolds as another dance: two becomes one. This jump is less a harmonious reel and more a boogie-woogie.

OPPOSITE: Various fountain designs, each with its top-knot centrioles, and the chromosomes picked out in red. Plan of the rill zigzagging between the miracles of life: one becoming two and two becoming one.

BELOW: One into Two, Two into One: conceptual sketch of life's miracle transformations.

BELOW RIGHT: Stages of mitosis depicted in teaching models and Liesegang rocks: Reading from the bottom up are the Prometaphase, then Metaphase, then Anaphase and finally the two phases together, (Telophase and the splitting of Cytokinesis): one has become two.

The Mitosis Rill and the six stages of mitosis, the tiny waterfalls, with their signs and symbols in rock and plastic. (The split rock underneath the fountain, and the twin model in the basin, One into Two, covers the pump.)

The Two into One Arch, seen from the side, the culmination of the six stages of the Mitosis Rill.

CURVED TOPS

Seats and eye-catchers at the top of each mound are the focus of movement. On Mound One, a spiral of movement turns into a white concrete path that continues the lines of the landform. Inside its membrane the cells cluster as Liesegang rocks and the teaching model of an animal cell, showing similar signs and elements. The model depicts organelles, such as mitochondria. Mound Two, near the trees, has a much larger seat with the chloroplasts picked out in green – those packets of photosynthesis that convert the energy of the sun into usable power.

Throughout this garden I have deployed these red-spotted stones because of their fascinating similarity to living cells. Indeed, the target-shaped circles are often mistaken for fossils. When split apart or cut smoothly by a diamond saw, the red-brown circles look as if they might be related to former sea-creatures such as ammonites. However, each rusty nodule is mostly a three-dimensional sphere, unlike the flatter ammonite, and despite appearances has never been alive. They are formed from iron deposits through a process similar to crystallization. The patterns, known as Liesegang rings, were named after the German chemist Raphael Eduard Liesegang, who discovered them in 1896. Sometimes as many as eight beautifully formed rings circle a purple centre; sometimes they intersect or grow out of each other, like cells splitting. Often they cluster together in sets like organelles attacking a foreign body, or delivering food to a desired location. The visual similarity between living cell and dead nodule may be fortuitous. Or it may show deep relationships between our mesocosm and the microcosm. Maybe, where similar forces of self-organization underlie them both, the formal links are not so accidental.

LEFT TOP AND MIDDLE: Mound One. The seat shows an animal cell.

BELOW AND RIGHT: Mound Two. The seat shows a plant cell. Liesegang rocks create a teaching model of the plant cell with its green chloroplasts. The similarities of form between the red rock nodules and the cell's organelles once again underline the analogies between microcosm and macrocosm, the Universe in the Landscape.

THE ENIGMA OF LIFE

It is easier to recognize life than to say what it is. Definitions abound and are more or less adequate, but never entirely convincing (see 'Twelve Properties of Life', below). For instance, if you make a list of defining qualities, you notice that there are many beings that are alive but only *partly* fulfil the criteria. Reproduction is one of these definers. Ponder the mule and the great-grandmother. Both are clearly living beings yet under normal conditions unable to reproduce. As if to further confuse the issue, consider crystals, clouds and computer viruses. All are not alive, but they are wildly reproductive. Such confusions lead to other thoughts. Life is a very worldly thing, inextricably part of the super-organism Gaia, or earth as a self-organizing system. It has to be defined with *many* criteria; and its distinction is to have some of these criteria developed to an uncommon degree, into quintessential qualities. Whereas the red spot of Jupiter runs on rotational power and thus looks alive through a telescope, real life essentially runs off the free energy of the sun or heat vents.

In discussing life, scientists emphasize energy exchange, the homeostasis of metabolism and temperature control. Living things hold off entropy; they are bounded entities able to keep their internal conditions harmonious by constantly using free energy for transformation. Organisms routinely take apart and reassemble their molecules. Somewhere I remember reading that each day 7 per cent of molecules in the human body are replaced, and virtually all of them in two weeks. Whether this is true or not I couldn't say, yet the idea points to what I take to be a quintessential property: the endless loops or cycles within life's process. These circular transformations of energy, information and reproduction deserve a sign and symbol in a garden, the enigmatic motif of a strange attractor, the language of life's self-organization.

Other thinkers emphasize the functional aspects of life: what it does as a whole, as an organism and in a group. Living beings evolve in a world that is developing, and here it is organized complexity that is the quintessential definer. All organisms equipped with a rudimentary nervous system are involved in a search, a struggle to predict what will happen to their environment and a desire to persist in their being. Thus they suffer, expend energy (or money) and believe or disbelieve. The higher forms of animal fear, think, act, react, change their mind, invent, love, die, reproduce, optimize their chances of success, transcend their circumstances or modify their environment to do so. In a word, their self-organization has a life-line, a trajectory, an orientation.

In the end, life is, for me, symbolized by the cell, since everything alive is either a cell or made from cells. Cells *are* Life, Life Cells – Life a Cell, Life Sells, Cells Sell, and it's a great expenditure, or A Sell of a Life.

TWELVE PROPERTIES OF LIFE

Life usually, but not always, has the following obvious properties: it reproduces, respires, ingests food and evacuates (metabolism). It grows and develops, stores and passes on information, shows a mixture of permanence and change, that is, evolution through genetic coherence and mutation. It has emergent properties such as semi-autonomy, feeling and thinking, and holistic aspects, such as the harmonious process of overcoming entropy. Homeostasis is another holistic property, both of an individual and of a species with its habitat. There are two big problems of defining life by its properties. First, it shares many of these aspects with non-living things such as a crystal and, second, it is an open-ended list. Perhaps emergence and surprise are life's most prized qualities.

	Crystal	Bacteria	Primate	Gaia
Reproduction	+	+	+	+
Metabolism	-	+	+	+
Overcomes entropy	-	+	+	+
Growth	+	+	+	+
Evolution	-	+	+	+
Self-healing	+	+	+	+
Homeostasis	-	+	+	+
Information processing	-	+	+	-
Feeling/thinking	-	-	+	-
Emergent properties	+	+	+	+

After James Lovelock, *Gaia: The Practical Science of Planetary Medicine* (1991).

LOOPS OF LIFE

The self-organization of the cell is an extraordinary example of self-creation, self-control and self-readjustment to the outside world, achieved through feedback cycles. This can be seen, poetically, as the feedback loops of a strange attractor, always attracted to a basin but taking a slightly different route each time. The basic cycles can be seen as two loops, adjusting inside elements and outside ones, thus:

Cells are like factories in their self-organization or autopoiesis. Or maybe they are more like farmyards or even cities, because of their rich complexity and the way they differ and specialize. If one expands the loop metaphor into a basic linear path, ending back at the beginning, it might have six or seven basic stages.

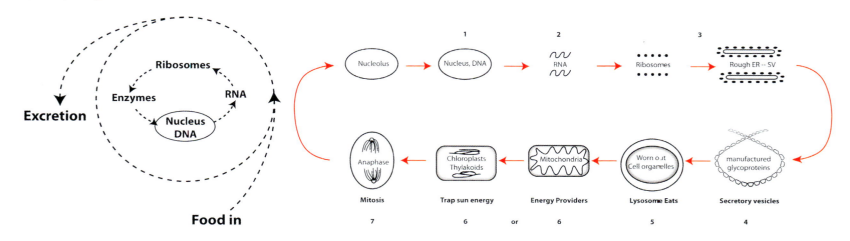

ABOVE AND OVERLEAF: Mound Three, at the top, has a strange attractor in the shape of a stretched figure 8. These self-organizing forms, here made from pennies, underlie much of nature, a metaphor for life's endless cycles – loops within loops. The dotted inscription reads as a continuous line: loopsoflifecycleinendlessstrangeattractors. The two strange attractor basins pull the pennies, and words, into a continuous curving loop of copper colour. The mounds are also conceived as strange attractors, continuously curving paths of turf and earth that are pulled towards their centre of gravity. This white top is thus not a seat, but rather a symbol of the whole scheme and the way life endlessly cycles in loops.

Loopsoflifecycleinendlessstrangeattractors: the top of Mound Three.

EVOLUTION CREATES SENSE

Evolution is obviously one of the defining properties of life, on page 232. But dead things evolve too, such as chemicals, beautiful crystals, cities and economies. Hence every subject is now framed in its evolutionary history, as arising out of a previous process and as part of a developing chain. Such a universal process should find its metaphor in a garden, and on Mound Eight I have fashioned one out of letters and connected rock fragments. These show the analogy of 'making sense', or how any one thing is part of a larger, coherent story.

But this raises the question of purposefulness. How much direction and coherence does evolution really have? We grant human purpose, the trivial or profound motivations that guide action, and life shows many goal-driven aspects even if a final teleology is questionable. Life obeys physical laws, and has feedback loops and many internal constraints. All these things guide it along limited paths, towards various outcomes. From this *internal* viewpoint it is purposeful even if, from the outside, as Winston Churchill said of history, it seems to wander aimlessly as a series of frozen accidents.

Let us take the internal view with its limited direction and ask how can one evoke this sense-making change? One cogent metaphor for this is language itself, with its grammatical rules and semantic meaning. Consider the following linguistic game and its analogy with genetic evolution. In every stage of evolution, the genes of an individual organism have to work as a significant whole; they have to be more or less correctly spelled, genetically, and have meaning. If not the organism will be aborted. Likewise, every species in a developmental sequence has to be coherently related to its bloodline, and also adapted to its context in a workable way, just as a word has to work reasonably well in a sentence. To continue the analogy, coherent word series are like gene sequences with no radical spelling mistakes. Genomes can tolerate only minor mutations, or few letter changes. Thus the following linguistic game. Transposing one letter at a time (below) – the single mutation of a character in a word – is like a coherent evolutionary sequence. Consider two strings of words:

LIFE	LIFE
LINE	LITE
LINT	KITE
PINT	MITE
PANT	MILE
PUNT	MILL
RUNT	HILL
RUNE	HELL
TUNE	CELL

Thus in eight spelling jumps, by changing only one letter at a time, 'Life' makes its 'Tune' or turns into a 'Cell'. Or, read upwards, the reverse sequence occurs.

Evolution normally is like this coherent development, always progressing from behind. That is, it usually works step by step, based on what has developed in the past. The large cells of animals and plants have internalized mitochondria and chloroplasts, or smaller, pre-existing cells that give them power. In the past, these might be picked up and swallowed whole in a symbiotic alliance. Two past cells would become joined as a new third. And then as the combination evolved it might get hung up on good solutions, on patterns that worked adequately or perhaps very well. Charles Darwin's original title for *The Origin of Species* included the words: *or the Preservation of Favoured Races*. Evolution is indeed preservative: the shark did not change much for 300 million years, nor did the spiralling ammonite. Being a killer shark is a pattern of nature that, given the context of eating other fish, could not get much better. Many other internal factors in evolution also preserve patterns, such as homologous structures and what are known today as Hox genes. The latter can be considered like nature's patents, very good ideas that work across many different species. For instance, we share the Pax 6 gene, the one that regulates the eyes, with virtually every animal. The pattern works well, and therefore this patent guides evolution along certain avenues of development.

As Darwin averred, nature is conservative. Look at the pattern of letters in the two series above. In the left one the combination 'nt' repeats five times, while on the right there are four 'ite's and 'll's in a row. Such common transposition of words came to my mind quickly, without much effort. Evolution uses a similar lazy (or conservative) strategy, working with what is at hand. The good clichés of nature have only to function adequately, or be better than the competing ones, not be perfect. The same is true of technical evolution and such things as the computer keyboard I am working on. Following the earliest nineteenth-century typewriter, the keys still have the same standard order, called QWERTY after its first six letters. This suboptimal pattern was worked out because it appeared to cause the least number of jamming keys, which was not always the case. Nevertheless, it won a commercial competition and became the standard solution for English and American typewriters ever since. It is now used on computers that have no movable keyboard! This frozen accident may last another thousand years: it is an example of lazy, conservative evolution.

Can evolution go anywhere? Can it explore all possibilities? As my two lines of concrete poetry suggest, 'Life' can lead in any direction as long as it is a four-letter word that makes sense, and is a sequence in the sense-making chain. If this metaphor is apt, then the resource of all possible four-letter words, and their internal structure, would channel evolution in some directions and not in others. I haven't a clue if, given enough time, it could cycle through all the four-letter words in English, but it would by definition have to follow sequences. In this sense, the one-change-letter-game would not show *one* final goal, a teleology, but rather evince a general teleonomy. Does evolution also show a predisposition to move in a *few* preferred directions?

The evolution of the universe shows such 'wide avenues of possibility', as the theorist Stuart Kauffman calls them, or 'chreods', as the biologist C.H. Waddington named them years ago. Constraints of physics, gravity, geometry and history obviously limit how big an animal can be, and which routes are open to development.

Letters and rock coherently transforming. 'LIVE' turns to 'DEAD' in ten transformations of a single letter. The two linear seats on the top of Mound Eight create a dialogue of words about the life and death cycles.

ONE STEP AT A TIME

In this landscape, the sequence of words presents a metaphor of evolution. When the sun is low and a raking light cuts across the letters, their meaning is revealed. To show that evolution and health depend equally on the growth of new tissue and the destruction of the old, I have transposed the words 'live' into 'dead' and back again, in two different ways, and put the different sequences on the two seats. They are picked out in white Corian, a synthetic material that nearly matches the concrete. This makes the words hard to decipher, like the intimate relationship between life and death itself. The two sequences are:

LIVE	DEAD
LIFE	LEAD
LINE	LEAN
LONE	LEON
BONE	LION
BOND	LINN
BEND	LINE
LEND	LIFE
LEAD	LIVE
DEAD	

ABOVE AND RIGHT: Two seats on top of Mound Eight. Once again words and Liesegang rocks are used as the nucleus of the cell to spell out a message, here the conservative nature of evolution, which changes one step at a time. This slow, developmental sequence is evident in the word series. The seat on the right shows the sequence from 'DEAD' to 'LIVE'. Evolution may also move very quickly, because it can transpose whole groups of Hox genes. Then the metaphor would shift from 'one step at a time' to a 'quick jump', and it is true that evolution can move on occasion very fast by shuffling whole gene sequences together.

BELOW: The Two into One Bridge, under construction by Mound Eight.

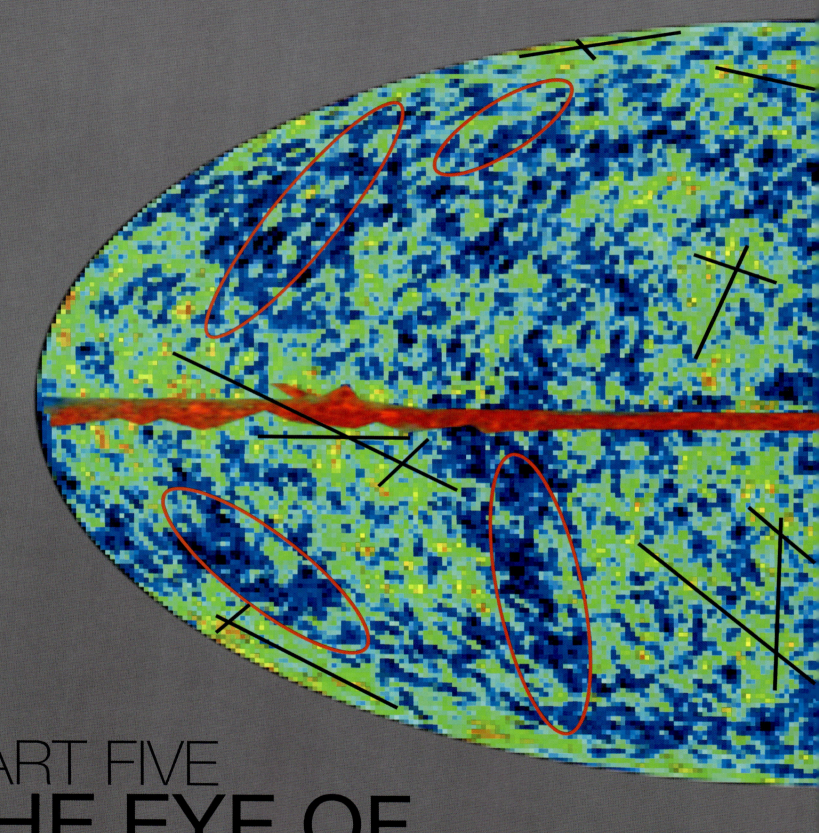

PART FIVE
THE EYE OF
THE UNIVERSE

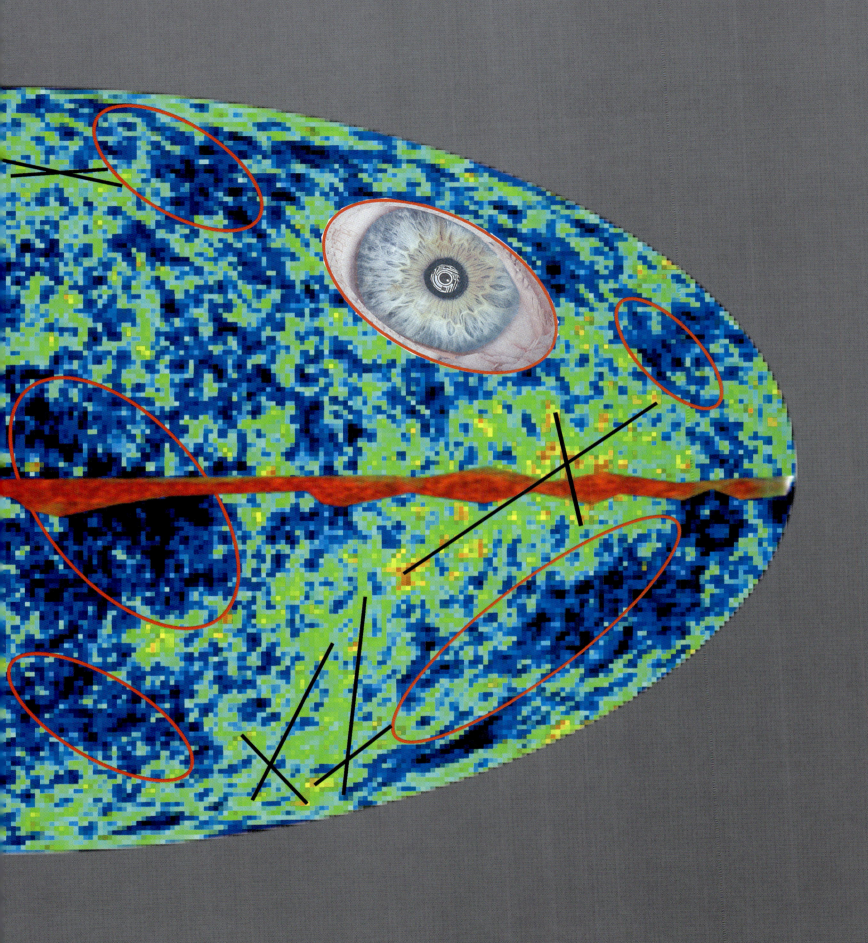

14: THE COSMIC AND THE SPIRITUAL

A Chance Encounter

The landforms in this book are designed around some ideas of nature, life and death. Such fundamental content begs the question of still larger ideas and, in these concluding chapters, I will address them with an approach I call the spiritual cosmic, to distinguish it from other views. As we will see, it is close to what many scientists have believed, including Einstein, who called it the cosmic religious feeling. Religious questions cannot be avoided when approaching the big issues or the quandary our time, and artists are often asked to fill the void left by the decline of religion. Today that often means the paradox of atheists being brought into the cathedral to give it the intense meaning it had in the past. This raises significant issues of belief. But while conviction and religion are important – and atheist belief as much as any other kind – I would rather see the big issues in the larger perspective of spirituality. After all, the feelings elicited by landforms (and other works of art and nature) went on for thousands of years, and long before scripture or doctrine, or even before the Standard Dogma of Genetics or the Standard Model of ultimate particles (see below) were a gleam in the eye of the Nobel Laureate. Spirituality and the feeling for the cosmos have priority over such beliefs. At least they do in historical duration, in breadth and, I will argue, in relevance.

My work is also inspired by concrete examples drawn from the fields of art and history. One question, in a post-religious age, is how we orient ourselves in a cosmic setting that is inhumanely large and apparently uninterested in our fate, and for me that issue can be explored directly through landforms, and also through chance encounters and humour. After all, the cosmos looked at from one angle can be rather comic, and it gives rise to the spirit.

One spring afternoon, when I was up in Fife inspecting the landforms next to the M90 motorway, a group of us, dressed in hard hats and fluorescent jackets, stopped to get a good view of one of our largest mounds. Called OB4 in coal miner's argot – the overburden or fourth pile of excess earth – it was very big, and very heavy (at 5 million tons), and meant to entice drivers going north to turn in and visit the artificial loch among other things Just behind it was the Final Void, another unintentional bit of coal men's poetry, where the seam of coal runs out. This phrase does not symbolize existential angst or a Zen love for nothingness; as far as I know it only means where they stop digging. And this void gives rise to a beautiful and terrifying precipice that overlooks the sublime moonscape of the extraction that goes on below. The whole scene, under the Big Sky, reminded me of the American West, and more particularly of those nineteenth-century paintings of the Grand Canyon. These colourful canvases, which could be 30 feet wide, would be 'performed' to assembled audiences seated as if in a theatre. The curtains were slowly drawn aside, revealing to applause the Spectacular Creations of Nature. This style of painting was called the American Sublime and it followed earlier, British versions of a similar romantic tradition. Aimed somewhere towards that psychic space between religious ecstasy, nature worship and a fearful agoraphobia, these paintings sparked off a spiritual mood; they do in me, at least, even in spite of their occasional corniness. The Grand Canyon, like the great oceanic experience, may look like a thousand photographs of itself, but it can still work its awesome grandeur.

At any rate, here in the artificial sublime we were, five coal men and my daughter and friends, all dressed in official safety clothing. We climbed out of our Land Rovers and I saw, puttering ahead, just at the bridge where the view is best, an elderly man. He was also dressed in yellow fluorescent jacket, and also was looking at the spectacle, including the Final Void. He sat on a mobility scooter, usually used by people who cannot walk. Soon recognizing that he wasn't one of us, in spite of our common dress, and feigning ignorance because I wanted to find out what the local people thought, I asked, 'What's happening over there?' He looked up from his battery-buggy and said, 'That's what they're making us, a public place and nature reserve with a lake in the shape of Scotland.' And added, optimistically: 'That's where I'm going to have a walk.'

His grizzled face and disability so clearly spoke the opposite that the words stopped me short.

View from Overburden 4 looking at the Final Void. The titles are poetic phrases used by coal men to refer to their landforms, and the final point of excavation. The foreground shows a boulderfield under construction that represents the part of Eastern Europe where the Scots settled in the seventeenth century, especially Poland and the Baltic.

Here was the dream, and PR, coming right back at me like a dart. Of course I welcomed the reply. We were repairing nature for the community and new use, but however idealistic our project it was not going to give him back his legs, much less a 2-mile walk. So I mumbled an evasive reply, 'That's great,' returned to our group, and sat silently in the Land Rover having a think.

Architecture, planning and landscape are all oriented to a future world, as I knew from forty years of writing about these things. They are necessarily shot through with idealism, the designs for a better world, and this optimism is something like a shared conspiracy between the client, designer and, perhaps, the politician. But society, and the four kinds of nature I have mentioned throughout this book, will slow plans down, if not scupper them altogether. In response, the professional idealism will sometimes turn into something else, a self-serving ideology. How could I be sure our project would not also go sour? It had been under way for seven years, delayed by the usual horse-trading, like all the big schemes I have worked on: the bargaining between local council, big business, laws interpreted by separate interests and the community. For every tiny victory in pushing through a design idea there was also a compromise, and then the reflection: 'Is it worth it? Is the sacrifice worth the greater possible opportunity?' How would I know? The projective act is not a fact: it's a gamble. The old man's idealism triggered these ruminations on the risks. With large landforms, built under extremely reduced circumstances, one never knows how the trade-offs will work out, until it is all over (maybe after you've hit the Final Void).

Recycling Different Natures

In any case, many of the landforms in this book come from necessities, such as recycling earth in different ways. To recap: I often use scrap metal, or worn-out Fourth Nature in a garden, and in the Renaissance a garden itself was seen as Third Nature. These are sometimes combined with vegetables and functional growth, what Cicero called Second Nature and wilderness, his First Nature. With landforms I have added another level to these useful distinctions, that is, Zero Nature, and the laws of nature. If necessity is the mother of invention, then recycling these different natures in different ways is often how necessity turns out.

In the past the custom and law was that one returned a coal site to farming, restored the fields to a flatness for cows, as if no one had ever dug 90-metre holes in the ground, and created lakes and huge earthworks. Basically a semi-pastoral ideal of Second Nature prevailed, a kind of denial that dirty mining had taken place, and that an artificial Grand Canyon had been momentarily created. Much money was spent returning nature to an idea of farming that is probably not even the reality in an age of agribusiness. So today there are alternatives and some clients are taking

risks, building new landscapes from industrialized spoil. About 40 per cent of my work comes from such necessities. Recycling these different natures has been the impetus with six or seven projects: Parco Portello, Northumberlandia, the Scottish Worthies, the brown coal site in the German town of Altdöbern, the Imperial War Museum North (that came to nothing in the end), a scheme at Crawick just getting under way at the time of writing and the Fife Earth Project.

Repairing the earth that has been exploited for energy, turning it to new social use – that is the goal. The human species is obviously involved in the eternal struggle for survival, in our case short-term economic growth at the expense of longer-term natural cycles, and no doubt burning coal plays a role in global warming. Forty per cent of this excess heating, it is sometimes said, comes from faults caused by architecture, my profession for many years. I am well used to hearing architects claim they can affect this trend (or make much of a difference to it), an exaggerated hope when they control and construct, maybe, 5 per cent of world building. Once

LEFT AND ABOVE: Primitive sculpture made from scrap, in this case supersize tyres 8 feet high.

RIGHT: Puget Sound, seen in the distance, was sold in a forced sale to the government in Washington DC by Chief Seattle for $150,000. In the foreground is the city of Seattle, whose name is the only remaining memory of this unequal treaty.

again it is idealism that may be turned into professional ideology. I have supported green building for years, especially when it leads to an expressive architecture, but such interventions are more symbolic than instrumentally effective. Likewise, as far as the greater ecology is concerned, my interventions in recycling the earth are token clean-ups.

Yet landforms do indeed pose larger questions, like all gardens and landscapes, about our relationship with different natures. Consider the argument of those who claim that the earth comes first, as it no doubt did 3 billion and many years before *Homo sapiens*. The Earth Firsters, as they say of themselves, brook 'no compromise in defence of Mother Earth'. We have a moral obligation to avoid species extinction – all species have intrinsic value – because they, like us, are part of the web of life.

Aside from the moral and legal issues, there are aesthetic and spiritual claims about our obligation to different natures. While these issues are complex, abstract and deserve more than a book in response, I like to think of them concretely, through examples and metaphor, the way I approach them with landforms. Take the issue of the 'web of life' and 'Mother Earth', two of the strongest ecological metaphors. A very poetic claim for these was made in 1854 by Chief Seattle, the head of many Suquamish and Indian tribes around Washington State's beautiful Puget Sound. In response to the American nation's proposition of buying land for peace, the Chief delivered one of the most moving ecological statements ever made. One version, put together by a film writer in the late 1970s, sacrificed accuracy for poetry, and for that reason it tends to be the one quoted.

'How can you buy or sell the sky,' the Chief asks quite logically, 'the warmth of the land? The idea is strange to us. If we do not own the freshness of the air and the sparkle of the water, how can you buy them?'

The filmic Chief goes on to celebrate the many aspects of first nature, wilderness, and those aspects that are hard to buy and sell. He continually returns to a point that the real Seattle emphasized: 'Every part of this earth is sacred to my people . . . Our dead never forget this beautiful earth, for it is the mother of the red man. We are part of this earth and it is part of us . . . [whereas] the white man . . . is a stranger who comes in the night . . . The earth is not his brother, but his enemy, and when he has conquered it, he moves on . . . *All things are connected* . . . This we know; the earth does not belong to man; man belongs to the earth.'

Allowing for the overstatement of a scriptwriter, these metaphors are not altogether wrong, either in terms of what Chief Seattle is supposed to have said, or their truth. It appears he did refer often to the sacred earth. Particularly he emphasized the way his ancestors and peoples regarded it as something to love and tend, and its beauty and connectedness to the rest of life. He was also realistic about the occasional stupidity of his followers, or at least the adolescents who liked war, and he knew that Indians were not perfect ecologists any more than the white man. But the truth of his message, it seems to me, is in its mixture and feelings. Whether coming from Hollywood or Puget Sound, it is a compound message of spiritual issues: the attitudes towards his ancestors and the land (aesthetic ones) the beauties he describes – and the more obvious moral and ecological issues. All of these are relative to each other, as well as intrinsic values in themselves. Most importantly, the values are experienced as a whole and together, so they are naturally expressed poetically, with feeling.

As feelings, they are hard to disagree with. It is when we analyse their various aspects, and grade them, that doubts begin. Deep Ecologists, for instance, challenge the idea of the stewardship of the earth coming from religion. In particular, the Bible emphasizes the dominion over the earth that God has given man, and this form of stewardship is a form of arrogance, of anthropocentrism. Non-human life, Deep Ecologists claim, has 'rights', not just the strongest species. Indeed various ecologies have 'rights', even if they do not have obligations and responsible consciousness (but then, nor do babies and children and those with Alzheimer's).

Various ecological movements have illuminated these parallel issues and rights and, it seems to me, their arguments again show the relative worth of competing values, the shifting way in which one comes first depending on the context. How does this relate to my interest in landforms and the various levels of nature? The claims for different natures vary according to temperament, and situation. Obviously, most people will find my calling scrap metal a form of Fourth Nature perverse, even though they may grant that industry today, and its overwhelming by-product – waste – is exuding from us like a metal forest of perspiration. Something useful must be done with it. And as for my petromania – my love of rocks, the dead minerals which reveal the artistic talent of Zero Nature – they may find it misplaced, even though they may grant that the earth's fantastic 'rock cycle' (the way subduction recycles continents and allows life to flourish) is most welcome. We have a natural tendency to regard dogs and flowers as part of nature, but not pollution and lumps of clay, even though parts of the Bible, and some biologists, say life started with this slippery mud.

So I am asking to extend a category for conceptual and physical reasons. Once we admit that the laws of physical nature created living nature, we are on the conceptual and spiritual journey to the various levels I have mentioned, and then on to the very mixed media that create landforms (as I outlined in the first chapter). If the Earth Firsters and Deep Ecologists have a point about the web of life and our implication with it, then that must extend to the rest of the universe. Indeed, the earth is hardly 'first', as sun worshippers from Egypt to Stonehenge knew for several millennia. Without a billionth part of the

sun's energy, over several billion years, there is no life, no 'natures one through four'. The same logic extends beyond our local solar system in space and time. The cosmos is before nature, before life, before the sun by some 10 billion years. So where priority of space, time, power and size are concerned – and following Chief Seattle where paternity is concerned – we ought to be Cosmic Firsters. It sounds absurd. As Woody Allen said, 'What has the universe ever done for me?' Well, it brought him into being, as a distant parent. What has scrap, or worn-out industry, done for us? It allowed us a better life, for a time. And then wilderness, gardens and the laws of nature? Count their benefits. Because our relationship to these different natures is entailing, intimate and mutually nourishing, we owe them a lot. Because they are also violent, unthinking and different from us, we do not owe them unconditional worship, in the sense that Chief Seattle seems

Sun and clouds over Stonehenge. Such ancient landforms heighten both the daily weather and the cosmic orientation.

to suggest. The universe creates beauty and takes it away, arbitrarily, but, as with a distant and occasionally senile relative, so we owe it the kind of honour, respect and love that comes from these deep relationships, but in a conditional way. As I said in the first chapter we are on a parity with it, as with the rest of the different natures.

It hardly needs emphasizing, but what I am proposing is not the usual orientation to nature, or the fundamental questions, or to science and religion. I am arguing for a different relationship to these perennial disciplines, for a different metaphysics than the customary ones, neither a materialistic nor idealistic worldview. It is what I have called elsewhere a 'critical spirituality'. But rather than put this position abstractly, as a philosophical argument – and one that informs my landforms – I prefer to suggest it by concrete works of art and landscape – to think with them.

Frank Gehry's 'cathedral of art' in Bilbao, the New Guggenheim, opened in 1997, catalysing the most recent stage of this modern metaphor for the museum, here a place that celebrates both the art and basic qualities of space and sunlight.

Religion Declines, Art Inflates

For more than 200 years, since religion started to decline in the West and a secular culture take root, art has become a kind of substitute religion. Matthew Arnold was one of many English writers to address the 'long withdrawing roar' of faith, and in Europe the artistic avant garde started its slow advance as the roar of the future, of what one of its leaders, Saint Simon, called Nouveau Christianisme. That call for avant garde artists to become the new priests was in 1825, and it was made because they were more in touch with feelings, 'the imagination and sentiments of mankind', than either the scientists or the old priests. By 1950, with Picasso and Jackson Pollock, the avant garde were becoming celebrity artists; by 1980, with the Centre Pompidou, the New Louvre and other *grand projets* in Paris, the 'museum as cathedral' had become established, and a cliché of journalists. The outburst of museum-cathedrals for the millennium was reminiscent of the batomania of the year 1000, when the end of the world did not occur and church building celebrated the fact. Since Frank Gehry's famous New Guggenheim in Bilbao in 1997, every major city wants 'The Bilbao Effect', and in a way that sentiment is the Nouveau Christianisme. Art, particularly avant garde and semi-spiritual art, works as a kind of religious icon.

The oddity of this situation has been much debated. A recent summary in London's *Times* by Rachel Campbell-Johnson ('Artists Ask the Big Questions – Let's Hear Them in our Churches') shows how bizarre it can be when Brit Pack Atheists are given the high altar for their 'transgressive games'. After discussing Damien Hirst and Tracy Emin's rather thin works, and Antony Gormley and Bill Viola's commissioned pieces, she recapitulates the trends of 200 years.

> Culture often takes the role of religion in our contemporary world. Galleries are modern-day temples, regularly attended by the people on their day of rest. Exhibitions are discussed with almost evangelical fervour. Art has become a cult. It is there to make us wonder how our lives may be raised above the level of mundanity. As we wander through museums, we ponder the sort of questions that theology once asked: Why is this here at all? What does it mean? How should we live in the face of our challenges? In an era in which religion is too often reduced to dogmatic squabbles, art reopens the mind and emotions to the wider questions of the world. As we push our prams through Tate Modern we are not so far removed from the medieval peasants who once stood gawping in cathedrals, learning their Bible stories from the stonemason's works. But now the balance of power has shifted. (*The Times*, 2 April 2010)

Pushing prams suggests museums are not only the new cathedrals, but they have also become shopping centres. Indeed, people gawp at works in the Tate Modern, as they walk on by, often for less time than they examine a product at Tesco's. Tracy Emin's neon sign at Liverpool Cathedral – 'I felt you and I knew you loved me' – has the same kind of deep, staying power as 'Have a nice day'. As Matthew Arnold predicted, modern art may be a kind of religion, but it is a poor one; and, as their income reaches heavenwards, celebrity artists have become, as priests, even poorer. This is a far cry from Saint Simon's elevated role for the avant garde. Indeed, another well-worn argument is that today money has become *the* religion, the transcendental standard that unites the globe and is accepted uncritically, tacitly, as a universal value.

Spiritual Orientation: The Universe as our Distant Parent

Such strange developments provoke unusual thoughts about the universe, and the cosmos is slightly more universal than the gold standard. They make one confront the shifting relations between religion, spirituality, science and the cosmos, what they might mean today and more importantly where they will be in the future. What will those relations be in another hundred years, when it is generally understood that the cosmos is 13.7 billion years big, and that the earth has suffered five or six mass extinctions? The narrative of science, although full of misplaced metaphors and incomplete in many important ways, makes the idea of a personal, interacting God, the one of positive prayer, look more and more like either a bad joke or a bad God.

Whatever the polls say about the decline of religion in the West, the absence of the young in church and the rise of fanaticism and consumerism, there are some clear long-term trends. Dogma, scripture, and checklists, such as the Ten Commandments, are on the way out and an enigmatic spirituality – including its expression in art – is on the way in. This practice may vary from New Age mysticism to Art Pilgrimage by the international élite, from mass-culture evangelism to an individual contemplating the sunrise. Spirituality cuts across categories of experience. Like the feelings of awe inspired by a great work of art, these experiences are not, at a certain point, distinguishable from other strong emotions: love, passion, ecstasy, aesthetic perception, feelings of wholeness and identification with

ABOVE: The Dalveen Pass, an inspiring, natural landform in southern Scotland. Animistic metaphors evident here – skin and bones, veins and arteries – have been the inspiration for the designs of Chinese gardens and landscapes.

BELOW: The sculptural forms of the Grand Canyon are typically seen through various metaphors. Some have a European ring, such as Isis Temple or Cheops Pyramid; a few have a more exotic designation, such as Krishna Shrine or Vishnu Temple. One remaining red-topped hulk is called The Battleship and other distinctive sites are marked out as The Indian Garden, Bright Angel Canyon and Freya Castle. Such naming can be found in any highly sculpted landscape whether it is Chinese, French or American, a normal response of personification.

nature's powers. This empathy used to be decried as 'animism', the sin of believing a hard landscape was alive. It is now more accepted as a normal neurological response to the metaphors inherent in the rolling land: its 'skin, bones and arteries' (some natural metaphors of value). While perceiving the landscape, projection and empathy are always hard at work. Moreover, brain scans show that the experience of love, spirituality and the reaction to powerful art all have a great deal of overlap. Indeed, in art and poetry one area of experience is described by the other two, and in certain cases, such as Bernini's *Ecstasy of St Teresa*, all three are merged.

This common experience is one reason why today, as religion declines, artists are being employed to bring back a transcendent feeling into the church, even if they are atheists. For them, the universe may be violent and meaningless, but it is still at times beautiful and wonderful, and they bracket these good points for their art. Beyond this convergence is the growing recognition that enigmatic spirituality is partly supplanting religious observance. Ritual lacks immediacy, and liturgy lacks credibility as the credo is recited with a mechanical drone, 'Credo in unum Deum' (I believe in one God). By contrast, art can be experienced with a 'willing suspension of disbelief': that is, without bringing up the difficult questions of belief and truth, a great advantage in an age sceptical of all beliefs (especially that of scepticism).

What about the positive belief in atheism itself? Recently this has led some to notable and dogmatic attacks on religion and spirituality. But it has also encouraged others to open up a more nuanced and tolerant debate. Those who do not believe in God are nevertheless claiming the rights and history of the spirit – l'*esprit* – and its several cognate terms, such as inspiration. This is perhaps easier for those in Europe than for Anglo-Saxons, for whom religion has largely swallowed spirituality. Notable among the new thinkers is the philosopher André Comte-Sponville. His lyrical polemic L'*Esprit de l'atheisme* was published in French in 2006 and in English in 2008 as *The Book of Atheist Spirituality*, with the subtitle *An Elegant Argument for Spirituality Without God*. 'I loathe fanaticisms of all kinds,' Comte-Sponville declares, 'including atheistic fanaticism.' Most atheists will say 'amen' to that because, as he mentions, 'Humanity is far too weak and life far too difficult for people to go round spitting on each other's faiths.'

He is a pugnacious defender of the non-faith and very apt to declaim his arguments – 'Being an atheist by no means implies that I should castrate my soul!' By soul he usually means his spirit, or brain, or psyche, or his thinking and feeling personality, the whole bundle of *being* human, a full person. For Sponville, the soul is a verb, a process, an activity that is essential to the human because it includes all experience.

The human spirit is far too important a matter to be left up to priests, mullahs or spiritualists. It is our noblest part, or rather,

our highest function, the thing that makes us not only different from other animals (for we are animals as well), but greater than and superior to them. 'Man is a metaphysical animal,' said Schopenhauer – and therefore, I would add, a spiritual animal as well. This is our way of inhabiting the universe, and the absolute, which inhabit us.

His 'absolute' is a hard concept to understand, but there is much to agree with in Sponville's generous and noble view of the spirit. It relates directly to the cosmic landforms that are the subject of this book. His inclusive view is based on the European attitude towards nature as the summary of immanent reality, the sum total of everything that exists, 'the All' as he says. The five levels of nature I have mentioned are included – Epicurus' *pan*, Lucretius' *summa summarum* (*Natura, sive omnia*) and Spinoza's *Nature*, not to mention Ludwig Wittgenstein's 'everything that is the case'. In his open-mindedness, European philosophy speaks across time with spirited passion. It is refreshing that atheists are now reclaiming the larger tradition of the West, and Sponville shows its links with Buddhism, Taoism and similar world views in the East. He also makes the important point that while all religions have a spiritual practice, not all spiritualities have a religion. The spiritual orientation is the bigger of the two, and more inclusive, and does not make dogmatic claims on its followers. So it is rather like the aesthetic sense that is now capturing the high ground, if only formally, inside the cathedrals.

This stimulating view seems basically right to me, except for a few provisos. First, while the spiritual orientation is very important, for me it is only one among others, and these include the aesthetic, the moral and the symbolic, on an equal basis. I would not elevate the spiritual as the noblest of all capacities, though it is the important unifying mode that emphasizes the basic truths.

Second, Sponville's atheism has its limits because of what it is against, because of the inherent negativity of the 'a-'. As I shall discuss, the scientific world view can modify the atheistic one in important ways, because it can acknowledge emergent qualities. Suffice it to mention here that many of the attributes of a Christian God – except that of a personal creator – are also attributes of the universe, including the positive ones. The laws of nature and emergence (immanence), for instance, are similar. The harmony, growth, order and creativity are parallel virtues. So in many ways the universe does most of the things Theos did. On a daily basis, for instance, gravity sustains us, as does oxygen for that matter. Atheism, like theism, through which it puts a cross, does not, even in Sponville's generous interpretation, open up enough of the parallels that the scientific world view is revealing. Theos and A-Theos both have to be transcended. The cosmos is more creative and interesting than either allow.

Because ours is *one* universe, with common laws throughout, and because there are many correspondences between the macrocosm and microcosm, we can feel a deep connection to it. Children, mystics and animals – if we may judge by the playfulness of a dog or the leaps of a whale – feel these connections spontaneously. They do not have to be taught. Most people also feel them at moments, when perceiving a special work of art or nature. No one can deny such feelings of identification and empathy, especially the cynic who exploits them. They precede thought. 'I feel therefore I think therefore I am,' as the neuroscientist Antonio Damasio has now corrected Descartes.

Scientists who ponder the laws of nature deeply, or those who dedicate their life to decoding the truths of nature, are often seen as on a religious quest. Indeed, as often observed, they may sacrifice themselves much more to such an ultimate reality than a theologian or mystic. One reason for this religion of scientific pursuit is the equation between God and the laws of the cosmos. As Paul Davies put it in *The Mind of God: The Scientific Basis for a Rational World* (1992), the equation works most of the time: the laws, like God, function everywhere in the universe; they are absolute and do not depend on anything else; they are eternal in the sense they have not changed since after the first microsecond of the beginning; they are omnipotent, immanent and above all creative. Cosmogenesis – the generative laws and development of the universe – is in effect a Genesis myth that is true, and therefore worthy of respect.

The second reason for a quasi-religious attitude in science is touched on by Einstein when discussing the 'cosmic religious feeling' among the great thinkers. His list of exemplars overlaps somewhat with that of Sponville, and it is worth quoting to get an idea of how strong and wide this cosmic religious motivation may be:

> It is very difficult to elucidate this [cosmic religious] feeling to anyone who is entirely without it, especially as there is no anthropomorphic conception of God corresponding to it. . . . The beginnings of cosmic religious feeling already appear at an early stage of development, e.g., in many of the Psalms of David and in some of the Prophets. Buddhism, as we have learned especially from the wonderful writings of Schopenhauer, contains a much stronger element of this . . . no dogma and no God conceived in man's image . . . Looked at in this light, men like Democritus, Francis of Assisi and Spinoza are closely akin to one another . . . How can cosmic religious feeling be communicated from one person to another, if it can give rise to no definite notion of a God and no theology? In my view, it is the most important function of art and science to awaken this feeling and keep it alive in those who are receptive to it . . . I maintain that the cosmic religious feeling is the strongest and noblest motive for scientific research . . . [of, for instance, Kepler and Newton]. Those whose acquaintance with scientific research is derived chiefly from the practical results easily develop a completely false notion of the mentality of the men who, surrounded by a sceptical world, have shown the way to kindred spirits scattered through the world and the centuries. Only one who has devoted his life to similar ends can have a vivid realization of what has inspired these men and given them the strength to remain true to their purpose in spite of countless failures. It is a cosmic religious feeling that gives a man such strength. A contemporary has said, not unjustly, that in this materialistic age of ours the serious scientific workers are the only profoundly religious people. ('Religion and Science,' *New York Times Magazine*, 1930)

This sounds like a just description of both the historical truth and a key orientation for many scientists and artists, not to mention mystics, philosophers and ordinary people. Yet, accepting Sponville's point that the spiritual is a wider category than the religious, I would rephrase Einstein's concept to 'the spiritual cosmic feeling'. And I have changed the order too, because in the end the spiritual is a feeling elicited by the cosmos, a quite spontaneous emotion that does not bring up doctrinal questions or scientific dogma. Belief and indoctrination are secondary. It is not necessary to be a Christian or subscribe to the standard model of vertical genetic transfer to respond positively to a cosmic landform. And that is what landforms can be, as we will see in the next chapter: forms that perform the universe.

Furthermore, because the *universe is in the landscape*, as my title has it, we are in some ways 'at home in the universe', to use the words of the scientist Stuart Kauffman (and the title of his 1995 book). We are born in it, we come from it, we have affinities with it, and we can understand its laws. Indeed we are quintessential universe stuff, in the sense that we feel and think its many aspects. But there is still, obviously, a big problem. As we reflect on the cosmos and understand some of its wanton cruelties, we appreciate our differences from the world. Ponder the five mass extinctions and the continual 'war of nature', as Charles Darwin put it, which decimates nine in ten species, or how indifferent nature is to an individual's fate. Such alienations are why I put forward as an orientation for art and design two basic positions: our *parity* with the universe, and a *critical* spirituality. Clearly, further implications also follow from both the estrangements and the positive connections. Over the next hundred years as the scientific world view becomes more understood, and pervasive, these connections will renegotiate our metaphysics.

In the West the deity was supposed to be a just and loving God, and as an omnipotent and omniscient creator he was in a position to look after everyone, personally. Against this standard of supposed fine-tuned justice, it would be naïve to think that the cosmos, which is indifferent to individuals, deserves complete identification. It may dispense all the good things: beauty, plenty, feelings. It brought us into being and often nurtures us. But, as a distant and sometimes wayward parent, it does not deserve total love; conditional love is quite enough. This ambivalent relationship to our parent brings me to issues of co-creation with the universe, and two different paradigms for such co-design. Their humour and insight continue to inspire my landforms.

The Egyptian garden of Nebamun, c.1400 BC. A pond, containing paired species, is ringed by a border of the sacred plants of Egypt and then fruit trees. The garden is strangely reminiscent of later Paradise Gardens. The Sky Goddess Nut, upper right, offers Nebamun some figs and dates.

Cosmic Landscapes in Culture and Nature

For the Italian Renaissance, as mentioned, gardens are a kind of Third Nature, *improved* by art. Even depictions of Egyptian and Roman gardens show them to be a kind of materialistic heaven, the perfected nature-abode on earth, and the Paradise Garden became a well known convention of the Persians and the Muslims, the Jews and the Christians, and many variations still remain from the Taj Mahal to the early botanic gardens. The latter were modelled on the idea of collecting a perfect specimen of each species to put in an eternal ark, just as Kew Gardens is doing today with its programme of DNA preservation. Religion, science and the garden are thus intimately connected. The Judeo-Christian idea that God created an ideal Garden of Eden, right after he created the universe, brings up the important relation between these two scales of nature. In this way history and fateful metaphysics connect our view of natures zero through four.

Ponder the human condition as if we were a species of ant. It is daring to believe that an insignificant creature could have any positive relationship to an indifferent world. Most cultures, in their

Francesco Bassano, the Garden of Eden just before the fall of man. Adam among the peaceful animals leans towards Eve in her primitive hut. God has created an ecological paradise of harmony broken only by the stormy sky and Adam's belly button.

origin myths, look on nature as if it were chaotic and our place in it little better than fleas (as a few Chinese myths put it). The Western tradition, based on Genesis, is much bolder, hubristic, even outrageously so, with Man made in the image of God and given a cosmic destiny! Ants change the world. The Creator comments on each one of the universal units – the day, the night, the sun, the moon – 'that it was good' (as if his audience might sometimes doubt this).

And so the paintings of Eden give the mixed message of eternal harmony set against a partial human frailty – an ideal relationship of ecology versus the violent thunderstorm of passion. These depictions are a type of cosmic landscape. A touching example is by Francesco Bassano, from the sixteenth century. Here God creates his Elysium and hands it over to the beasts of the field, and they seem to get on

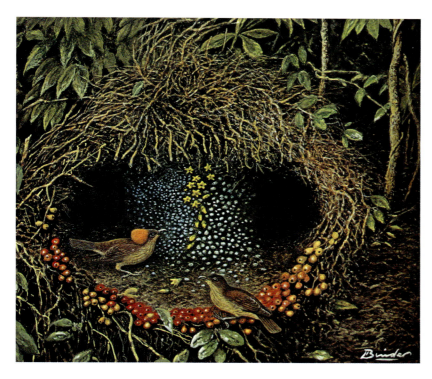

The male bower bird attracts a mate into his nest by constructing an attractive home made from berries, shells, flowers and even industrial scrap such as bottle caps. (From Karl von Frisch, *Animal Architecture*, Harcourt Brace Jovanovich, New York and London, pl. 99. Photo @ Dr. Max Renner, Munich.

reasonably well – the lion does not eat the lamb – no Darwin here. It is an ecological heaven, the perfect recycling of a wilderness garden, no decaying compost heaps or scrap metal, every picturesque detail composed just so, as any prize-winning gardener would hope on the opening day of the Chelsea Flower Show. But the stormy sky foretells Adam's future as he moves, longingly, towards the perfect primitive hut built of wattle and daub. Forbidden sex enters the cosmic picture, shifting the subsequent trajectory of Western metaphysics and the story of Genesis. 'And he saw that it was good' takes a turn for the worse.

This duality, nature good *and* bad, underlies the contradiction in Western identity, of theology versus nature red in tooth and claw. Bassano depicts it not only in the quandary of open sex versus human self-consciousness: it is also marked on the body of Adam and Eve. As in most pictures of the first garden, Man has a belly button, therefore a parent and therefore a bloodline, and therefore we are not just the *ex nihilo* creation of God.

As others have observed, the telltale mark of the belly button contradicts the metaphysics of sole creativity. Evolution *and* Darwin are both in the garden before the Fall. The ideal ecology is already disturbed by another nature: lust. One implication is that God cannot create the perfect pre-lapsarian paradise; even He has to co-create with nature. Alternatively, 95 per cent of Western painters are confused on theological matters (I have counted fifty Edenic

scenes without belly buttons). Or, third, it is only a matter of taste, and that without the usual hole in their stomachs Adam and Eve would look rather odd. Whatever the case, it is the first implication that concerns me. Co-equal creation underscores the truth of the parity between us and different natures. As gardeners try the impossible task of forming a perfect nature they actually create a dialogue with its several layers. 'Nature *improved* by art' means what gardeners soon discover. When they embark on a design, growing nature makes another move, physics and entropy may enter the equation and only if they are lucky and inventive can they turn these changeable realities to good account by reinventing their plot. This dialogue between the ideal wilderness garden *and* evolution is built into Bassano's picture, as in so much Edenic art.

Furthermore, and just as importantly, ideal wilderness gardens are constructed by non-humans, for instance bower birds. Typically the male bower bird will sport his crest and advertise his aesthetic prowess at the entrance to the garden. He will surround it with a wattle and daub fence and, as in the Edenic garden, thatch his house. Where the keystone over the gate would attract attention, he places cherries and shiny fruit. He strews the floor with a path picked out in brightly coloured flowers (so pleasant to walk on or nestle into), uses throw-away scrap such as bottle caps or beetle jackets, if they have a complementary colour, and designs a circular lair with perhaps a trysting place in the back. All this aesthetic work is done to get the female bird – a good reason for constructing a garden. How many nesting species, hibernating animals, termites and ant colonies make a 'house and garden'? Enough to show these are generic activities, and not just a publishing genre. They precede our attempts and, like God's version of Eden and the paintings from Egypt, show that aesthetics and gardening are *universal* motives. Or, rather, they extend to other species and suggest that any sentient creature might be pulled along these attractive routes by the allure of beauty and meaning.

I find these conjectures very inspiring. Again they tie us into the other natures and relate us to the universe as the quintessential species. The idea that aesthetics and cultural meaning *come before us* in time and are built into the cosmic code is logical, and now a truth that increasingly finds corroboration. The reason is obvious. Any complex adaptive creature would benefit from beauty and meaning. Biologically they might be adaptive features like the peacock's multicoloured tail. Creatures such as the bower bird and evidence from prehistory point in this direction. For instance, it appears that Neanderthals mourned and buried their dead, and it looks as if some other non-human species – elephants, chimpanzees and grey whales among others – do similar things, leaving behind aesthetic and significant tokens. And for thousands of years before the birth of Classical religions, such a spiritual tradition existed among many people along the Atlantic seacoast, as we shall see.

15: LANDSCAPES OF COSMIC CONJECTURE

Ritual Landscapes

Recently archaeologists, like ambitious land artists, have expanded our view of individual monuments such as Stonehenge, by seeing them as part of the larger landscape. The shift in perspective from the object to its overall context view has enabled them to decode some of the most plausible meanings. The results are both exciting and conjectural, since no writing survives to prove one theory right and another wrong. Somewhat like today's cosmologists reading the polyvalent signs from their particle accelerators, looking for the

LEFT: Stonehenge at sunset. The solar corridor connects the sunrise on 21 June to the sunset on 21 December, a cosmic orientation in this and other ritual landscapes.

BELOW: The Domain of the Living, the henge at Durrington Walls, is connected via the River Avon to the Domain of the Ancestors, Stonehenge. Thus a single ritual landscape of over a mile is conceived as a journey from life to death, from wood to stone, from contingency to permanence. Diagram after Francis Pryor, *Britain BC* (Harper Collins, 2003).

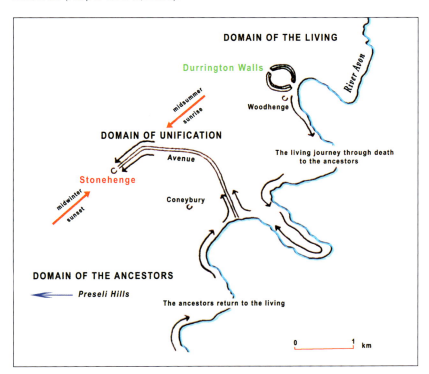

elusive Higgs Particle, they infer answers from the overall evidence. According to the in-joke, a fact is not a fact until proven by theory, or, more accurately, until it is consonant with well-tested ideas. With prehistory the new theory is that Stonehenge and other such sites are part of a ritual landscape, an area conceived in aesthetic and symbolic terms. Some archaeologists deny this, and there is only circumstantial evidence. But when I return again and again to the ancient landforms, they convince me of such perennial motives. These nurture my own practice, which is the reason for a short digression into the land art of 3000 BC. In some respects these ritual landscapes are similar to sculpture parks today, or to earthworks developing everywhere, even if the ritual is now no more than a day out with the kids.

The aesthetic and meaning of Stonehenge have engaged speculators ever since the henge fell into disuse, some time before the Roman occupation of Britain. Today the speculation is as lively as it was 2,000 years ago, eliciting different theories, even contradictory ones. Where the Dark Ages saw Stonehenge as created by a race of giants led by sorcerers such as Merlin, some archaeologists today believe it was a regional hospital (extending its reach to Switzerland) because of the wounded and suffering pilgrims who were buried near by. Also, there is evidence that it was the centre of a Euro-Scottish cult. Large numbers of pilgrims were drawn on annual summer feasts from both the north and east trade routes. They met in the largest turf henge at Durrington Walls, where there are also very large wooden posts forming palisades. The ritual included not only feasts and celebrations in this Domain of the Living, but a movement down the River Avon, perhaps carrying bones and ancestral symbols. They were interred at Stonehenge, the Domain of the Ancestors (see left). Thus a wooden upright, signifying a previously living person, is turned into a permanently reified stone ancestor.

This is a plausible inference, but some interpretations are well established. Even today Stonehenge is a place to celebrate the summer solstice on 21 June, the longest day of the year, as it was in the past. But surprisingly, it was also a monument to focus on the shortest day of the year, in the winter when the sun set in the south-west. It turns out that the solar corridor, an axis connecting the two cosmic lines, works equally well both ways. Investigators are divided on which alignment has priority.

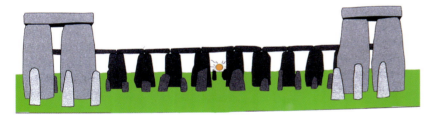

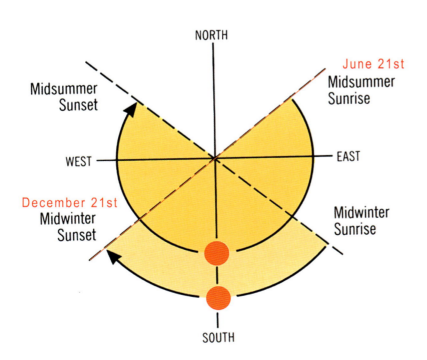

On a general level a plausible interpretation is that Stonehenge was a theatre of power where the elites reaffirmed their mastery of cosmic understanding, particularly the sense of when to plant and when to reap. Or, if one is looking for a more democratic version of events, the landscape was, from about 7000 BC, a place where all members of the local tribe were buried with a certain social equality. The 'henge', which is technically a ditch and circle of earth, or a landform in my terms, reaffirmed the interdependence of the tribal members. Initially, at the beginning of construction, such landforms supported a community in its participation with nature's rhythms.

You might try to rank its *primary* purpose. As hospital or solar instrument? Oriented to the summer sunrise or winter sunset? An elite or a democratic institution? While this may be unknowable, archaeologists have agreed on what is for me a most important point: that Stonehenge is the culmination of a sacred passage through the 'ritual landscape'. We may not know exactly what the rituals were, but through the recent excavations by Parker Pearson we can be sure that, as the people moved from the wood of Durrington Walls to the stone of Stonehenge along the river way, it was a meaningful landscape. As with most landforms, the sky predominates over things that both nature and humans have made. It captures in one theatre the cosmos, the earth and the human drama. And over 2,000 years the meanings probably changed step by step, like most evolutions.

What about the aesthetic intentions? Some are fairly clear. The careful placement of the stone circle is on the brow of a low hill and at the end of an avenue oriented to the north-east, along the solar corridor of the midsummer sunrise. The big Sarsen stones have been artificially dressed and, late in their career, carved with phallic symbols and axe heads. Some stones have been polished in places, and shaped on four sides so that they taper in entasis like those of a Greek temple. Some lintels are curved and flared. Several uprights have strong flutes or grooves to emphasize their verticality. The estimate is that these visual refinements took fifty masons working ten hours a day almost three years, a kind of absurdly accurate figure. It is illogical because the stonework was done over several generations and during this time the significance of the henge most likely changed. For instance, the Sarsens and the blue stones were moved to different places because the latter referred to the healing stones of the ancestors, both in colour and origin. This coherent change is important for the coherence of meaning.

The archaeologist Michael Pitts calls this cultural formation, along the Western Atlantic, 'Hengeworld' (in a book of that name). The site shows continuous work from 7000 to 1500 BC – a very long time. At the very least, henges and geometric

OPPOSITE: A solar corridor connects the north-east–south-west axis to the key sunrise on 21 June and the sunset on 21 December, the high point of summer and the moment of promised renewal. Diagrams after R. Castleden, *The Making of Stonehenge* (Routledge, London, 1993) and R.J.C. Atkinson, *Stonehenge and Neighbouring Monuments* (English Heritage, London, 1987).

RIGHT: On the stones are several symbolic and aesthetic signs and refinements. These include axe heads, phallic custs and flared lintels. Diagram after Mike Pitts, *Hengeworld* (Random House, London, 2000).

RIGHT BELOW: The grooved refinements, one of many aesthetic signs.

landforms with stones were built for 3,500 years, more than double the period of Christianity and seven times that of the recent global civilization, modernity. For nationalists, in search of identity, there are humorous conclusions. If length of cultural continuity were the measure, then the British should be called 'the circle people', because their form of living, burial and worship was, for a large part of that time, in round houses and landforms. They built many more circular constructions than other European peoples.

Yet Hengeworld has deeper implications for the present, and its co-design with nature and a dynamic cosmos. One lesson is the development of meaning across vast stretches of time. The landforms accepted new readings and allowed open semiosis, or the communication of changing meaning, while providing continuity. This consistency amid change is like the whispering game, the way words in a message are passed from one ear to another around the table and coherently decoded by sense-making interpretation, even when the sounds are too faint to fully understand or the message unclear. Our search for meaning reimposes new meaning. Like the molecules in a string of inherited DNA, which I depicted in sculptural seats on the Life Mounds (page 236–9), the elements of Hengeworld had a coherent use that made sense with each re-use.

Catastrophe and Response

Another lesson of this world is its similarity to the dynamic and uncertain cosmos. The metaphysics of our time is coming to terms with the implications of a self-organizing universe, in which there is a general emergence of order out of chaos and complexity out of simplicity. This overall positive trend was the orientation of my work shown in *The Garden of Cosmic Speculation* (2003). But the further consequence of a self-organizing universe was not particularly stressed in that book: creative destruction and destructive creation. The gardening equivalent of this is a flood or a drought that kills off the planting scheme, or at the larger level the mass extinction of life caused by any number of tipping points.

Natural catastrophes were part of everyday life in Hengeworld, when the average lifespan was about thirty years. Seasonal renewal was only somewhat predictable, with sudden cold spells, and climate change was always a deadly threat. This tense relationship to different natures is rather like ours, with our uncertain relationship to global warming and a global economy beyond much control. I find such a delicate association with nature depicted most strikingly on the northern islands of Scotland. Here on the Orkneys 5,000 years ago the people enjoyed a few warm periods and, because it was relatively

Brodgar standing stones looking both ways, to a causeway and Stenness, above, and the north inlet, right. Some 29 of over 60 huge stones remain in this Orkney Domain of the Ancestors.

free from predators, they often thrived in relative social peace. The stone circles and ritual landscapes that were constructed show a direct relationship to wilderness that is still palpable today. The Brodgar and Stenness circles are made from thin, knife-like stones that cut the sky and horizon like primitive acts of defence and defiance, of celebration and passion, as if they were both secure and insecure. The scene is still wild enough (even with the sheep grazing) and close enough to water on all sides to feel the primitive meanings, viscerally. As with Stonehenge, water plays a key role in ritually connecting two parts of the bigger plot, the journeys back and forth between life and death. Landforms and wilderness orchestrate this journey across a very thin causeway that was often flooded and disappeared. It disconnected and reconnected life and death. The overall feeling is of a world built against a precarious but wonderful cosmos.

At the time I was beginning to understand this ancient meta-physics, a series of accidents, some of them natural, led me to building an echo of Hengeworld. Fortuitously it was by a river which floods from time to time, but with catastrophes that were more humorous

than deadly. Called Fishenge, because the earth henge is designed to push the water away from a fisherman's hut, it was built as fast as possible. Necessity, as often, was the whiplash of invention.

The first stage in this saga was the destruction of a weir below which salmon used to rest before making their next jump up the river. This small waterfall was destroyed by the authorities to make way for the railway bridge over the Nith (see pages 94–5), and since this ruined some of the best fishing on the river, the powers that be agreed to compensate for this loss by creating a series of artificial croys. These diagonal breakwaters, made from large boulders, were supposed to slow the river down and create new pools for the salmon to rest in. They were thus made to create good places to fish, but it did not work according to theory. The catches went down, the fishermen complained, the government wanted more rent from the fishing rights and the River Board gave me two weeks to clear all the boulders. Catastrophe, surprise, gun to the head, response. Thus, from a series of well-intentioned fiascos, Fishenge was born.

In plan it is two triangles of relocated boulders, skewed to create a tense and fragile balance. They are bisected by an avenue that focuses north-east on the key moment of sunrise, 21 June. The turf mounds also rise and fall in synch with the boulders to skew the perspective even more, adding to the dynamic tilts. Inside one triangle is a spiral and the other a line of rocks, a galaxy as it were seen top down and from the side. Once again the galactic form, the largest shape in the cosmos, became the inspiration for design. The logic and reality were compelling. Because prehistoric cultures always referred to *their* ideas of the cosmos, and since the River Board gave me just two weeks to design and build, I reverted to *our* standard cosmology. It is not high art but perhaps, to misquote the Futurists, the primitive art of a new sensibility.

Catastrophe and response continued to play a role, as they must have with ancient henges. In the first year a larger-than-average flood knocked over boulders and littered the site with the flotsam of trees, bushes and even discarded plastic. I responded to this with an angled earthwork that channelled the water away from Fishenge, and that was fine for a while. But the following year, a larger flood raised the whole water level dramatically for three days. This effectively turned the rock structure into a momentary 'Riverhenge' and that, in turn, recalled the excavations of Francis Pryor, an archaeologist and author I admired.

In the 1990s Pryor had discovered 'Seahenge' on the Norfolk coast – a wood circle of fifty-five posts with a huge, upside-down oak tree at its centre, built quickly in a ritual around the year 2049 BC. Our river flood not only recalled this speedy construction but also reminded me of the ephemeral rock art of Andy Goldsworthy. Characteristically, Goldsworthy will build a small tower of round stones precariously stacked one on top of another. This obelisk of wobbling granite is located just at the edge of the sea between the order of the land and the chaos of the waves. It faces the incoming tide defiantly, before

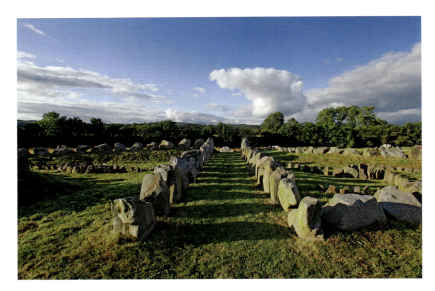

Fishenge normal view and flooded and, right, the conceptual plan. The layout shows a galaxy of rocks seen as a bulge in cross section and a three-armed spiral from the top. The galaxy was thought to be the largest structure in the universe until the 1950s, when galactic superclusters came into focus. By the mid-1980s the stick figure, at the top of the drawing, called the little green man, was thought to be the largest cosmic form – each dot being a galaxy – and thus it became a partial model for the design. The stickman is the Coma supercluster. But now even larger superclusters have been decoded, so now it is only a trace in the plan. The axis of Fishenge is focused north-east on a white granite rock, and the propitious moment of sunrise on 21 June, over the distant hill.

Riverhenge, above, versus Fishenge. Henges and stone circles are in constant dialogue with the clouds, the horizon and a changing or violent nature.

collapsing as it always will. Goldsworthy turns such transitory acts into permanent photographs, and today the art world happily stores them behind everlasting frames. Overcoming evanescent time seems constant to both the past and present art; yet there is also a difference.

At Seahenge, Pryor calculates that, with 200 people involved in the speed-ritual, 'it is fair to say that its construction was also its use. It was built to draw people together.' That was true of henge construction in general, a simultaneous building of monument and community. This forms a contrast with the individual perception and collection of works of art today. However, contemporary artists and prehistoric people do have an orientation in common. They both carry on a dialogue with nature, and each side makes a move responding to nature's countermove. And, presumably, they both assume that neither side of this equation is in complete control, nor perfectly understood. The metaphysics of prehistoric Britain was based on a continuous response to an uncertain nature, and an aesthetic of contrast and parity with the cosmos. Maybe we add to that metaphysics an attitude of amused, and bemused, irony.

Back to Metaphor

Whatever our differences with this prehistoric past, there are important lessons to be drawn for landforms. Return to the two stone circles on the Orkney Islands I have just mentioned. Although separated by a mile from each other, across a causeway that sometimes is cut off, the Brodgar and Stenness circles are intervisible, and clearly part of a single ritual landscape. Recently the 'largest cathedral of prehistory' (of as yet unknown use) has been found between these two monuments. It is just one more connection of a complex system being excavated, and there are clearly some exciting discoveries soon to be made. But already apparent is that the landforms – the henges, stone circles and burial mounds – were like Stonehenge. They were oriented to the cosmic points, the rise and fall of the sun and moon at key moments of the year, and to the local topography. Distant mountains form a natural circular bowl, and their peaks and troughs tap out the passage of these cosmic spheres. Their pinnacles become rhythmical marks on a giant sundial and moondial, but laid out on a heroic scale, typifying the theme of this book, the 'universe in the landscape'. Conceptually, the two stone circles miniaturize the horizon. They are earth bowls within the greater bowl of hills and the largest bowl of the sky. These reciprocal circles and forms – sun, moon and cloud – are usually captured in a landform. For instance, here in the Orkneys the midwinter sun sets between the two peaks of the distant mountains called the Hills of Hoy, an adjacent island, and this is marked by the slant of the stones and the solar corridors.

In retrospect, the point is obvious, but I missed it for a long time. Landforms basically perform the distant landscape and wilderness (First Nature, in my scheme). Half their visual field includes the cosmos (or Zero Nature) because of what you see captured – the sky, the sun, the moon, the planets such as Venus, and above all the clouds. On a good day, as these photos reveal, landforms and the weather become one, and nature's changing sculpture complements that of the earth. Because my eye was focused on the construction below, as architects usually are, I didn't appreciate these undesigned natures and how important they are for landforms. They complete the picture and the meaning. Imagine a landform inside a gallery: dead boring (or bizarre).

The prehistoric earthworks reveal the greater dimension, and in this sense are spiritual instruments that extend the view outwards to the next larger question. They refer to moods and meanings that are less denotative than connotative, a point that I have touched on in the first chapter when interviewing the scientist Martin Rees. It is worth repeating his words: 'I *don't* believe we can ever have more than an incomplete and metaphorical understanding of the deepest aspects of reality. That's why, although in some senses a religious person, I am not in favour of dogmatic religion, and suspicious of anyone who claims to have more than a vague and metaphorical understanding of deeper reality. I know it is hard understanding even a hydrogen atom. I think because of the limitations of our brains we have to learn in a limited way through metaphors which encapsulates *part* of the truth.'

This is partly true of our understanding of history and archaeology, specifically the meanings of the stone circles of Brodgar and Stenness. Metaphor is a way of decoding our relationship to the past and the universe. I have already mentioned a recent theory of what Stonehenge and Durrington Henge may mean, as a ritual landscape connecting the journey of life into death along the River Avon. This idea, proposed in the 1990s by Mike Parker Pearson, has reached something of a consensus among archaeologists. In 2009 Tony Robinson narrated, in his inimitable manner, a film for *Time Team* on Channel 4 called *The Secrets of Stonehenge*. As he turned piles of dust into interesting TV, he broached the big question of what those secrets were, and how the different materials of Stonehenge and Durrington Henge revealed them.

> Tony Robinson: What did you think the significance was that Durrington had a wooden circle whereas Stonehenge had a stone one?
>
> Mike Parker Pearson: It was coming to the key realization that the materials they were using were important to them in a symbolic and metaphorical sense.
>
> TR: And what did you think these metaphors meant?
>
> MPP: Well, for timber it is something like a human life. It begins, it ends and it decays, whereas stone is something that is permanent and goes on forever, it is a metaphor for the eternal after life.
>
> TR: But you've got these two metaphors *geographically* very close together.
>
> MPP: Yes, that's the really interesting thing. [The wooden Durrington circles] are less than 2 miles upstream from Stonehenge. So instead of seeing them as two *separate* sites, one sees them as two *halves* of the same complex.

According to Parker Pearson, the same may be true of the connection of Stenness to Brodgar. Again there is a journey across water, from the domain of the living at Stenness to the domain of the ancestors at the giant Brodgar Ring, where 3,000 people could congregate. The evidence that the former was the place of feasting and celebration – with its hearth, four poster and pits full of pig and cattle bones – is as clear as the local house to which it bears some similarities. Brodgar was obviously the place of final resting, with very few signs of domestic activity and its surrounding burial mounds. Like the palisade and cursus walls of division

bowl of sky

ABOVE: Orientation to south-west and setting sun, in red, left, between the distant Hills of Hoy. The two stone circles of Brodgar and Stenness are almost connected by a pointing finger causeway, and are both partly oriented to the midwinter sun setting between the distant mountains, visible in the photo right. This was also the midwinter focus for the largest burial mound in Scotland, Maes Howe. The setting sun shines down a long solar corridor on 21 December and illuminates the interior of the grave, as well as crossing the hearth at Stenness, cosmic connections of life to death.

LEFT: The changing weather and clouds are captured by the nearby stone circles. In the distance can be seen the Hills of Hoy, the focus for the midwinter setting sun. In the centre of the circle is a central pit, a hearth for feasting and behind it a four poster for excarnating the bones, and a pair of rocks oriented to Maes Howe. This last grave is in the shape of a dome or bowl like the bowl of the sky and so much other contemporary symbolism. The distant bowl of the horizon marks the passage of the sun and moon, while the stone circle completes these time pieces.

at Stonehenge, there is a strong demarcation between these two domains, but here it is made by a thick wall of stone. This is part of the 'cathedral' now being excavated. Further evidence may make the case for this interpretation of the two separate domains even stronger. But, as with quantum physics and other mysteries of the universe, all we may ever understand is a statistical probability of what it all means. No written Rosetta Stone is there waiting to be found and, in any case, over the thousand years of active use the meaning of these monuments will have changed.

Most importantly, the meaning is bound to have been polysemic and metaphorical all along. Ask archaeologists the question 'What is the meaning of Stonehenge?' and one will hear different 'secrets' that are 'plausibly true', so many different ones that it proves the point: the stone circle meant several things and these meanings changed as the form evolved, as it developed from the circular henge pits and the circular grave mounds. If you could ask original members of the circle tribe, that is the ancient Brits, what they meant, and give them enough time for an answer they might say: 'The sun, the moon, the passage from life to death to life, the community festival,' and then go on for another few minutes enumerating the uses and overtones.

In effect, these spiral and circular forms, and their decorative counterparts carved in rocks, are like most visual metaphors of value: they crystallize multiple associations. One of the most exciting detective riddles today is the meaning of the cup and ring marks. These were cut in rocks up and down the Atlantic seaboard, over thousands of years. Connecting the Stone Age peoples of northern Spain to southern Norway, this extended culture used rock art to communicate various messages now lost to us. When one comes across a series of concentric rings, many with a single vertical cut leading to the centre of the bull's eye, one conclusion springs to mind. These signs resemble a passage grave seen from above in plan, or conversely, when lying down on the floor looking at the circles of stone corbelled on the ceiling. So one meaning may be 'ancestors' place' or 'our home'.

But, as the lawyer Ronald Morris found, after studying cup and ring marks for many years, some general meanings are also likely: 'religious', 'magical', 'astronomic', etc. Collecting over a hundred such interpretations, and grading them one to ten, he came up with a scale of likelihood. Twenty-two per cent were plausible explanations, 53 per cent were possible, in some cases, while 25 per cent were zany – the 'Freemasons' earliest marks'. The search goes on to crack the code(s) and, once you are sucked into the game of hunt the symbol, absolutely captivating. If you know where to look, if you understand the code of where these signs are likely to be placed – overlooking important landscapes of transition – then the cup and ring marks can be literally unearthed by scraping away the moss. One self-trained expert has already discovered a lot though this insight.

In the end, however, the meanings may turn out to be more projective than denotative, more like enigmatic signifiers than religious scripture or road signs. As Martin Rees said about deep reality and the truths of the universe, they are best approached through metaphor. This is, by definition, general and only partially true. For me that is what landforms do very well: they crystallize multiple metaphors about deep reality.

LEFT: Magnificent symbolic decoration: spirals and concentric circles were pecked into stones at the Pierowall chambered cairn, Orkney, third millennium BC. Like the decorative signs in Ireland and the cup and ring marks all over the Atlantic coast at the same time, these shapes probably had precise but changing meanings over two thousand years. Their connection to the sun and moon, the spiral bowls of burial, the domed graves, the stone circles and a host of analogous curved forms means that they are likely to have a general metaphorical significance: death and rebirth, the cosmic bodies, etc., as well as particular social meanings. For instance, eight concentric circles on a large signpost stone might mean 'large hamlet, my property'. Or they could have many other specific meanings, depending on the context. This stone is now in the Orkney Museum.

RIGHT: One of many billboards of rock art at Achnabreck, in western Scotland. These constitute perhaps the largest single collection of prehistoric cup and ring marks. Characteristically clusters are located on a high hill overlooking an important river boundary. This suggests some kind of territorial signpost as well as a spiritual meaning.

Cosmic Relations

Our relations with the cosmos have affinities with those of 5,000 years ago. The builders of the great stone circles are kindred spirits in the search for a new relationship with nature. They too faced an uncertain world and a fast-changing climate. Their highly symbolic and social monuments show the human continuity with nature and their ancestors. For us also the cosmos has a spiritual significance, as I have been arguing, of a distant but beneficent parent. We relate to this very big thing in strange ways that are not easily defined, because it is both fascinatingly mysterious and the ground of our being. We are literally, and metaphorically, grounded in the cosmos.

We cannot think and feel outside the universe, and, like a fish in water, have to grasp this interiority even if we can imagine being outside it. Since the universe is omnipotent and stupefyingly large, it commands respect, and since science gives us only a fuzzy picture of its 100 billion galaxies (or is it 100 billion superclusters?) we are in the comic position of a clown made super aware of exactly how puny his knowledge is. For me this is one more reason to believe in the cosmic comic (or is it the reverse?), the serious idea that the spiritual has to be rooted in the human spirit, and that includes humour.

The mixed attitude, serious laughter as a spiritual mode, is brought home to me as I contemplate a recent landscape project at Cern, the organization in Geneva responsible for a host of cosmic discoveries and worldly spin-offs. These include finding the basic subatomic particles: the quarks and other ultimate building blocks of the universe. Cern is also responsible for creating the World Wide Web, set up in order for scientists to handle the trillion bits of information that flow from each experiment. Even this has its humorous side. Perhaps, since the particle accelerator has recently smashed protons together, at the time of writing in summer 2010, we have already discovered something amazing. Maybe we have seen back to the birth of the universe, or found Dark Matter, or created mini black holes, or even found the holy grail of this expensive search. We might already have pinned down the elusive Higgs boson, the so-called 'God particle' that brings it all together. That religious moniker is what the Nobel Prize-winning physicist Leon Lederman called it in 1993, in a popular book of that name.

Have all these discoveries been made – the origin of the universe, the Higgs field, God? Ironically, we will not know for months, until long after the explosions and each trillion-bit shower is carefully analysed on the web by 100,000 joined-up computers. That is a post-coital experience, maybe typical of today's ultimate reality.

In any case, the quantum world of the super tiny *is* really paradoxical, and it underlies everything, including all matter and thought, all being itself. No wonder that religious metaphors are being used, like the Holy Grail, and spiritual issues are being raised, like the vanishing distinction between body and mind. As Niels Bohr famously said many years ago, when quantum physics was first understood in the 1920s,

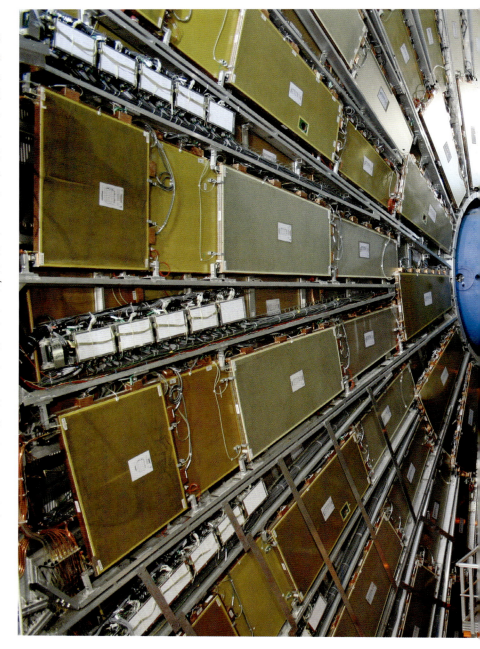

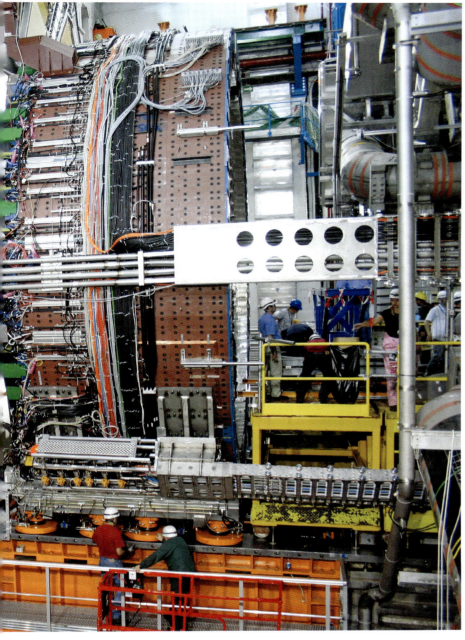

Cern has many experiments under way, but its most famous is being conducted by the Atlas detector, shown above in its seven-storey cavern, being worked on in June 2007 when I first visited. Other experimental centres are also located in the 27 kilometres of tunnel and they take part in this underground circle of high energy. Shown here are the red magnets that accelerate the super-cooled protons to 99.9997828 per cent of the speed of light, that is, the speed limit of the universe. Also, below, are metal tubes through which the atomic particles are bent, including the copper-coloured one that handles the big hadrons. Is this a twenty-first-century, underground stone circle?

'anyone who is not shocked by quantum theory has not understood it'. It is called 'weird and crazy' because particles routinely occupy two different places at once. All atomic and subatomic particles have this uncanny property, as do even some combinations of them.

Working with the people at Cern is for me like working with the coal men: inspiring, because the work is so basic, so fundamental and practical, even when using the most advanced equipment in the world. Imagine constructing a 27-kilometre tunnel seven storeys down to fire protons at anti-protons, almost at the speed of light, in order to create conditions that may explain the universe. Then imagine spending months looking through photos, or now having computers do this, to find one sliver of evidence among the debris. It is a primitive method of decoding the universe, but it is our way. The machine aesthetic that results also characterizes our time. It is a mixture of pure abstract forms and clunky compromise, glistening steel tubes and a riot of wiring, diagrammatic beauty and messy afterthought. Beautiful and ugly, simple and infinitely complicated to the outsider, this oxymoronic mixture reveals a basic truth about our search for the ultimate. Fundamentally the aesthetic system contrasts high-tech machinery with multiple colour-coding, the latter absolutely necessary for understanding the complexity. Note the central tube of copper colour. It is where the protons and anti-protons race through the 27-kilometre ring, which happened to be open for repair when I visited. It was the crown jewels and a car muffler, the Holy of Holies as exhaust pipe.

Quark theory was named by the physicist Murray Gell-Mann in the 1960s to reflect the uncanny nature of this basic reality. Gell-Mann took a drinking phrase from James Joyce, of an Irishman in a pub giving a kind of drunken toast for more booze – 'three quarks for Muster Mark'. He believed only three invisible and unthinkable bodies underlay all atomic particles. The maths and experiments proved it. And then the shattering explosions more or less showed it. 'Three quarks for Muster Mark', indeed, even if at Cern we now 'see' and 'know' there are six.

I suppose Gell-Mann's literary joke was an appropriate metaphor for these trapped concepts that never reveal themselves 'naked', but are always present as mathematical inferences in every explosion. Let us christen inferences that are invisible as 'inferations'. Over the next forty years linear accelerators built up a bigger picture of how these quarks and other ultimate particles, like electrons, hang together. The great search for rock-bottom reality, which started with the Greeks over 2,500 years ago, led to what was called by the 1980s the Standard Model. One should not underrate this solemn phrase because, like its first cousin, the Theory of Everything, a great deal of effort and money were spent proving its parts – even if the whole is rather shaky. In the last forty years 50 billion dollars were spent. One by one, after many explosions, all seventeen of the inferations turned up. They were more or less where the theory said they should be found. It was like having a theory of a loaded roulette wheel, then betting huge sums of money on each roll of the ball and hitting the number that was predicted. The Standard Model was a great intellectual achievement and perhaps the most impressive collective endeavour since going to the moon.

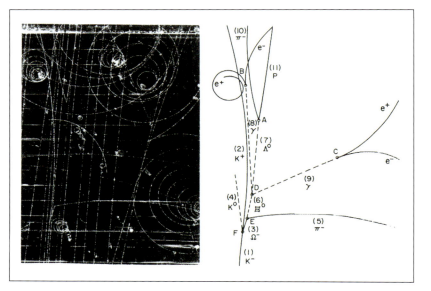

Naturally, since all grand theories of nature that look correct ought to be monumental icons in a garden, I constructed a large seat oriented due north, where one could contemplate this ultimate insight. All the eight red posts, a basic family of quarks, face the northern horizon like people looking at the cleft in the hills, just as the sarsens at Stonehenge face north-east and the rising, midsummer sun. So far so cosmic. To show the Standard Model and the supposition that everything in the universe spewed forth from an initial fast expansion of spacetime, I constructed the back of the seat with a lot of ready-made industrial objects – salt and pepper globes, spiralling superstrings, beautiful junk – and made the culmination of this flaring shape into the Standard

LEFT: Explosions revealing quarks in the 1960s through the traces left in a cloud chamber. These spiralling particles and anti-particles are here turned into a three-dimensional sculpture that is reflected in two dimensions, over water, just as they were seen and measured in photos. This language of zero nature was built in the year 2000. The quarks are noted on the red posts. For instance the proton (P) has a plus one electrical charge. It is made from two up quarks (2U) and one down quark (1D). Since the value of an up quark is plus two thirds and a down quark is minus one third, the sum equals one which is the electrical charge of one proton.

RIGHT: The Standard Model emerges from the fast hot-stretch of spacetime and the origin of the universe. It shows the family of six quarks, above six leptons, and to the right the five force carriers. The elusive Higgs boson is surrounded by dashes, and an eye, upper right, searches to find it: a diagonal line connected to another tiny eye that looks north. What is north? Edinburgh, and where Mr Higgs lives, an elusive physicist.

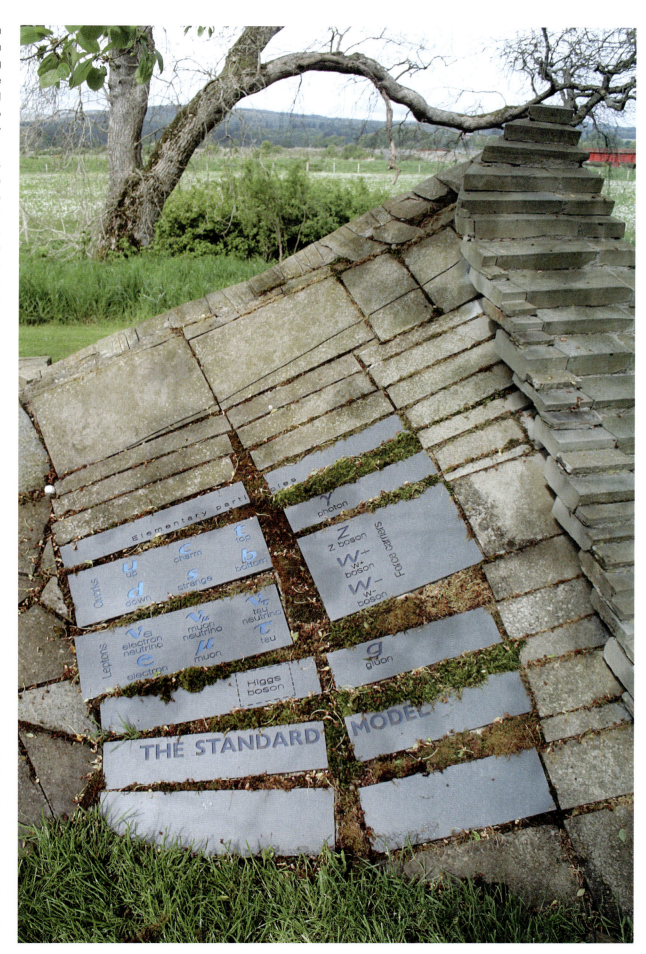

Model. The problem is that while the model appears correct, and heretofore has always produced the sought-for particle more or less where it should be, after billions of dollars and many years of looking no one can find its necessary keystone – the Higgs. The God particle will not turn up, maybe, and if it does not then most of the bets are off, and the Standard Model falls to pieces – which is how it is shown, held together by moss, symbol of the priority of nature over theory. We see humanity locked in mortal struggle with the cosmos, both given parity, both equal. Higgs and theory – falling apart or coming together?

Also due north is a tree with its branches and twigs forming little curls and spirals. To underline the connection of the microcosm to the macrocosm, I planted a circle of shrubs called *Corylus* 'Contorta' and *Salix* 'Tortuosa'. Their contortions are like the exploding particles, spirals of energy that whirl inwards, or around and about, helter-skelter.

Actually, as all this was being constructed and planted I found out that the modest physicist Mr Higgs was as elusive as his namesake. Far from being the usual egotist with a particle named after him, he was not a celebrity, nor did he seek fame, nor had he written a bestseller invoking the deity. Shy and retiring, he even tried to give others credit for the invention, and when no one could find the missing boson he called it ironically 'The Goddam Particle'. This is far from untrue. The Higgs boson, and Higgs field, are said to give mass to every other particle in the universe, and slow them down like molasses. So, if Cern and its large accelerator of 27 kilometres cannot find it, the theory is in big trouble, and all the money will have been misspent.

As you would guess, the scientists at Cern, like hedge funders, have taken a positive view of both sides of this question. Either way they win. If they find the elusive Higgs then their mission is accomplished and the reductive paradigm is fulfilled. *Per contra*, if it does not exist then things are even more interesting than imagined, and it is back to the drawing board. Cern has many scientists, up to 2,500 from sixty countries, working on such experiments and the reigning mood is refreshingly upbeat. As an institution this multinational is more of an Enlightenment body than the usual global corporation of today. Optimism and a collegiate atmosphere prevail as scientists from different cultures work on the fundamental questions, hoping to find what they are looking for, or even something better. Whichever the case, working with them is like working with the coal men, in unchartered territory where I am unsure of the outcome in terms of the landform, the content or the quality. They have already, however, produced the elusive Mr Higgs and sat him on my particle seat. If it is not quite the cosmos in the landscape I am pursuing, then at least it is the cosmologist. He left his retreat in Edinburgh and came to lunch one Sunday in April 2010. It makes me reflect back on the bower bird and his strong motive for building a garden – to get the bird, to capture an elusive moment.

LEFT: Mr Higgs contemplating The Standard Model, 2010.

RIGHT: A shrubhenge of *Corylus* 'Contorta' (hazel) and *Salix* 'Tortuosa' (willow), the universe in a landscape of spiralling plants.

Mystery at the Heart of the Universe

Cern asked me to look at their landscape in Geneva around The Globe, a wooden structure designed for the Swiss Expo of 2002, which was moved to the public entry of their sprawling campus. This symbolic centre is at a potent juncture. It lies just on the French-Swiss border, right by a tangent of the 27-kilometre accelerator and next to Atlas. This is, as it sounds, the world giant among particle detectors, illustrated on pages 270–1. The design challenge was as exciting as it was daunting. For my content-driven approach what could be better than a commission to interpret with gardens, and top scientists, some fundamental aspects of reality and get closer to 'the universe in a landscape'. But I did not know if luck and creativity would alight simultaneously in the right place at the right time – that is, whether I was up to the task. Moreover, two immediate hurdles were obvious.

Cern had grown like Topsy over the last fifty years. Since the site was criss-crossed with tramlines and building projects, it was running out of protected, natural landscape. How could one construct a peaceful heart in the middle of Heathrow Airport? Any garden or retreat will soon be overwhelmed by urban reality. Secondly, The Globe, although an ideal sphere, imposed geometrical consequences. It sent out a series of concentric circles like landscape waves emitted from a zero point. One has to respond to this absolute form with circular buffers to the traffic and pollution – something I was happy to do – and then pie segments, because the adjacent space is so limited. Such constraints led me to a strategy of protective skins, the layers of a green island, for the ceremonial heart of Cern, with a further buffer of landforms around The Globe. The metaphorical concept developed as a green onion with other onions inside, or an oasis in a hardscape of building and traffic.

The sketch of the site (right) shows the way we hope to pull the fragments together as the green heart of Cern, conceived as a field with the sculptural remnants of outdated machines, and a new Uroboros (see below). Even the parking lot might combine landscape and superannuated accelerators. Some of the old equipment is stunningly beautiful, even if clunkily propped on concrete slabs. Once again it is Fourth Nature, industrial scrap turned into art. One landscape strategy is to mix the latent art of advanced testing – its hardware – with various gardens, even including the parking lots. After all, these potentially beautiful artefacts give Cern one identity the public is coming to love, and in spawling suburbia it sorely needs it.

But the main way Cern can gain visibility and public understanding is to concentrate on its fundamental goal: searching for the mystery at the heart of the universe. It is this captivating journey that is the basic content and, if their authorities grasp the opportunity, it should give way to a new iconography that puts them on the map. There is no question that this Vatican of Science, with the visage of Heathrow Airport, desperately needs urban definition. It calls for a

The Globe, an ecologically driven structure designed by Hervé Dessimoz for the 2002 Swiss Expo and re-erected as the centrepiece of Cern. Because of the spherical shape, sliced horizontally about one-third up from its base, workable outbuildings were necessary, and because of circulation, the site had to be cut into a series of pie segments and surrounded by a buffer to noise and traffic. The site sketch below shows a green oasis across a highway (yellow) and the connection of pathways (blue) uniting a previously disconnected set of buildings. An iconic bridge, right, could become the symbolic gateway to Cern and France. In the future The Globe and other globular instruments of experiment (brown) might be opened to the public and connected by a landscaped walk.

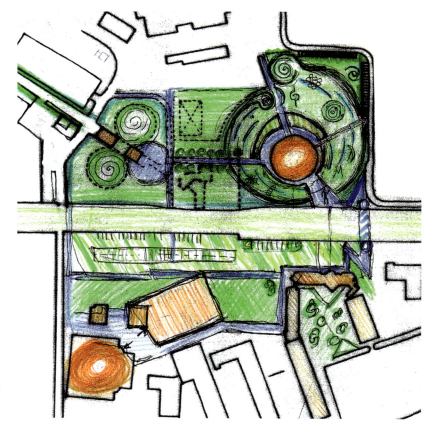

RIGHT: A copper 'frequency cavity', one of 128 that were located on the 27-kilometre ring. These accelerated electrons and positrons; the copper sphere at the top stored the microwave energy that pushed the bundle of particles faster and faster. The glistening sphere like The Globe has a generic beauty but it is pinioned on clunky concrete like a dumb specimen.

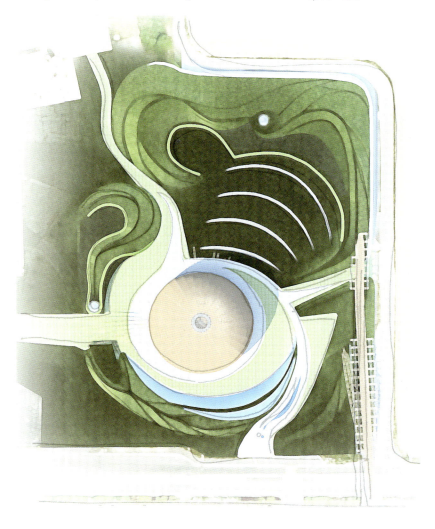

sensuous landscape, identifying sculpture and an iconic architecture that, together, could convey Cern's hugely ambitious goal.

A short summary of this content is necessary, since it formed the basis of my landscape proposal to the Director General of Cern, Rolf Heuer, and above all because it remains the basic question facing science, not to mention the rest of the world. Do we live in one universe with a closely correlated set of laws or a multiverse with an emergent set of by-laws? Another basic question that stems from this search is: How does the human fit into the magisterial picture, especially since we know how the universe evolved, more or less, after the first few seconds? The hint of an answer can be found in the recent history of physics, and its search for unifying principles.

Since the nineteenth century, when electricity and magnetism were discovered to be aspects of a single force, the goal has been to decode the superforce that scientists, especially Einstein, assumed underlies everything. Electromagnetism was the first synthesis of the Grand Unified Theory (GUT), also known as the Theory of Everything (TOE). These and other acronyms often sound as if they had fallen out of the human body; maybe they are meant to. In any case, some of great discoveries at Cern, in 1981 and 1983, pushed the synthesis further, when electromagnetism was found to be linked with the weak force of the atom. The combination became known as the electroweak force. Such unification of very different forces occurs only at incredibly high energies, those present just after the origin of the universe, or those that now occur inside big accelerators.

An unlikely logic drives explosive discovery. Since speed translates into energy and is proportional to it, and since the velocity of light is the speed limit of the universe, and since things become infinitely big when they are accelerated to this pace, and since opposite particles, which meet, annihilate each other in an explosion, thus creating further energy – then, all of these facts make it reasonable for physics to grow intellectually through ever greater destructions. In effect, with super-explosions physicists 'see' all the way back to the first microseconds of the universe, and can tell the story forward from this point when there was just pure concentrated energy, a hot plasma expanding *faster* than the speed limit of the present cosmos. Known as inflation, this excess acceleration supposedly gives us the perfectly balanced forces and constants we see today, the miracle of fine-tuning.

Whatever the actual case of the universe, a lot of theory and evidence point, towards the ultimate goal of finding one, unified superforce. Presumably from this, all the other four forces, and perhaps more, have evolved. The Holy Grail of science assumes these forces are perfectly resolved together, and that they froze out one by one as the universe cooled. Such existing patterns are explainable by perfect mathematical theorems, like superstrings, those ultra-tiny, coiled bands, which look so elegant and vibrate away in higher-dimensional space. Not only do these theories have the beauty and simplicity that characterize natural laws, but they *demand* a place for the very one that is so hard to integrate into the overall picture, gravity. Thus these aspirations and views come together at Cern: to see both the unification of physics and the origin of the cosmos, at the same time.

The problem is the vanishing horizon. After teetering on the edge of such a breakthrough for forty years (when GUTs and superstrings were first mooted) that edge has moved on and on. At the moment, it appears beyond the ability of big accelerators and big science to reach. Thus some cosmologists, such as Martin Rees, are beginning to doubt our abilities. He often now says: 'A "true" fundamental theory of the universe may exist but could just be too hard for human brains to grasp' – or, for that matter, for our accelerators to test. Other heretical thoughts add to the perplexity. Perhaps there is no possible grand unification possible; perhaps nature is an *ad hoc* assemblage of partial laws – by-laws as Rees calls them – and there is no superordinate unity to nature, no God of Einstein, no Final Theory of Everything, no TOE.

In that case, mystery would remain a stubborn and enticing friend. It would inspire ever-greater explosions – call them the flaming passions of science, the deep desire of collision – with ever-vanishing blandishments. Then we would come to see Mystery Herself as the attractive goal, or rather the younger sibling of her big sister, the Unattainable Empress of Everything (U-EE).

This answer is, of course, just another metaphor, and not a solution to the big puzzle. And it is bad taste to remain complacent with an enigma and give up the big search, especially since the former's mystery depends on the latter's subtlety. Hence my proposal to Cern is a landscape based around a metaphor that includes the big questions in its layout. This is derived from another metaphor, the Cosmic Uroboros, which has gained acceptance among scientists since Sheldon Glashow proposed it in the 1970s, when he was on the hunt for the GUT. This shows a snake eating its tail, an emblem of infinity itself derived from the ancient Egyptians and Greeks. Entailed in this symbol is the unity of everything, all things material and spiritual, which constantly evolve and eat each other, the eternal cycles of destruction and recreation. Many scientists have accepted Glashow's new version of the snake, because it is a comprehensive picture of the way the smallest size is connected to the largest.

Around the coil, from the left side where quantum physics rules, to the right side and the snakehead where relativity physics is on top, are the sixty powers of ten – everything that is, all sizes from quarks to galactic superclusters, and bigger and smaller than that. Physicists love this diagram because it helps explain where different forces reign, where different theories concentrate and, if you think about it, how these forces vary in their action. For instance, the electromagnetic forces are positive and negative by necessity, electrons are attracted by protons but are repelled by each other, while gravity is always positive and accumulative. Although unspeakably weak in comparison to the other three forces, gravity always adds up positively to become, in the end, the supreme ruler.

This cosmic diagram has many other fascinating truths embedded in its ring. For instance, as the authors Nancy Abrams and Joel Primack point out, the lower right-hand side – where we exist – has a special implication not only for the universe but for us. They show these comprehensible sizes in white, extending from the ant through us to the mountain, the earth and the sun. They call this

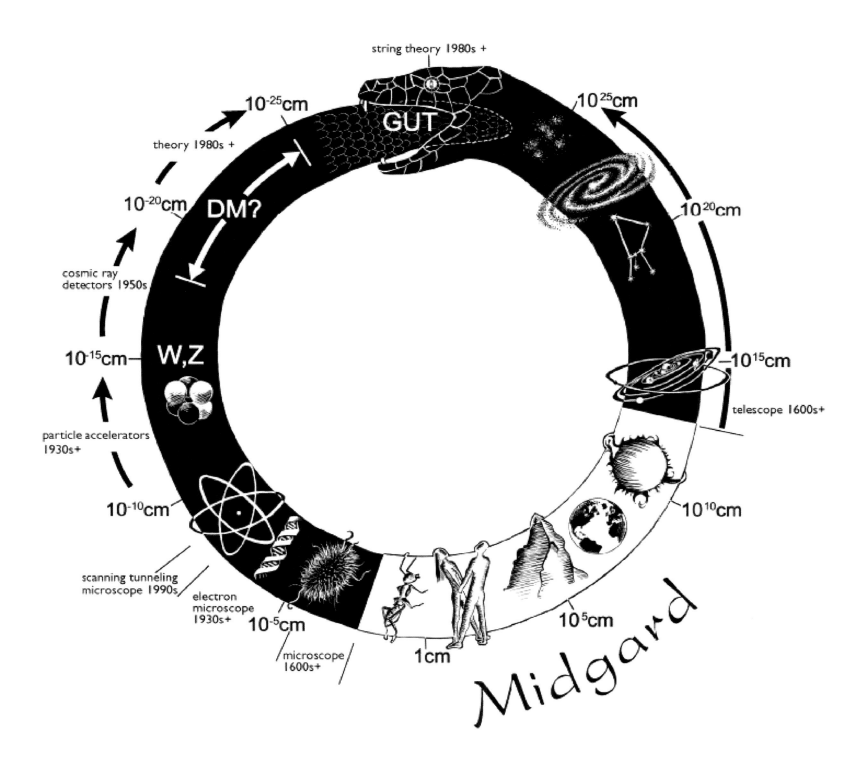

The Cosmic Uroboros and Midgard. The snake eating its tail, symbol of eternity for the Egyptians in *c.*1600 BC, is a cosmic metaphor that has been adapted by many eminent scientists today, among them Sheldon Glashow, Bernard Carr and Martin Rees. Note the way the Grand Unified Theory (GUT) is in the head that swallows the tail, and superstrings pop into its mind above. This very interesting emblem has many important implications that can be pondered and questioned, and it relates directly to the diagram near the outset of this book (page 32, right). But to think the universe can be described by a snakehead theory is as strange as to think that this concluding diagram can swallow my introduction. (After Nancy Abrams and Joel Primack *The View from the Centre of the Universe* (Fourth Estate, 2006).)

visible area Midgard, after the Old Norse mythological island of stability, which exists in a sea of big giants and small fish. That is also the spectrum of sizes where all cultures grow up, and classical physics reigned. It is the area where the universe is human-scaled and architects work in feet and inches, where things work according to our eyes and intuition. But slowly, in the 1600s we saw with telescopes that Midgard was not the centre of the universe, and then a few years later with microscopes that cells were smaller than ants. By the 1930s, particle accelerators had extended this vision downwards while many types of telescope – not to mention theories – extended both views enormously. We have today seen to the edge of the atom and, aided by the 'inferations' I have mentioned, seen pretty well down to 10^{-25} and up another fifty powers of ten to 10^{+25}. Looking one way we infer quarks and dark matter (DM in the diagram), and the other way, the black holes and web-like super-clusters of strange attractors. These invisible but existing structures hold the whole caboodle together. I say caboodle because we do not know it is a universe any more than we know it is a multiverse; the inferations go both ways, equally.

What has all this to do with the theme of this book, *The Universe in the Landscape*, and the design for Cern? The answer is implied in my modification of the Cosmic Uroboros, and its relation to the plan around The Globe. From a pragmatic point of view the biggest recommendation for the diagram of size is that it is so largely accepted by the scientific community. It can therefore work as a generic and iconic plan that enjoys a consensus, something necessary for the public iconography of Cern. But several aspects need questioning, not surprising for a diagram which is 3,000 years old. The fact is that there is no universal snake and, as far as we know today, no theory that successfully eats its tail. The whole relationship between the very big and small is shrouded in *veils of infinity*, and that treacherous number, infinity, is exactly what comes up every time a scientist tries to force quantum and relativity physics together. Endlessness falls out of the merger of the two truths, and when physicists see such infinities arise they drop their theories.

This is one reason I have placed a series of question marks at the joint between the two irreconcilable ideas, each of which is among the most respected and tested notions of science. Also, my version of the Uroboros shows another dimension than the growth from small to large: that is, the dimension of time. It is true that the universe grows in size from a quark into an atom more or less in a linear fashion. But then something strange happens to the Uroboros. After the first 100 million years the atoms cluster into gases, then stars and galaxies. Time, as measured in the evolution of complexity, or red in my version, jumps from the very small atom to the very big sun. From there it proceeds to evolve greater complexity – follow the red arrows – from suns to planets to mountain ranges, then to life, DNA, ants and finally people. Complexity evolves in jumps and

UROBOROS IN SPACE-TIME …

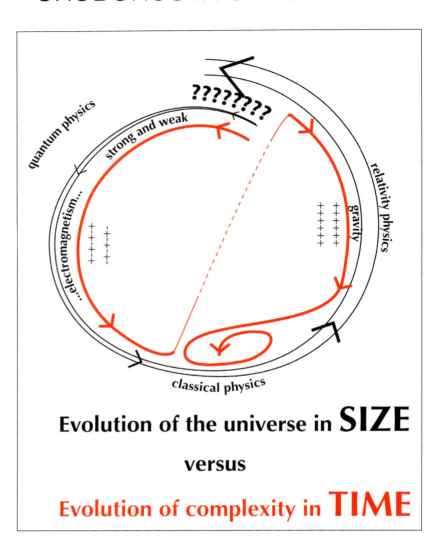

Evolution of the universe in SIZE

versus

Evolution of complexity in TIME

Uroboros in Space-Time generates the plan around The Globe. The diagram above shows the way size develops in a linear way from small to big, while evolutionary complexity, in red, jumps around and spirals within this system. Compare to the Uroboros on page 279: here there is a big question mark about the relationship between the head and tail. How do quantum and relativity physics match up? Their merger produces infinities, a sure sign that some basic idea is missing; or perhaps that the emergence of the big from the small is not resolvable in a single theory. The plan, right, has a fortuitous place for this new cosmic diagram: note that the public entrance, lower right, is where the human is located, and the two interlocking question marks is where the diagonal route to Atlas exists, where the experiment goes on into the very biggest explosions in search of the very smallest things. The green earth berm surrounding the site like the snake coil provides an acoustic and psychological shelter, while the narrative from small to large suggests a future iconography of planting, rills and landscape delights.

... BECOMES COSMIC RING

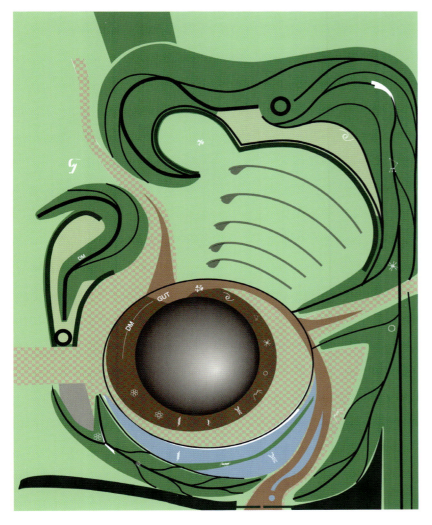

zigzags, as shown in the Universe Cascade. Thus the narrative of the universe is not a simple growth in size as the Uroboros first suggests, but more a spiral and twist between the big and small.

Beyond that the evolution of complexity also brings out a very important point for us: the place of the human in this immeasurably big and complex cosmos. It takes big numbers in time and size before culture can exist. The universe has to be venerable enough to have second-generation stars before it can generate complex chemistry. Maybe life could have emerged when the universe was 4 billion years old, but we know it took at least 10 billion before life grew on earth. The necessary sequence of events from the explosion of supernovae to the collision of planets has to occur before the complex molecules of oxygen and carbon are transmuted into life, and this takes what is called deep time by biologists. Creative explosions must occur, just as they do at Cern, before anyone can figure out how ultimate matter works.

In other words, as far as we know the size, balance and age of the universe have to be close to the way they are before it can produce feeling and thinking beings like us. The cosmos which looks inhumanely scaled at first turns out, once again and on second glance, to be a distant parent that is both surprising and touching. It must grow to such scale before it can give birth to those who can think about and celebrate its virtues, and that is one more reason to find the universe in a landscape, or a garden. And it is why for Cern I have modified the narrative of the Uroboros and adopted a set of interlocking question marks as symbols for the pleasure of the search. Future theories and a possible grand synthesis are today unknown, but we can be sure that the mystery at the heart of the universe will continue to pull and push us on like a very demanding lover.

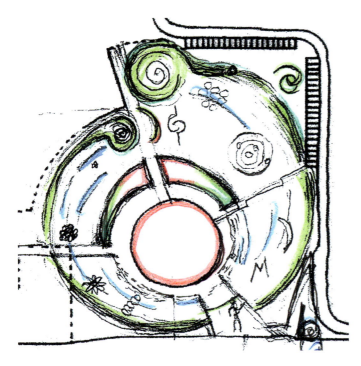

Interlocking question marks, mounds for Cern. They could unite the very big with the small, but as a metaphor they replace the head and tail of the snake. Cern is asking the big questions of the cosmic origin, but the Cosmic Ring, not the sanke, relates to our contemporary metaphysics, as it does to the physical 27-kilometre ring.

The Cosmic Ring now surrounds The Globe. Renderings and design were made with Lily Jencks. Building and bridge were designed by Hervé Dessimoz and Christophe Favre of Group H, Geneva. Conceptually the scheme is now the hybrid seen in the plan, lower left, the Building-Landform, a mixture developed from the mound sculpture of previous work. The Cosmic Ring and the Cosmic Eye, right, are the basis for a new Cern iconography!

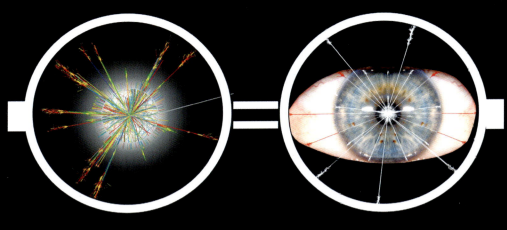

Cern Collisions = Eyeconology

INDEX